Dr. Martin A. Larson was born in Whitehall, Michigan, March 2, 1897. Following service in the Navy in 1918, he graduated from Kalamazoo College in 1920, where he distinguished himself in track, forensics, and scholarship. Studying under fellowships at the University of Michigan, he was awarded an M.A. in 1921 and a Ph.D. in 1923 for research into the sources of Milton's theology. After teaching a number of years at two universities, he established his own business in Detroit, from which he retired in 1950, to devote himself to research and writing.

His work has been cited, reproduced, or published in newspapers throughout the United States and in countless magazines at home and abroad, including *USNWR, Reader's Digest, Saga, Playboy, Pageant, The Humanist, Church & State, Fortune,* and others. He has published ten books, of which *The Modernity of Milton, The Religion of the Occident, Church Wealth and Business Income,* and *Praise the Lord for Tax Exemption* are best known. Recognized as an authority on tax-exempt property and income, he has appeared on radio and TV programs. He is a member of the National Advisory Council of Americans United for Separation of Church and State. He makes his home with his wife in Phoenix, Arizona.

WHEN PAROCHIAL SCHOOLS CLOSE

Martin A. Larson

WHEN PAROCHIAL SCHOOLS CLOSE

a study in educational financing

Robert B. Luce, Inc.   Washington — New York

CONTENTS

70273

Part Two
Conclusions and Commentary

Part Three
Two Centuries of Controversy

Appendix

One of the most persuasive arguments for government subsidies to church schools has been that if such schools should close their doors and transfer their students to public schools, these institutions would be overwhelmed. This might result in considerable damage to the educational program. Why not, therefore, forget the church-state issue and feed some public money to the church schools, just enough, perhaps to keep them in operation? Would not this be cheaper than to let these schools close and transfer all students to public schools?

There were, however, those who insisted that this argument was false and misleading, that in the long run one system of schools would prove more economical than two or several systems. How could one be sure of the answer? Why, obviously, by studying the results in communities where the church schools have been closed and their students enrolled in public schools. Facts are always the best basis for decisions.

But were there communities where this had happened? A quick survey indicated that the largest parochial school system, that of the Roman Catholic Church, had been steadily declining since 1965. There were, in fact, quite a number of communities in which these denominational schools had been phased out altogether. There were others in which sizable closings had occurred with residues remaining in operation.

The work of Dr. Martin A. Larson constitutes the first scholarly effort to scrutinize and analyse these situations and others with an eye to finding exactly what has happened in school financing and the general community's educational program of various representative cities. We believe his report is significant and will be of much use to educators, legislators and community leaders throughout the nation.

Glenn L. Archer
President, Americans United Research Foundation

Introduction

When the Directors of the Americans United Research Foundation decided to sponsor a research project dealing with private and public schools, their costs, and what happens when a public system is required to absorb gradually or suddenly a large or a considerable number of parochial pupils, the present writer was pleased to accept this commission; and the present report is the result.

Since it seemed that a resumé of the historical public-private school controversy and a view of it in perspective would be constructive and informative, we attempt in Part Three to re-create this in considerable detail. We have traced the development of American education, public and private, secular and sectarian, from the beginning, and have tried to understand the influences which have shaped their evolution; and we have reproduced considerable data and commentary as well as many statements, pro and con, expressing a variety of viewpoints which have appeared during a century and a half of conflict and confrontation.

In Part Two, we offer a number of comments and conclusions which flow directly from our research and historical study and which deal specifically with the parochial schools and their relation to the general community. We make an analysis of projected enrollments until 1980 and the capacity of the public schools to meet whatever contingencies may arise; the actual costs to public schools when they absorb parochial pupils; why Catholic schools began to decline about 1965-66; and what the alternatives will be should we begin to finance sectarian and other private schools as is done in certain other countries.

Since our principal purpose was to discover the precise and practical impact upon a public school system when called upon to absorb a large influx of parochial pupils, Part One analyzes the experience of 16 carefully chosen and representative cities, most of which have met and solved this problem. However, since we are also interested in the general cost of education, we have investigated several school districts where there have been few or no transfers, in order to compare their costs with others which have absorbed heavy influxes of parochial pupils.

In this quest, we have travelled from one end of the country to the other and have interviewed literally hundreds of people: students, teachers, principals, superintendents, administrators, and officials at state capitals; heads of small Protestant parochial schools and of elite private academies and boarding schools; nuns, brothers, priests, laymen, and directors of large Catholic systems. We obtained, digested, and organized vast quantities of statistical material in order to prepare tables which include an analysis of property taxes, and the extent to which these have risen because of school expenditures. We have computed the various sources of revenue: the local property tax, the state and county foundation funds, and subsidies from all other sources. The local tax, which usually supplied from 50% to 60% of school costs, however, varied widely: from 12% in Albuquerque to 80% in Milwaukee.

Choosing cities for analysis was a crucial consideration. Of the hundreds in the country, only a small proportion were potentially productive of significant results. There would, for example, be little purpose in doing a city where only 2% or 3% of the total enrollment was in Catholic schools: and since this is the situation almost throughout the South, we could not find any city to analyze in that area. Even the El Paso Catholic diocese, which claims 174,333 communicants in a population of 654,213, had only 7,500 pupils in its own schools. The Fort Worth diocese claims no more than 65,172 Catholics in a population of 1,237,713; and a school enrollment of 2,463.

In literally hundreds of cities, therefore, the ratio of pupils in Catholic schools is so small that if they were to enter the public system at once, the impact would scarcely be noticed.

Since Catholic school enrollment in the nation as a whole was about 11% of the total in 1965 and since it had declined about 30% by September, 1971, a city with approximately that ratio and experience would represent the norm. For this reason, we chose San Bernardino, Bakersfield, Duluth, and Kansas City.

On the other hand, we selected Boise and Fargo, in which Catholic enrollment remained stable between 1965 and 1970, to discover what had happened to the tax rate and school costs. We analyzed Scottsdale, Arizona, not because of any transfer of private pupils to public schools, but because the enrollment in the latter increased by 1,300% in twenty years. How has this expansion been handled and what has happened to property taxes? What has been the cost of new facilities and the greatly expanded

4

personnel? You will find the answers in the following pages. Albuquerque, New Mexico, was an intriguing object of investigation because its public schools not only increased by 265% in twenty years but also absorbed one-half of a large Catholic enrollment between 1955 and 1971, a period during which the latter declined from 14.9% of the total to 4.9%. Cities like Omaha, Nebraska, Denver, Colorado, Springfield, Missouri, Fort Wayne, Indiana, and Buffalo, New York, and many others were rejected because transfers in them from parochial to public schools had not become significant before mid-1971.

The most remunerative research would necessarily be conducted where large Catholic enrollments had either been drastically reduced or terminated entirely. For this reason, we chose Helena, Montana, and Pueblo, Colorado, where all Catholic schools have been closed; and Green Bay, Butte, Dubuque, Detroit, Milwaukee, and St. Paul, in all of which the public schools have absorbed heavy transfers from the Catholic over a period of years.

We have, therefore, placed under the microscope every possible situation. Nothing could happen, even in a large city like Philadelphia or New York, more drastic than what transpired in Helena, Butte, and Dubuque.

Since this report explains exactly what occurred, it also offers a preview and a blueprint of how any school system, in the event that it should be confronted with a similar crisis, might be able to meet the challenge.

At various points in this study, we have discovered facts pointing to certain conclusions on a number of sensitive issues:

(1) That communities which have many parochial schools and other forms of exempt property in large amounts have substantially higher tax rates than those with few private schools; we have concluded that this situation stems from the fact that the same power structure which creates a large system of private schools also fosters a social system which pours its wealth into exempt rather than into taxable property.

(2) That wherever the public schools have been severely undernourished, the primary cause has been the existence of a large system of parochial education; since the parents patronizing this, have refused to vote bonds for the public schools, the latter have been impoverished.

(3) That when parents transfer their children from the private to the common schools, the community achieves unity, and votes money for the latter by overwhelming majorities.

(4) That, whereas the public schools absorbed about 18 million pupils between 1950 and 1965, and did so without serious difficulty, they are now, on the contrary, facing a definite loss of enrollment because of the falling birth rate, which began to decline in 1962-63; and that they will be able to maintain their attendance during the Seventies only if private

5

schools close in considerable numbers.

(5) That the question involved in parochial aid is probably the most crucial, important, and far-reaching church-state issue that has ever faced the American people.

Since, in the interest of brevity, we use various terms without defining them which may be unfamiliar to some readers and employ initials or abbreviations to designate certain agencies of government, we offer the following glossary:

PTR: Pupil-teacher ratio, the number of pupils for each classroom instructor.

PSR: Pupil-staff ratio, which includes administrators, counsellors, etc.

ANB: Average number belonging, which includes all children of school age in the community.

ENROLLMENT: This includes all actual registrations.

ADA: Average daily attendance, the average number present in the classroom.

VO-TECH: Vocational technical institute, usually operated by boards of education for job or industrial training; it is separate from the academic educational structure.

BA or BAs: Bachelor of Arts, or persons holding the degree.

MA or MAs: Master of Arts.

AU: Americans United for Separation of Church and State.

CEF: Citizens for Educational Freedom, a Catholic-oriented parochiaid lobby.

PAROCHIAID: Any direct or indirect public subsidy for parochial or other church-related pupils or schools.

PAROCHIAL: Parish-related, as a school operated by a parish church.

RELIGIOUS: A term used as a noun and applied to members of orders in the Catholic Church who have taken the vow of chastity, poverty, and obedience.

PER-CAPITA TAX: The average amount paid by each person in a community as his share of a general levy upon property whether or not he, as an individual, actually pays it.

MILLAGE: The number of mills imposed as a tax upon real estate or personal property for each hundred or thousand dollars of assessed valuation: for example, with a millage of 143 and an assessment of $4,500, the tax would be $643.50.

ESEA:	The Elementary and Secondary Education Act of 1965, under which a great multiplicity of federal programs are carried on in public and private schools.
USDA:	The United States Department of Agriculture.
PL 874:	Public Law 874, under which federal subsidies are granted to relieve impacted areas.
NDEA:	The National Defense Education Act, under which the federal government makes grants to areas with large military installations.
HEW:	The Department of Health, Education, and Welfare.
OEO:	The Office of Economic Opportunity.
SDA:	The Seventh-Day Adventist Church or denomination.

In this study we have sought to achieve complete objectivity; to present every side fully; and to permit all controversialists the most accurate expression possible of their views.

We trust that the statistics included at the close of each case-study will not interfere with the readability of our reports but will, instead, make them easier to understand. For this reason, we have placed them where they will be available for quick and easy reference. We could have omitted them entirely or relegated them to the Appendix. We felt, however, since facts are the ultra *sine qua non* in this study, that many readers would wish the pertinent statistics to be quickly and easily available.

During the sometimes arduous labor of gathering the material for this book, I have been sustained by the generous and unfailing encouragement of Dr. Glenn L. Archer, President of Americans United Research Foundation. And I wish particularly to express my deep appreciation to Dr. C. Stanley Lowell, consultant to the Foundation, for his constant aid in supplying documents, making important contacts, obtaining information from a great variety of sources, and offering constructive suggestions which have been incorporated into the text. I wish also to thank Dr. Virgil M. Rogers, nationally renowned educator, and Mr. Edd Doerr, Managing Editor of *Church and State* magazine, for their careful reading of the manuscript and their extremely helpful and valuable appraisals.

Finally, I would like to express my gratitude to the hundreds of people who have graciously given me of their time in interviews and who have supplied me with statistics and other information in all the cities covered in this study.

Martin A. Larson

Part One

An Analysis of School Systems

In April, 1969, the Most Reverend Raymond Hunthausen, the Roman Catholic Bishop of Helena, announced that all Catholic schools in the city would close in June, thus consigning almost one thousand parochial pupils to the already overloaded public system and increasing its enrollment by about 17%. This was news of national import; and, since it followed by only three months the defeat by a single vote in the State legislature of a bill which would have granted massive parochiad, it seemed to some an ultimatum that unless subsidies were forthcoming, there would be a general "dumping" of Catholic pupils.

A Classic Situation

Helena, capital of the state, is a well established, prosperous community which has grown slowly but steadily over the years. Its population was 17,581 in 1950; 20,227 in 1960; and 22,557 in 1970. Since bond proposals had been defeated, the public schools were crowded and in straightened circumstances. A classic situation therefore existed: how would lay Catholics react? How would the schools handle the sudden influx? Would there be hostility or conflict? What would happen to the tax rates?

In 1965, there were four Catholic schools in the area, with an enrollment of 1,266. However, in 1966, St. Mary's, with 205 pupils, and in 1967, St. Ann's in East Helena, with 154, closed their doors. The Catholic high school, adjacent to the Cathedral, which had 160 pupils in 1965, was replaced by the modern Central High, built at a cost of about $1.8 million and designed for 800. However, the enrollment never exceeded 350; for two years interest on the $1.2 million mortgage had gone unpaid; without public subsides, the school could not continue.

There is little reason to believe that the old Cathedral elementary with almost 600 pupils in 1968-69 was in financial difficulty: centrally located, it had a staff of 11 religious and only 3 lay teachers. We can understand why the Church offered to sell its new high school; but when it decided to close the well-attended, flourishing, and economically operated grade school also, this was an unexpected and stunning development.

Mr. A.G. Erickson, superintendent of the Helena public schools, explained that the Church wished to sell and the Board of Education was willing to buy the new Catholic high school facility. A bond issue of $2.4 million was approved by a vote of 85 to 15 to finance its acquisition. The Church received $1,510,000 for a property with a replacement value of about $2 million.

Mr. Erickson declared that the great majority of Catholics were delighted; and their youth, warmly welcomed into the public schools, entered into their studies in the new environment quickly and with enthusiasm.

Asked how the crowded public system was able to absorb a sudden increase of 17%, Mr. Erickson stated that there had been no trouble at all and that the former Catholic high school was gradually filling up.[a] "We leased the old St. Mary's for one year, and spent about a million dollars of our bond issue making additions and improvements to eight elementary schools," he explained. "In September, 1970, we had space for everyone—in fact, for the first time in years, we had surplus room."[b]

Had it not been necessary to hire more teachers?

"Yes, fifty, and we had about forty applications for each position."

Were any of the former Catholic teachers engaged?

"Only a few. Some of the sisters went elsewhere to meet the needs of the Church. But there was a music teacher I wanted. She accepted a contract, removed her garb, but remained in her order for one year. Then she resigned from it, married, and is now a fixture in our system."

---

a.   Enrollment in the facility had grown to 670 in October, 1970.

b.   Although Mr. Erickson did not mention it, there is another very important facet to consider: the declining Montana birth rate. While the population increased from 674,767 in 1960 to 682,133 in 1970, the 18,219 births of 1957 dropped to 11,974 in 1967. This means that in 1973, something like 6,000 fewer pupils will enter the schools than in 1963; and the cumulative result must be that during the Seventies, the elementary enrollment in the state will be at least 30,000 less than in the Sixties. It may even drop from a high of 127,853 in 1968 to about 90,000 in 1977-78.

Were the Catholic students welcomed?

"With open arms."

Has there been any friction over religious differences?

"Never!"

How have Catholic parents reacted?

"Most of them were already sending their children to the public schools. Now almost all of them are happy, not only because of their great financial savings, but also because the more they see of the public schools, the better they like them."

Since the closing of the Catholic schools in Helena quickly became a *cause celebre*, it merited a feature article in the *American School Journal* of September, 1969, under the headline "Helena. . .Took 97 Days to Find Room in the Public School System for 1,000 Catholic School Youngsters." The crisis, declared the author, was complicated by the fact that a special levy of $1,000,000 was already being asked. In this case, however, convincing the taxpayers was not too difficult, since the community was united. The article points out that everything was done to make the new students happy: among other steps taken, permission was obtained to waive athletic eligibility requirements so that new students could compete at once; high respect was openly expressed for their previous education. "Before school ended last spring, joint elections were held for cheer leaders and drill teams that included newly enrolled Catholic students. Public school guidance counsellors have been hard at work helping the newcomers select courses and feel more at home. . . Our advice to other school boards faced with the closing of parochial schools would be: Keep calm and remain objective, give priority to the human values of sympathy and compassion for the systems that are being wiped out. . . It takes some introspection together with intestinal fortitude to work out such situations successfully. And when they are reached to everyone's general satisfaction, you'd be surprised how much more cohesive your community is."

Since we were deeply concerned over the Catholic viewpoint, we interviewed Father Ernest Burns, diocesan Assistant Director of Catholic Education. He stated that Church schools in Montana received no help of any kind, such as textbooks or transportation, from local or state sources; and only minimal aid under Title I and II of ESEA.[a]

---

a.   The *Biennial Report* of the State Superintendent of Public Instruction for 1967-68 states that private schools received $26,697 under Title II; and that $2,929,776 was expended under Title I, of which at least $150,000 must have gone to Catholic schools.

Asked why the Church closed its schools in Helena while they seemed to be doing well in Boise, Idaho, Father Burns declared that it was a matter of priorities; that more and more Catholic laymen were deciding that they would rather have a new T-V, a car, or a house than a Christian education for their children.

When we inquired whether this reflected some disillusionment with Church education, Father Burns stated candidly that errors had been made in the past, such as taking children of six or eight to confession and repeating the same formulas over and over and thus creating a feeling of intense boredom. Religion, he declared, should not be taught to little children and different methods should be used with teen-agers. He added that, in his opinion, the Catholic elementary schools should be phased out and that the Church should concentrate on secondary education.

Asked whether Catholic educators emphasize the primacy of the Church, he replied: "Of course we do!"

He stated that the loss of religious and their contributed services was the greatest difficulty encountered by Catholic education. Twenty years earlier, he said, a lay teacher in an elementary school was almost unheard of; now about half the staff are laymen, and they cost much more. He explained that sisters are paid from $2,200 to $2,600, while priests and brothers receive about $4,500, in addition to fringe benefits. They must pay for their own food and clothing and prepare their own meals. Lay teachers were paid almost as much as they would be getting in the public schools. He stated that there is no retirement plan for lay teachers and that the religious make contributions to their orders to care for members who have retired from active work.

Tuition, according to Father Burns, averaged about $125 to $150 in elementary schools and $300 in high schools. Parish churches made up deficits by subsidies to their own schools and contributed to the support of diocesan high schools. Per-pupil costs varied widely, but averaged about $250 in elementary and $350 in secondary schools for operation alone.

Asked what the Catholic laity thought of closing all the schools and selling Central High, he stated that although a few objected strenuously and two or three offered substantial sums of money to continue their operation, most of them were in favor of what had been done. He agreed with Mr. Erickson that there had been no difficulty at all in the public schools as a result of the transfers.

Asked what would be necessary for the Catholic schools to survive and prosper, he declared that such things as free lunches, textbooks, and bussing would not suffice. "What we want," he said, "is to have the salaries of our teachers—even if they are nuns—paid exactly as if they were in the public schools."

School Financing in Montana

Montana is one of the few states which have no sales or use taxes; and yet the real estate levies are quite moderate. This situation is made possible, at least in part, because the state sponsors two programs in support of local education:

(1) The school Equalization Aid, which draws appropriations from the General Fund as well as from gas and oil leases and royalties, in addition to 25% of all individual and corporation income taxes; and

(2) The Interest and Income Fund, which derives revenues from a variety of rentals, grazing fees, land sales contracts, legacies, and leases.

In 1960-61, $17,060,447 of state funds thus became available; in 1965-66, this increased to $26,278,777; and in 1967-68 to $33,625,060.

Between 1960-61 and 1967-68, the ADA in Montana schools increased from 136,113 to 160,659; the total cost of elementary and secondary education from $79,024,607 to $136,554,321; per-pupil state aid from $125 to $209. Meanwhile, however, the local property tax remained the mainstay of popular education: this was $57,711,525 in 1960-61 and $92,597,769 in 1967-68. It should be noted that the statewide per-pupil cost of $895 was much higher than in cities like Helena and was caused by low enrollments in small communities and the heavy cost of transportation in sparsely settled rural areas.

State Equalization Aid, based on ADA, finances both elementary and secondary education; the Interest and Income Fund is used for elementary schools only, but is allocated on the basis of the Average Number Belonging, including those in private schools; but all the money is used for public education. For this reason, the common schools receive less per pupil after absorbing parochial pupils than before.

The Impact Upon Property Taxes

Since proponents of parochiaid hold that subsidies for private schools would save taxpayers a great deal of money, the experience of Helena since 1968 assumes crucial significance. The school millage had remained stable for several years preceding 1965; but during the next three years—when there were virtually no transfers—it increased from 92.14 to 124.46. We need not, therefore, be surprised that it rose to 159.14 in 1970, when the full impact of school closures was reflected in the tax rate. Since the taxable valuation is 12% of appraisal, the tax on a $20,000 house was $429.60 in 1960, $443.83 in 1965, $526.10 in 1968, and $637.82 in 1970. In 1968, $298.70 of this was for schools; in 1970, $381.94, an increase of $83.24.

When asked what portion of the school millage—which increased 34.28 points between 1968 and 1970—was due to the transfer of pupils, Mr. Norman Matthews, County Treasurer, estimated that half of it should be charged to this. Assuming that this is correct, the owner of a $20,000 house would pay $41.62 in additional taxes because of the transfer.

But, as Father Burns intimated so clearly, the Catholic parents with children in parochial schools constitute the other side of this coin. Let us take a family with two children in elementary and one child in a secondary school. Direct tuition would be $600 a year, and subsidies to the parish church and the diocese possibly an equal sum, a total of $1,200. It would seem, therefore, that a Catholic family with three children in Church schools now retains for its own uses more than $1,100 which was previously expended for private education.

Although an exact, comprehensive analysis of Helena school costs over the past decade could not be made because the elementary and secondary systems include entirely different areas[a] and because financial reports preceding 1965 are not comparable for either, we do have statistics concerning teacher compensation, which constitutes the largest element in school costs. In 1960-61, salaries averaged $5,000; in 1965-66, $6,200; in 1970-71, $9,300, an increase of 86%, while the millage increased 89%.

Within the Elementary School District No. 1, which is virtually coterminous with the city of Helena, the per-capita property tax for all schools was $51 in 1960-61, $83 in 1965-66, and $143 in 1970. We have also complete financial data concerning school costs for 1967-68—before the transfers occurred—and 1969-70, when their full impact had been delivered. State aid continued at about the same ratio; but local property taxes fully doubled—from $733,963 in 1967-68 to $1,502,553.97 in 1969-70. When we add to this the revenue from the County Equalization Fund, we find that local taxes supplied $2,012,220 or 59.1% of the school budget in 1968 and $2,869, 200, or 58.8%, in 1970.

However, since the high school pupils are bussed into the city from surrounding areas, and since the overall attendance increased by no more than 17%, it is obvious that most of the added cost must be charged to general inflation. We should note also that the total per-pupil cost in Helena ($648) for 1970 is not only much less than in the state as a whole but well below the national norm of $858.

---

a.   There are only two high school districts in all Lewis and Clark County, that in Helena being by far the largest.

14

Finally, we can only add that the salaries of 50 new teachers would not at most exceed $400,000; nor would interest and amortization on a $2,400,000 bond issue be more than $250,000 in a budget totalling $4,874,100—an increase of about 13%—most of which went for capital expansion and improvement, long overdue, with or without transfers. The actual operational per-pupil cost for each of the 1,000 pupils absorbed into a much-improved system was therefore $400.

However, since state aid increased by $500,000, we find that local taxes increased by only $150,000, or $30 per family. This may be restated by saying that while 4,000 families paid $150,000 more, approximately 1,000 of them paid $350,000 less.

TABLE I[a]

Taxation in the City of Helena

Item	1961	1965	1968	1971
Taxable Value	$13,254,848	$18,235,552	$16,187,783	$20,305,642
Millage	179.00	184.93	219.21	265.76
County	31.11	29.06	30.01	35.32
State	8.00	9.00	8.05	8.30
Schools	85.21	92.14	124.46	159.14
City	54.88	54.73	56.69	63.00
Total Tax	$2,372,618	$3,373,577	$3,546,174	$5,401,300
School Tax	1,029,459	1,680,357	2,012,220	3,228,659
Per Capita	$51	$83	$89	$143
On $20,000 House	$429.60	$443.83	$526.10	$637.82
For Schools	203.50	221.14	298.70	381.94

a. Data in this and all following tables in Part One taken from official documents obtained from various sources such as state superintendents of public instruction, local boards of education, county auditors, and other government officials, the *Official Catholic Directory*, local Catholic education offices, etc. We omit the citations since these would render the text unduly cumbersome.

T A B L E II

School Expenditures and Revenues

Item	1967-68	%	1970-71	%
Enrollment	6,800		7,888	
Total Expenditures[a]	$3,401,615	%	$4,874,101	%
State Aid	1,208,592	35.5	1,719,581	35.3
County Equalization	1,278,256	37.6	1,366,648	28.0
Local Property Tax	733,964	21.5	1,502,554	30.8
Miscellaneous	180,803	5.4	285,318	5.9
Per-Pupil Revenue				
From State	$178		$214	
From County	188		189	
From Local Tax	108		186	
From Federal (Est.)[b]	59		59	
Per-Pupil Cost				
Local and State	474		589	
Total, including Fed.	533		648	

a. These expenditures include only funds received from State, County, and local sources; federal contributions, which averaged about 8 or 9%, were additional. When the federal subsidies are included, per-pupil cost rose as indicated above.

b. The estimated total federal contribution in 1967-68 was $400,000; in 1970-71, $460,000.

Schools in a Declining City

Butte was chosen for analysis because here also a unique development had taken place. It is a city decaying at the center; many of the buildings, including churches, are dilapidated, and some, with windows broken, stand exposed to the mercies of wind and weather. In spite of declining population, however,Church schools had been expanding for decades; and, until 1965, there seemed no reason to doubt that they would continue to do so. Public schools were cramped for space and hampered by obsolete facilities; one bond issue after another had been rejected. Then an extraordinary thing happened: the Catholic Church closed its 8 elementary schools in June, 1969.

The city sits on what was once known as the "richest hill in the world," which in its day supplied half the copper used in the United States. Thousands of men from central and southeastern Europe streamed into its mines, where they labored at low wages. With them, they brought their religion and their culture. But the years have wrought profound changes; the lodes are no longer so rich, and now great machines rend the earth to redeem its metallic treasures. A city that teemed with nearly 70,000 people in 1927-29, dropped to 33,251 in 1950, 27,877 in 1960, and 23,171 in 1970. However, since Butte School District No. 1 includes most of the 40,000 people in Silver Bow County, many of the children are bussed over considerable distances. At the edges of old Butte, modern and comparatively affluent suburbs have sprung up in recent years, which contribute materially to the tax-base.

Butte is, or at least has been, overwhelmingly Catholic; but several of the older churches built by this denomination are now occupied by com-

17

municants of other faiths, while others stand as ghostly reminders of days past.

The story of Catholic school expansion and decline is in itself intriguing. For many years, the Church operated eight elementaries and two diocesan highs. In 1940, the total enrollment was 2,407; in 1950, 2,808. From 1961 through 1965, it averaged about 3,600, but gradually declined to 2,626 in 1968; in 1969, the number of pupils fell abruptly to 1,177, and further to 1,017 in 1970-71, who attended either a junior or a senior high school. In the meantime, an even more dramatic development was taking place in the public system, which enrolled 6,593 in 1955, 6,880 in 1961, 7,798 in 1965, and 9,770 in 1970-71. Between 1964 and 1971, public school enrollment, including 1,232 at Vo-Tech, which did not even exist in 1964, increased by 2,153. In 1955, the public-private school ratio was 74%; in 1964, it dropped to 66%; but by 1970-71, it had risen to 89.2%. It is obvious that any difficulty in transferring parochial pupils was eased by the falling birth rate, which first exercised a noticable influence in 1970-71. Had there been no Vo-Tech or any transfer of students, the public schools would have declined in enrollment by at least 1,600 between 1964 and 1971.

Since, for 20 years, the Catholic schools had shown every promise not only of permanence but of continued expansion, precisely what was it that began to develop about 1965-66? It could not have been a sudden loss of financial resources among Catholic laymen, for they were certainly at least as affluent in 1968 as in 1961 or 1965. Many of the younger generation had indeed been moving from the dingy surroundings of the central city into the outlying areas; and we can only conclude that they had either become disenchanted with Catholic education or had decided that temporal considerations should take precedence. At all events, it is certain that they did not send their children back to the old buildings, or finance the construction of new church schools amid their lately completed and presumably heavily mortgaged homes.

Father Robert O'Donnell, Principal of the Catholic senior high school, stated that tuition in the two junior highs was a straight $100. In the senior high, it was $200 for the first, $175 for the second, and $150 for the third pupil from the same family. The eight parishes contributed $240,000 for the support of the three schools. In the junior highs, all teachers were sisters; in the senior high, eight of the faculty were Christian brothers, fifteen were sisters, and fifteen were lay teachers. The latter started at $6,100 with a maximum of $11,000. Sisters received $2,200 and brothers a little more than $4,000. All were certificated and the majority were MAs.

As fringe benefits, lay teachers received health and medical care, but had no tenure or retirement program. Brothers lived in lodgings provided by the diocese and there were three convents to house the sisters. The diocese paid for repairs, upkeep, and utilities—the religious paid for their own clothing and groceries and prepared their own food.

Father O'Donnell stated also that the Butte Catholic schools received no aid from the state or the city. Title II of ESEA supplied some books and visual aids; and help under Title III and IV was to be sought by a committee that had been formed for the purpose.

Operational per-pupil cost was about $375 in the high school, but less in the junior highs.

Asked what disposal had been made of the eight elementary school buildings, he explained that one had been leased to the Board of Education and another to the federal government; two were being utilized as junior highs; one by the diocese for religious instruction and another for church offices. One was being sold to the Anaconda Copper Company for remodeling.

Mr. Charles C. Davis, Superintendent of the Butte School District No. 1, which includes about 90% of the people in the County, was highly informative. How many pupils, we inquired, have been transferred from the Catholic to the public schools?

"In 1968, almost 400, and about 850 in 1969."

How had this problem been met?

"We leased St. John's school for $35,000 and have two new elementary schools on the drawing boards."

What about bonds?

"There was one issue in 1966 and another in 1968 which gave us nearly $4,500,000."

Had additional millage been necessary for operation?

"We were voted 25 extra mills in 1969. There will be another election on June 11, in which we are asking for 35 mills above the permissible budget, which would be $1.8 million."[a]

What is your per-pupil ratio?

"About 24 to 1."

Then more pupils could be absorbed without more teachers?

"If we had to."

How are the schools financed?

Had the staff and salaries been increased sharply?

"In 1961, we had 292 teachers and an enrollment of 6,880; now we

---

a.   The vote on June 11 was favorable.

have 450, with an enrollment of nearly 10,000. We added 45 teachers in 1969 to care for 850 transfers from the Catholic schools."

Do teachers from out of state receive full credit for teaching experience?

"No–if they have 20 years, we credit them with 5."

What is your salary schedule?

"It ranges from $4,932 to $11,930."

Isn't that rather low?

"We had 800 or 900 applications for 45 positions."

"The state gives the District the power to budget a maximum of $450 for every elementary and $622 for each high school pupil. Its Equalization Fund is allocated on the basis of need, and every city and county must raise the remainder by local taxation. The state allocates subsidies from the Income and Interest Fund for every elementary child, but all the money goes to the public schools. However, any increase beyond a prescribed millage must be approved by the voters."

Are federal subsidies included in the maximum per-pupil budgets?

"No, federal programs are kept in an entirely separate budget."

Miss Margaret Leary, Business Administrator of the District, explained further how State Aid operates. The Foundation Program, also called State Equalization, is based on the ANB rather than the ADA and covers a minimum of 80% of the former. The allocations from the I and I Fund are based upon the total school census of the District. In Butte, payments were $442,819 in 1968-69 or $36 for each of 12,300 children, of whom only about 6,000 were in the elementary public schools. The ADA-ANB allocations in 1969-70 totalled $1,521,179, or $190 per ADA.

Miss Leary supplied a mass of statistical data, partially reproduced in Table II. During the nine years following 1957, virtually no bonds were approved.[a] During 1966 and 1968, however, two issues were voted, totalling $4,476,760. The value of the school plant increased from $9,510,000 in 1961 to $17,228,477 in 1970-71, when it carried an outstanding debt of $4,796,776; and the cost of debt service rose from $466,871 to $913,722.

We note that while the State contributions increased from $843,488.67 in 1961-62 to $2,163,988 in 1970-71, the combined city and county tax remained the principal source of school income: as the per-capita tax rose from $63.89 to $108.46, this supplied $1,927,960 in

a.   The only issue approved during this period was one for $350,000 on July 1, 1962.

1961-62; $2,864,638 in 1965-66; and $5,737,923 in 1970-71. Meanwhile, the gross property tax increased from $139 to $294 per capita, with totals of $5,959,888 and $11,783,564 respectively.

Federal Subsidies

Mrs. Rita Melvin, in charge of ESEA programs, provided documents showing that $1,665,095 had been expended altogether since 1966. The breakdown between public and private school allocations was not complete; but, where they were made, indicated that about 30% was spent on programs for the latter—which would be about $550,000 in 5 years.

The Impact of Transfers on Costs and Taxes

It remains to discover how the drastic shift from private to public education has affected school costs and property taxation. These have indeed risen; the total budget for the District increased from $2,872,610 in 1961-62 to $4,163, 231 in 1965-66 and to $7,874,051 in 1970-71. Per-pupil costs, including debt service and all federal programs, rose from $417 to $806. The operational cost alone, however, rose only from $325 to $650.

When we realize that there has been a great expansion in the elementary and secondary school plants; that an excellent Vo-Tech has been established; that 2,500 parochial pupils have been absorbed; and that per-pupil costs are still more than $200 below the national average, we may well regard with admiration the remarkable achievements of the Butte public school system.

In 1961, a house appraised at $20,000 paid a tax of $454; in 1965, $476; and in 1970-71, $539. Assuming that assessments remained comparable, this means that the 2,500 parochial pupils were absorbed at an annual cost of $63 to the average home owner.

And let us note that in Butte, as in Helena, there is a silver lining. Since there is no sales tax, the owner of a median home in 1970-71 paid only one-third as much in total city, county, and state taxes as did his counterpart in Boston, Buffalo, or Milwaukee. And when he had paid this, he was virtually through with all, except federal, taxation.

Nor should we forget the parents who have maintained the parochial schools so faithfully and so long. If the average cost on the elementary level was $300 and on the secondary $500, including normal debt service, the total would be $1,250,000, or $625 for each of 2,000 families. Since the additional cost incurred in absorbing 1,500 parochial pupils in 1968 and 1969 totalled only $335,000 ($35,000 for a lease and $300,000 to pay the salaries of 45 teachers), the per-pupil cost in accomplishing this transition was less than $250, approximately half of which was paid by the state.

We can scarcely imagine a situation more serious than that facing Butte and its schools between 1966 and 1970. A deteriorating community with a declining population and an educational system enrolling 7,800—which had long been starved—was asked suddenly to provide facilities for 2,500 additional students. The gallant manner in which the whole community rose to the challenge is a tribute to the American spirit. Scarcely anything else could have happened so to unite the people in a great and common cause. Should all remaining parochial schools close, the shock will be mild in comparison to what has already been endured. From its ordeal, we believe that Butte has emerged much stronger and with a far greater realization of brotherhood.

TABLE I

School Enrollment in Butte

Year	Total	Public	%	Catholic	%
1940				2,464	
1950				2,808	
1955	9,923	6,593	74.0	3,330	26.0
1961	10,507	6,880	66.0	3,627	34.0
1964	11,228	7,617	67.9	3,611	31.1
1965	10,239	7,788	69.4	3,441	30.6
1969	10,954	8,328	76.0	2,626	24.0
1970-71	10,947	9,770	89.2	1,177	10.8
1971-72	10,910	9,900	90.9	1,010	9.1

TABLE II

Financial Statistics of Butte Public Schools

Item	1960-61	1965-66	1970-71
Property Valuations	$30,189,042	$32,911,740	$52,903,583
Tax	5,959,888	6,493,447	11,783,564
Millage	188.84	198.18	224.40
School Budget			
General	$2,234,576	$3,508,710	$6,354,524
Total	2,872,610	4,163,231	7,874,051
Debt Service	466,871	554,612	913,722
Total Property Tax			
For Schools	1,927,960	2,864,638	5,737,923
Millage	63.89	57.04	108.46
State Aid	$848,488	$1,177,294	$2,163,998
Value of Sch. Property	9,510,655	15,732,494	17,228,477
Bonds Outstanding			4,796,776
Per-Capita Tax	$139	$152	294
For Schools	47	67	144
For Av. Family	188	268	576
Tax on $20,000 Home	454	476	539
For Schools	156	219	290
Per-Pupil Cost			
For Operation	325	450	650
Total	417	534	806
To State	103	151	253
To County	93	163	197
To Local Taxpayers	117	140	210

San Bernardino, California

A Case of Classic Normality

Some 60 miles east of Los Angeles lies San Bernardino, which had a population of 63,058 in 1950, 91,922 in 1960, and 106,676 in 1970. Considerable construction was in progress, including a new city hall and civic center; as a whole, the city presented a definite appearance of prosperity.

This city was chosen for analysis because it reflects what has been happening educationally in our most populous state and, in fact, on the national scene. Whereas Protestant schools have held their own or even expanded, the Catholic lost about 30% of their enrollment nationally between 1964 and 1971. San Bernardino is, therefore, a classic replica of what has been occurring and may develop in the average American city where Catholic parochials are gradually being phased out over a period of years.

Statistics Concerning Taxation

Mrs. Joselyn W. Cox, Auditor-Controller, supplied voluminous documents concerning taxation. While assessments increased during ten years from $132 to $201 million, the millage escalated by about 50%, the per-capita tax from $118 to $238, and the per-capita school levy from $72.62 to $142.33. Property owners contributed $6,682,706 to the schools in 1960-61; $9,744,326 in 1965-66; and $15,229,724 in 1970-71. Meantime, the bonded indebtedness increased from $13,235,000 to $31,650,000 and the physical value of the school plant in the United School District from $30,651,291 in 1965 to $52,507,826 in 1970-71. The millage to cover

amortization was only .696, which imposed a property tax of $1,398,960, or $10.38 per capita.

Financing the San Bernardino Schools

The District operated 42 elementary, 12 junior high, and 5 senior high schools in 1970-71. At the District headquarters, Mr. James E. Wheeler and several of his assistants in Business Administration were most cooperative. The statistics shown in Table II for 1960-61 are for the San Bernardino Schools; those for 1965-66 and 1970-71, are for the Unified District, which does not differ substantially from its predecessor either as to schools or area covered.

During the decade following 1960-61, enrollment increased from 32,323 to 37,907; the number of classrooms from 1,004 to 1,641; the certificated personnel from 1,271 to 1,635; the average salary from $6,800 to $10,118; the total salaries from $8,758,660 to $16,593,166. Per-pupil cost increased from $467 to $780; the pupil-classroom ratio dropped from 32 to 23.2; and the pupil-teacher ratio from 27.4 to 25.3.

The principal sources of income were (1) the local property tax, which yielded $15,947,483, or 49.37% of the budget in 1970-71, and the State allocations, which supplied $14,785,543, or 47.77%. Federal subsidies, channeled through State agencies, dropped from $2,691,328 in 1969-70 to $835,556 in 1970-71. In 1960-61, these were $700,346 and in 1965-66, $941,124.

Under the State-aid program, a minimum of $125 was paid to all schools for each pupil through the 12th grade. However, only the most opulent received so small a subsidy: in San Bernardino, the average was $353; local sources provided $421, which included amortization of debt, an item not specifically shown in the overall budget.

Special Programs

Dr. V.V. Knisely, Assistant Superintendent of Instruction, stated (1) that there was no provision for shared or released time: Mormon and Roman Catholic students received religious instruction in their own facilities before or after school, or on week-ends; (2) that Catholic schools received federal funds totalling $2,955 during the current year under Title II of the Elementary and Secondary Education Act of 1965; and the public schools about $37,000; (3) that the non-Catholic private schools had grown slowly but steadily during the decade following 1961; and (4) that the students transferred from the Catholic schools between 1965 and

1971 had made no noticeable impact whatever upon the public schools.

Mr. Neil Roberts, who administered Title I ESEA funds, stated that two Catholic schools—Guadalupe and St. Anthony—had 160 identifiable, disadvantaged pupils who could qualify for special programs. For each of these, approximatley $300 was spent—a total of $48,000, of which $39,000 went to the virtually all Mexican-American Guadalupe. In six elementary public schools, about 4,000 pupils qualified for special programs, for whom more than a million dollars was allocated in 1969-70.

There was no bussing of parochial pupils at public expense in San Bernardino in 1970-71.

The Private Schools

The following non-Catholic private schools were in operation:

		Pupils
Secular:	The Montessori	40
	The Council of Retarded Children	132
Protestant:	Fairview Junior Academy (SDA)	240
	Valley Christian (Nazarene)	150
	Sterling Christian (So. Baptist)	61
	Grace Christian (Brethren Bible)	145
	Highland Av. Lutheran (L.C.A.)	184
	San Bernardino Christian (Faith Bible)	114
	Total Protestant	894
	Secular	172
	Total Private Non-Catholic	1,066

The table on page 27 traces the growth and decline of the Roman Catholic schools in San Bernardino.

Thus there were 3,006 pupils in the non-public schools in San Bernardino in April, 1971.

Since the Protestants nationally enrolled only about 5% of the total non-public enrollment, their ratio here (30%) was unusually high. Furthermore, they have experienced a steady growth; are currently in excellent condition; are staffed with competent and dedicated teachers; and are expected to continue a steady expansion. Conceivably, in a few years the majority of parochial pupils might be in Protestant schools.

All of these (except the Seventh-Day Adventist Fairview Junior Academy) operated in church plants. Since their costs for maintenance and capital outlay were negligible and since their teachers received salaries averaging only 40% of those paid in public schools, per-pupil costs were sometimes less than $250. It seemed doubtful, however, that teachers of such dedication could be obtained in sufficient numbers to man the schools, should they expand greatly.

School	Enrollment					
	1955	*1961*	*1964*	*1965*	*1970*	*1971*
Holy Rosary	700	667	602	565	340	340
Lady of Assumption		283	304	304	288	228
Guadalupe	310	411	392	386	384	384
St. Anne's	373	491	562	540	370	334
St. Anthony			433	382	262	262
Bernardine: Ele.	305	196	176	176		
High School	356	411	500	480	362	362
Aquinas High School		350	312	333	290	30
Totals	2,044	2,809	3,281	3,166	2,296	1,940

The Catholic Schools

During a tour of the city, we inspected all Catholic schools.

(1) Our Lady of Guadalupe had an old stucco building, with 8 or 10 rooms, a chapel, and a small playground. It was staffed with 10 sisters and no lay teachers either in 1964 or 1971; enrollment was 382 and 384 during those years.

(2) St. Bernardine, near the center of the city, was a girls' high school, which formerly operated an elementary division also. The enrollment, which was 676 in 1964, fell to 362 in 1971. The buildings were to be razed during the year and the site sold for commercial redevelopment. In September, 1971, there would, therefore, be no Catholic girls' high school in San Bernardino.

(3) St. Ann's, located in an upper middle-class area, had a large playground, a fine chapel, and airy, well-appointed classrooms. It was on a par with the public schools. Yet its enrollment dropped from 562 in 1964 to 384 in 1971.

(4) St. Anthony's located in a poorer area, had 30 pupils who qualified for Title I programs under ESEA in 1970-71; Holy Rosary, which had a small facility across the street from an enormous parish church, had an enrollment of 667 in 1961, which fell to 340 in 1971.

(5) The Aquinas High School was far inferior in equipment to the nearby San Gorgonio (public) High School. Since its 1970 enrollment of 290 dropped to 30 in 1971, it seemed as if this also were being phased out.

An observer could scarcely fail to note that, while the public schools of San Bernardino were substantially equal in quality in all areas, those operated by the Church depended upon the clientele they served and reflected their respective poverty or opulence. Thus, St. Ann's is wealthy and Guadalupe is very poor.

It was also evident that, with the exception of Guadalupe, which was virtually all Chicano, there was almost no minority ratio in the parochial schools. In the public sector, the neighborhood school was the governing norm, with pupils attending the nearest facility: 19% had Spanish surnames, 15.2% were Negro, and 64.9% were labelled "non-minority." Black pupils and those with Spanish surnames were found in all schools in greater or lesser ratios.

In 1964, the PTR in the Catholic Schools of San Bernardino was 38 compared to 27.6 in the public schools; in 1971, it was 29, compared to 25.3 in the latter.

Although we have no financial reports from these Catholic schools, we can make an estimate of their operational costs. Let us assume that the cost of lay teachers averaged $4,000 in 1964 and that it then cost $1,500 to maintain a religious; that these costs increased to $7,000 and $3,000 respectively in 1970-71; and that the non-teaching costs rose from $50 to $75 per pupil. Since there were 3,281 pupils with 69 religious and 18 lay teachers at the former date; and since these numbered 1,940, 37, and 30 respectively in 1971, we can make the following computations. The per-pupil cost for operation alone would have been $103 in 1964 and $241 in 1971.

In 1965-66, there were about 4,300 pupils in the private schools of the city, who constituted more than 10% of the total enrollment. In 1970-71, this number declined to 3,006, or 7.3%; and the Catholic ratio alone fell from 8% to 4.7%. With the closing of St. Bernardine, there remained only 1,600 in September, 1971—a ratio of 3.9%.

As we have already noted, the absorption of 1,300 pupils since 1965 made no impact whatever upon the public schools. What would happen should this gradual phaseout continue? And what would be the result should all Catholic schools close at once?

In 1965-66, there were only three public senior high schools, which enrolled 6,896 pupils in 219 classrooms. When the Cajon was completed in 1971, it enrolled 1,015 students, but the enrollment in the older schools declined by 701; there were 7,022 pupils in 286 teaching stations—an average of 24.5. If each had 30 desks, there were at least 1,573 not in use. Even if the entire St. Bernardine and St. Aquinas enrollments were to transfer to the public schools, the average number in each classroom would be only 25.9, where all would have the advantage of magnificent facilities. It would not be necessary to hire any additional teachers or construct any additional classrooms.

There were less that 1,600 pupils in all Catholic elementary schools in January, 1971. What could happen is indicated by the public Ramona-Allesandro, which had 1,127 pupils in 1966 but only 742 in 1971. It could, therefore, absorb the entire enrollment from Our Lady of Guadalupe, located across the street, and still have room for more.

In 1965-66, 42 public elementary schools had 738 classrooms and 21,853 pupils—an average of 29.6. In 1970-71, after replacing 4 schools, there were 21,633 in 938 classrooms—an average of 23. Since elementary classes may enroll up to 33, unused capacity exceeded 7,000. Should all Catholic pupils enter the public schools at once, the transfer would not be noticeable, for it would only increase the average class size to 25

Furthermore, the declining birth rate, first noticed in 1962-63, has now become decisive. In spite of increasing population, the elementary enrollment, which was 22,226 in 1965, fell to 21,623 in 1970-71.[a]

Finally, the $50,000 now allocated to Catholic schools under ESEA programs would go to the public schools. But of far greater importance is the fact that State ADA apportionments to the Unified School District would be increased by at least $750,000 and could reduce the levy on local real estate by that amount.

From the purely financial point of view, therefore, it would be highly beneficial to the taxpayers of San Bernardino if all pupils were to enter the public schools.

---

a.   Mr. James Wheeler has informed us that total 1972 enrollment is 3.5% below that of 1970-71 and that an additional 4% decline is projected for 1972-73.

T A B L E I

Real Estate Taxation in San Bernardino

	1960-61	1965-66	1970-71
Valuation	$132,252,240	$170,760,930	$200,655,128
Total Tax	10,823,523	16,512,582	25,526,973
Total Millage	8.1837	9.6648	12.2228
County	1.7950	2.2300	3.0024
City	1.3357	1.6278	1.6326
School	5.0530	5.7070	7.5878
School Property Tax	$6,682,706	$9,744,326	$15,229,724
Per Capita Tax	$118	$154	$239
Tax on $20,000 House[a]	409	483	611
School Tax on It	253	285	379
Per Capita School Tax	78	91	142

a. Since valuations are theoretically 25% of "market" value or appraisal, a $20,000 house would be taxed at $252.65 in 1960-61; $409.19 in 1965-66; and $611.14, in 1970-71.

TABLE II

The San Bernardino Schools

	1960-61	1965-66	1970-71
Enrollment	32,323	37,716	37,907
Value of Properties		$30,651,291	$52,507,826
Bonded Debt	$13,235,000	19,780,000	31,650,000
Classrooms	1,004	1,226	1,641
Elementary	567	738	938
Junior High	260	269	417
Senior High	177	219	286
Average Class Size[a]	32	30.7	23.2
Staff: Total	1,271	1,470	1,635
Teachers	1,185	1,364	1,498
Pupil-Teacher Ratio	27.4	27.6	25.3
Revenues: Total	$15,434,455	$20,536,589	$31,947,483
Federal	700,346	910,571	273,699
State	7,088,915	9,478,488	14,785,543
County	31,695	333,693	611,761
Local Tax	6,442,076	8,281,925	15,947,473
Other	1,177,423	1,531,912	329,007
Expended Budget	15,108,437	20,338,909	29,558,472
Teacher-Salaries	8,758,660	11,270,710	16,543,166
Lowest	4,350		6,600
Highest	9,000		14,604
Average	6,800	7,600	10,118
Pupil-ADA Cost, including Debt. Serv.	467	539	780

a. These statistics indicate maximum use of facilities in 1960-61; but great expansion of decade shows that ample room existed in 1970-71 for the absorption of thousands of additional students.

4.   **Bakersfield, California**

Bakersfield, seat of Kern County, is situated in a large and fertile valley, where fruits ripen in profusion, sustained by irrigation waters from the mountains looming in the East. Its population was 34,784 in 1950, 56,848 in 1960, and 67,955 in 1970; and the peripheral area has grown even more rapidly.

At the court house, Mr. Al Lorenzetti, Assistant to the Auditor-Controller, spent hours on end computing the composite tax rate for the county, city, and schools for the years 1960-61 and 1965-66 so that a comparison could be made with the current year. This data is reproduced in Table I.

The average 1970-71 millage for code areas within the city was about 13.3, of which 3.5 went to the county, 2.57 for city operation, 3.65 for the city elementary schools, 2.31 for high schools, and .6131 for junior colleges and peripheral educational programs. Those living in the code areas outside the city enjoy millages averaging about 10.5. Between 1960-61 and 1970-71, the millage for education increased from 4.77 to 5.96; the total property tax in the city for this purpose from $6,406,149 to $9,641,428; and the per-capita tax for this item from $112 to $157. The tax on a $20,000 home in Bakersfield was about $665 in 1970-71.

The Elementary School District

At the Bakersfield City School District Education Center, Mr. George C. Palmer, Associate Superintendent, and several of his assistants, were most helpful in providing the information set forth in Table II concerning the Elementary School District which includes the junior high schools and extends beyond the city limits. Real estate in its area is assessed at

$183,136,530, while that in the city itself is rated at $142,581,140.

While elementary enrollment between 1960 and 1970 dropped from 24,146 to 23,880 (Mr. Palmer stated that it had declined by 1,500 since 1967), two new schools were added, many improvements and additions were completed, and the value of the school plant expanded from $24,406,061 to $32,112,152. By adding 219,000 square feet, space has been provided for more than 3,000 additional pupils. Total employees increased from 1,273 to 1,925; and certificated instructional personnel from 821 to 1,086. The pupil-teacher ratio declined from 29.4 to 22, while per-pupil cost rose from $368 to $690; and the average salary of certificated employees rose from an average of $5,700 to $8,813. As in other California communities, the principal revenue came from state and local sources; the latter yielded $2,918,833 in 1960-61 and $5,320,340 in 1970-71; the state, which supplied the District with $5,350,109 in 1960-61, paid it $9,184,180 in 1970-71. In the meantime, total revenues grew from $8,274,380 to $15,501,403.

The Bakersfield operation differed from the San Bernardino in two respects: (1) federal funds, which totalled $967,228 in 1970-71, were much greater; and (2) a higher ratio of total income—about 60%—came from the state, compared to 48% in San Bernardino.

According to statistics supplied by the Chamber of Commerce, the Negro ratio in the city was 10 or 11%; but in the metro area, only 7.4%. Those with Spanish surnames, however, constituted about 19% throughout and probably accounted for the generous subsidies from ESEA and the State.

The Joint Union High School District

Our analysis of Bakersfield was complicated by the fact that there are two distinct systems: (1) the elementary, of which about 30% is beyond the city limits and includes the junior highs; and (2) the Joint Union High School District, which serves about three-fourths of Kern County and has a tax base more than four times that of the City itself.

Data concerning the high schools will be found in Table III. In 1960-61, there were 9, with an enrollment of 14,452. During the following ten years, while the population increased by 16%, four magnificent new schools were erected with a combined capacity exceeding 7,000; enrollment increased by 37%, to 19,609. Per-pupil cost rose from $565 to $868. Overall per-pupil cost was $826, including debt service: this is well below the national norm.

33

Although secondary classes may enroll 29 pupils and still qualify for ADA apportionment, the certificated staff-pupil ratio declined from 22.8 to 22 since 1960. In some schools, the ratio was as high as 25, in others as low as 15 or 17. It seems evident that the existing plant could absorb some two thousand students with few or no additional instructors.

Subsidiary Programs

There was no provision for shared or released time in Bakersfield or Kern County.

One Roman Catholic (Guadalupe) and four public elementary schools qualified for allocations under Title I of ESEA. Guadalupe received $41,850 during 1970-71; the others $875,129. Under Title II, there was an allocation of $22,647.89, of which something over $20,000 went to public and the remainder to the Roman Catholic schools, except for $86, allocated to St. Johns Lutheran.

The Catholic Schools

(1) Christ the King is a 4-grade school in the County, but in the Bakersfield elementary school district. Its facilities are minimal.

(2) Guadalupe, with an almost totally Mexican-American enrollment, was equipped with a chapel, medical center, and storage facility. Although more than $42,000 of ESEA money was expended there in 1970-71, its enrollment fell to 265 from a peak of 475 in 1964.

(3) Our Lady of Perpetual Help was the Catholic elementary showplace. Even though it had a large playground and many airy classrooms, its enrollment of 417 in 1964 fell to 241 in 1971.

(4) St. Joseph's Church has operated the St. Lawrence School, 5 miles away, for years. Pastor Antonio Gonzales stated that his congregation consists of more than 2,000 members; that the school, with a capacity of 550, had 422 pupils in 1964, but only 180 in 1970-71. The tuition was $200 for the children of one family, and the congregation had been subsidizing the school with $40,000 a year. He intimated that the basic problem was not money, but the refusal of parents to enroll their children; and for this reason the school would be closed in June, 1971. About 40 of the pupils would transfer to other Catholic schools, while the remainder would enter the public system.

(5) Garces Memorial School presented a somewhat aging but still opulent appearance. In 1964, it had 550 students: in 1971, only 360. There was a chapel, a spacious playground, and a large concrete stadium.

Pastor Gonzales stated that it had been established by the Christian Brothers (of Ireland), but is now operated as a diocesan secondary, the only one remaining in the area. Tuition was $375; few sisters were available; and there were no longer any brothers. Drives for parish subsidies had met with little success; and only 115 applications for fall matriculation had been received.

(6) The St. Francis school was very large, had an ample playground, beautiful lawns, a good auditorium, and 15 spacious, well-appointed classrooms, which compared favorably with those in the public system. The parish church, located a few blocks away, was also in the midst of a median, well-kept neighborhood.

However, the story of St. Francis is another tragedy; in 1964, there were 680 pupils, with a staff of 11 religious and 6 laymen; in 1971, there were 317, with 6 religious and 6 lay teachers. Since per-pupil costs should not exceed $175 and since the school is operated by a wealthy parish, we can only assume that parents have transferred their children for reasons other than economic to the public schools. It is not likely that either the church or the school was burdened by any debt. The fact is that enrollment continued to rise until 1965; and the decline and disillusionment following that date have been, and continue to be, factors of the highest significance.

Summary

In 1964-65, the private, elementary schools of Bakersfield enrolled 10% of the total; 90% of these were in Catholic schools. The ratio fell to 5.3% in 1970-71, of whom 22% were Protestant. After St. Lawrence closed, not more than 3.2% were in Catholic institutions.

Although Protestant schools in Bakersfield enrolled only about 420 pupils—less than 1.5% of the total—they were in excellent condition and gave every indication of viability and expansion. Of these, the Bakersfield Academy with 345 students and operated by the Seventh-Day Adventists, is easily the most important.

The decline of private education in Bakersfield was, therefore, confined to the Catholic schools, which enrolled 2,611 in 1964 and only 1,440 in 1971--a loss of 41%. The resulting transfers were absorbed without the slightest difficulty; as Mr. Palmer pointed out, should 1,500 more occur on the elementary level alone, it would only restore the enrollment of 1967 and there would still be ample room. As already noted, the high schools could absorb up to 2,000 more students in existing facilities.

Furthermore, while absorbing more than 1,000 Catholic transfers, the public elementary schools declined in enrollment by 266, during a period in which $5 million was spent for additional space sufficient to care for 3,000 pupils.

Furthermore, should all Catholic schools close, the ESEA funds now allocated to them would accrue to the public sector; and the State appropriations would be increased by $600,000—sufficient to finance the construction and operation of a new school with 50 classrooms serving 1,200 pupils. However, since the evidence indicates that this would not be necessary, the State subsidy could be utilized to reduce the millage for both elementary and secondary education.

T A B L E I

Bakersfield and Kern County Taxation

	1960-61	*1965-66*	*1970-71*
Assessed Value of County			$894,173,220
County Tax	$15,234,586	$19,905,079	31,360,063
Bakersfield Assessment			142,581,140
City Tax: Total			19,010,398
For El. Schls.	3,619,345	4,803,867	6,346,804
For High Schls.	2,785,800	2,882,300	3,293,624
Per-Capita for All Schools	112	126	157

TABLE II

Bakersfield Elementary Schools

Item	1960-61	1965-66	1970-71
No. of Schools	34	35	36
Enrollment	24,146	24,338	23,880
Certificated Staff	821	900	1,086
Median Salary	$5,700	$7,200	$8,813
Pupil-Staff Ratio	29.4	27	22
Assessments	$133,583,812	$165,055,880	$183,136,530
Value of School Plant	24,406,061	25,795,788	32,112,152
Sq. Ft. Added: Total	1,564,955	1,572,879	1,783,260
In Year	136,067	17,204	126,730
Value of Improvements	$2,152,117	$413,205	$2,897,959
Bonded Debt	3,976,000	1,086,000	2,700,000
Total School Revenue	8,274,380	10,788,803	15,501,423
Federal	5,437	901,337	967,228
State	5,350,109	5,409,466	9,184,180
County		141,255	8,111
Local Property	2,918,833	4,331,351	5,320,341
Per-Pupil ADA Cost	368	456	690
To State	237	267	389
To Local Taxpayers	130	182	237
Expenditures: Total	8,983,557	11,106,761	16,489,875
Administration	286,927	292,117	497,875
Instruction	5,824,669	7,940,347	12,881,457
Operation-Maintenance	1,066,136	1,226,797	1,567,763
Capital Outlay	1,184,803	872,198	481,678
Other	621,022	775,302	1,061,102

37

TABLE III

Kern County Joint Union High School District

Item	1960-61	1965-66	1970-71
Enrollment	14,452	18,355	19,609
Schools	9	11	13
Capacity			22,500
District Assessment	$489,136,520	$537,780,840	$651,706,140
Tax Levied for Schools	9,978,385	9,303,512	15,054,408
Total Schools Revenues		12,188,917	20,401,189
Federal		356,680	717,805
State		3,489,241	5,924,797
County		152,853	133,822
Local Property Tax		8,190,143	13,624,665
Expenditures: Total		12,218,223	20,054,616
Certificated Salaries		7,190,186	12,271,289
Operational		4,617,277	7,202,375
Capital Outlay		410,760	580,952
Bonded Debt	5,030,000	4,655,000	7,700,000
Certificated Personnel	607	766	849
Salaries:			
Low			$7,017
High			14,634
Pupil-Staff Ratio	22.8	22.5	22
Per-Pupil Cost	$566	$626	$868
Combined El.			
and Sec. Per-Pupil Cost	437	538	826

5.   Albuquerque, New Mexico

The Historical Background

Albuquerque was chosen for analysis because its school enrollment increased 265% in 20 years; and because it absorbed, during the Sixties, more than half of a large Catholic enrollment.

Named after a Spanish nobleman and redolent of its Mexican heritage, Albuquerque lies astride a plateau near the Continental Divide. Since it became a part of the United States only after the war with Mexico in 1846-48, it is not surprising that Spanish names are ubiquitous and that Oldtown, dominated by the Church of St. Felipe de Neri, built in 1735, is typical of the old culture. The 1970 census does not identify the Chicanos; but that of 1960 lists 43,790 persons with Spanish surnames in a population of 201,189. Father Albert Schneider stated that, in four of his parish schools, 90% of the pupils were Hispanic.

As late as 1900, the city had only 6,238 people; for several decades thereafter, it grew very slowly, having only 11,020 in 1910, 15,157 in 1920, 26,570 in 1930, and 35,444 in 1940. Throughout this period, the community remained predominantly Mexican-American, with the Catholic Church a dominating social and religious force.

During and following WW II, however, Americans discovered Albuquerque; and the city grew from 96,815 in 1950 to 242,411 in 1970, with a metropolitan population of 316,000. In 1971, there were 21 Catholic parishes in the bustling and burgeoning city; however, the telephone directory listed well over two hundred other churches, many of which, judging by their external appearance, were blessed with affluent congregations. Interesting also were the many Protestant churches (*iglesias*) in Mexican neighborhoods.

Education in Albuquerque

Table I traces the evolution of school enrollments. Between 1950 and 1971, the public expanded from 23,387 to 84,691. In 1910, when about 2,000 pupils were receiving instruction, 648 were in three Catholic schools, about 30% of the total. In 1950, they enrolled 3,390, but the ratio had fallen to 12.6%. In 1961, they reached their peak with 9,045 pupils, 13.7% of the total school population. Then began a gradual shrinkage, not only in ratio but also in actual attendance: to 8,676, or 10.4%, in 1965; 7,184, or 8.3%, in 1968; and to 4,395, or 4.9%, in October, 1971.

We should note that School District No. 12 embraces all of Bernalillo County and a portion of Sandoval, with a combined population of nearly 350,000. The Catholic schools covered in our survey are in the same area, as are seven or eight other private institutions, which, according to the United States Office of Education, enrolled 1,450 in 1965 and 1,889 in 1968.[a]

Table I reflects the increased birth rate following WW II, which, added to an increase in population of 145,000 or 150%, in 20 years, augmented public school enrollment alone by 61,305. Since the Catholic fell by 4,650 during the decade following 1961, we may assume that this fact accounted for about 8% of the increase.

During its halcyon period of 1961-65, the Catholic educational system consisted of 14 elementary and 4 high schools with an enrollment averaging 9,000. However, after 1968, St. Anne's elementary, as well as St. Mary's and Lourde's secondaries were closed. After 1969, St. Vincent's Academy, Holy Family, Immaculate Conception, San Jose, and Sacred Heart all followed suit. In 1969, the beautiful Holy Rosary school, with extensive playgrounds and other facilities, was built in an affluent west-side suburb. But in June, 1971, this also ceased operation.

In the fall of 1971, only nine Catholic elementaries remained; and there was only one high school—the excellent Pius X; but even this had a reduced enrollment. Whereas in 1965, there were four secondaries with an enrollment of 1,712, in 1971, there was only one junior and one senior high with a combined enrollment of 853. Several of the schools still operating, such as San Felipe, St. Francis, St. Charles, St. Therese, and Holy

---

a.   Cf. the *Nonpublic School Directory* of 1965-66 and 1968-69.

Ghost, had become quite or very old and must be considered obsolete. The oldest, San Felipe, had only 325 pupils compared to 615 in 1964.

A Near-Miracle of Economy and Achievement

Tables IV and V contain comprehensive data on receipts and expenditures in the public schools for 1959-60, 1966-67, and 1971-72. Since the system had accepted more than 30,000 additional pupils during the Fifties and almost as many more in the Sixties, we would naturally expect that enormous expenditures, reflected in heavy per-pupil costs, must have resulted. We find, however, that this is not the case. The Administration Building of the Board of Education has been expanded again and again since 1953 to meet the growing demands of the system it operates.

There are now 78 elementaries as well as 9 senior, and 22 junior highs in the public school system. Almost all have modern and superior facilities.

This excellent plant has been completed without heavy taxation. Costs have, of course, risen; but they have been and are much less than in many cities where there has been no expansion and where few transfers from private to public schools have occurred. In 1959-60, the overall per-pupil operational cost was $325; this rose to $433 in 1966-67 and to $632 in 1971-72. (This contrasts with an average of $375 in 1960 and $858 in 1971 nationally.) However, still more remarkable is the fact that when we add the cost of debt-service, the totals are only $370 for 1959-60, $504 for 1966-67, and $703 for 1971-72. And even when we add the federally financed programs, the total rises only to $743.

In older states, many of the schools may be from 60 to 100 years old; they are obsolete, inadequate, and often without recreational facilities. As a result, there may be as much need for replacement as there is for construction in expanding cities like Albuquerque; and the cost of razing old buildings, acquiring larger sites, and building modern schools may well be much greater than that of acquiring land and constructing new plants for the first time in burgeoning cities.

Personnel and Salaries

We should also remember that thousands of qualified teachers are fleeing the old and dilapidated metropoli and seeking employment in the growing West. We find therefore that current salaries in Albuquerque ranged only from $6,100, to $12,648, and averaged about $8,500—compared to $12,250 in Detroit. There were dozens or even hundreds of applications for every vacancy that arose; and the PTR, which remained constant at about 27.5, was a significant factor in holding down per-pupil costs. Whatever the reasons may be, it is certain that Albuquerque has constructed a remarkably superior educational plant in twenty years while keeping the cost of schooling at 75% of the national norm.

Bonds and Budgets

There is another factor in the financial situation which holds down the long-term cost of expansion in Albuquerque: the requirement that all school bonds be amortized in five years. In 1960, unpaid balances on outstanding bonds totalled $10,177,146; in 1966-67, $15,635,000; and in the fall of 1971, $22,170,000. However, at the latter date, the system had $12,644,183 of unspent cash on hand, while improvements and new construction were proceeding as rapidly as possible.

In 1971-72, the operational budget was $53,655,292; and the cost of debt service, $5,895,445. Less than 10% of the total cost, therefore, went into expanded facilities, for which outstanding bonds required interest payments of $925,000.

Financing the Schools

An examination of Table II reveals some significant facts: first, that the total tax in Bernalillo County in 1970 was $37,701,903, which was $118 per capita, or $472 for a family of four. Since assessments are one-third of appraisals, the levy on a $20,000 house, at 74.11 mills was $470 and on one appraised at $30,000, $705: less than one-half that in Milwaukee.

The total collected for school operation was only $1,073,200 in 1959-60, $1,918,947 in 1966-67, and $6,811,271 in 1971-72. However, at the latter date, the County supplied a total of $10,378,009 to the schools, the difference being for debt service.

We find, therefore, an important difference between school financing in New Mexico and that in most other states, where the local property levy pays from 50 to 60% of school costs, or even more; but in Bernalillo County this supplied only about 6% in 1959-60, 5% in 1966-67, and 13% in 1971-72.

This has been possible because of the generous State contributions. In 1959-60, these totalled $13,543,514 for School District No. 12, or 75% of costs totalling $17,883,410; in 1971-72, $41,415,699 of a budget totalling $57,856,740, or 70%, came from the same source. This was $489 out of the $703 expended for each pupil.

The State was able to subsidize education so generously because (1) there is a state property tax, which yielded nearly $5 million in Bernalillo County; (2) because the State has permanent investments which produced about $20 million in 1970; and (3) because it had an income in that year of about $18 million from land and mineral leases. Of all this income, 80% is earmarked for education. There were also substantial revenues from gross receipts and compensatory taxes, as well as from income and other levies. Total State income in 1969-70 was $234,594,000, of which $33,455,000 was earmarked specifically for schools. In 1970-71, the budget allocated $136,745,000—more than half of the total—for elementary and secondary education: this averaged $457 for each of 299,000 pupils so enrolled.

We should note also that the federal government, in addition to ESEA programs, made significant direct contributions to the cost of public education in New Mexico under PL 874, 864, and other subsidies. These totalled $3,401,295 in 1971-72 in Albuquerque alone—an amount approximately equal to one-half of the funds derived from local property taxation for current operation.

Subsidiary Programs

(1) Twenty-five public and five Catholic schools participated during 1970-71 in Title I ESEA programs, which involved 16,166 pupils in the former and 1,112 in the latter at a total cost of $1,776,865, of which approximately $120,000 went for projects to benefit parochial pupils.

(2) Under Title II of ESEA, $93,981 was allocated to the public schools and a proportional sum for the Catholic.

(3) Lunch reimbursement from the USDA totalled $1,267,617 in the 1970-71 year in the public schools. It was probably proportional in the parochial.

(4) There was no released- or shared-time program in School District No. 12.

(5) The State reimbursed the public schools for the full cost of transportation, which totalled $1,480,826 in 1970-71, and which served 25,000 or 26,000 pupils. There was no subsidized bus service for pupils attending nonpublic schools.

(6) The State supplied textbooks to all schools, public and private; and did so for the pupils in District No. 12 in 1970-71 at a cost of $708,052.

At the diocesan center we interviewed Father Albert A. Schneider, Director of Catholic Elementary and Secondary Schools in the Santa Fe Diocese, who is the pastor also of the St. Francis Xavier Church and

School in Albuquerque. We were surprised to find him in civilian attire, and were much impressed with his graciousness and candor. We marvelled here, as elsewhere, that a large system could operate with an administrative staff consisting of two or three persons. At the Board of Education, there must have been 150 or 200 employees.

Father Schneider stated that in a typical elementary school, tuition is $50 a year for the first pupil from a family, and $10 for additional children, no matter how many; and that per-pupil costs range from $150 to $300, depending on the proportion of lay teachers, the area in which the school is located, and the amount of debt. He explained that the budget at St. Francis was $35,000; that the school had 230 pupils and 8 teachers, of whom half were sisters, and whose salaries were $1,500 in addition to fringe benefits. Salaries of lay teachers averaged $5,000. The school paid $2,400 a year for medical insurance, but there was neither tenure nor a retirement program. Since the school had no debt and since the pastor himself did much of the repair and maintenance work, the per-pupil cost was held at about $150.

Father Schneider estimated tuition at Pius X at $300 and per-pupil cost at $700; lay teachers there received about 80% of the salary schedules prevalent in the public schools. He stated that the parishes of the city subsidized this high school according to an established formula; that the facility had an outstanding debt of $600,000; and that, in addition to tuition, it required revenues of about $250,000 or $300,000 a year.

He confirmed that there was no released- or shared-time program; and that private schools had to supply their own transportation. He stated also that most parishes did not participate in the subsidized lunch programs; but that their schools shared proportionately with the public in Title I and II ESEA programs. He stated also that the state supplies each parochial pupil annually with textbooks costing $8.00. Since there were 4,631 parochial pupils in 1970-71, this subsidy totalled $37,000.

We asked Father Schneider why it was that Catholic schools expanded so rapidly between 1950 and 1961, and why they had been losing enrollment during recent years. This, he observed, was a "dangerous" question; but he considered the principal cause an accumulation of financial factors.

Nevertheless, he ventured, there were other important reasons. For example, the Ecumenical Council of 1962-65 caused a great many doubts among the Catholic clergy as well as the laymen concerning Church authority and the ultimate source of faith. At one time, only dissident laymen voiced objections or criticism; but since 1965, many of the priests and the religious have done the same, and those with the "loudest mouths" have received the widest hearing.

There is, therefore, a widespread ferment and questioning throughout all the segments of the Church. Laymen, particularly, are seriously questioning the old priorities. Some seem to think that there is no future any longer to consider.

What are these priorities?

The things that are important in life and the Church. As long ago as 1965, many Catholic laymen shouted with glee at the prospect of closing the parochial schools; but some of them, seeing what is going on in the public, would like to return their children to the religious instruction of the Church. But there are other priorities: many would rather spend their money on what is called the Good Life than on a Christian education.

How generously do Catholics contribute to the Church and for its schools?

According to Father Schneider, one fact should be clearly understood: it is a complete myth that Catholics contribute generously to the Church or for religious education. As an average, parishioners do not give more than 1% of their income for parochial education; and their total contributions do not exceed 1.5%. In a typical parish with one thousand families, we can expect 400 or 500 to give 3% regularly; another 300 or so will give sporadically, about 1 or 1.5%; the other 30% give nothing at all.

Even if they attend Mass regularly and go to confession?

Even if they do that.

Summary and Conclusions

As we left, the thought occurred that by transferring more than 4,500 of their children to the public schools, Catholic laymen had relieved themselves of financial burdens in Albuquerque totalling at least $1,000,000; and that, since the per-capita property tax for schools rose only to $38.43 in 1970, it was highly unlikely that more than 5% of this, or $1.60, could be charged to the cost of transferring Catholic children to the public schools. Let us assume that a typical Catholic family had two children in a parish school and a son at St. Pius: the cost of their education, paid by Catholic laymen, would be at least $1,000. By transferring these children, among 4,500 others to the public schools, this family pays an additional $10.00 a year in property tax on a $20,000 house.

Our investigation in Albuquerque prompted the following observations:

(1) Should every private school in the area close, only 45 pupils would be added to the average public; and each teacher and classroom would have an increased load slightly in excess of one pupil.

(2) Should the population remain static, the falling birth-rate will cause enrollment to decline. Should the city continue to grow at the rate of the

last twenty years, the problem of school enrollment will be met exactly as it has been during the past.

(3) Since the state pays the school district more than $450 for every pupil enrolled, the absorption of transfers could actually be accomplished with profit to the District.

(4) The Albuquerque system had more than $12 million cash on hand in 1971, earmarked for expansion and improvements.

(5) Should the remaining Catholic schools close without warning, the impact upon the public would scarcely create a ripple in the community.

(6) Since the voters have approved bond issues in the past, there is no doubt that, should Catholic closures continue, they will favor them in the future.

(7) Since all bonds must be amortized in five years, the educational plant of Bernalillo County will be free of debt in 1976 and costs will be reduced, unless, of course, more issues become necessary.

It is therefore incontrovertible that a rapidly growing community can, without oppressive taxation or undue cost, provide excellent schools, not only for a quadrupled population in a space of twenty years, but can do so without undue cost. It can also accept a heavy influx from private schools without the slightest disruption or difficulty.

TABLE I

Public and Private School Enrollment in Albuquerque

Year	Population	Public	Catholic	% Cath.	Other Private
1910	11,020		648		
1920	15,157		573		
1930	26,570		1,425		
1940	35,449		1,601		
1950	96,815	23,386	3,390	12.6	
1955		36,532	6,409	14.9	
1961	201,189	56,789	9,045	13.7	
1964		72,047	8,688	10.7	
1965		74,677	8,678	10.4	1,450[a]
1968		78,889	7,184	8.3	1,889[a]
1970	242,411	83,214	4,621	5.3	1,340[b]
1971-72		84,691	4,395	4.9	

a. These totals from the Office of Education in Washington.
b. This total is from the State Superintendent of Public Instruction and may not be complete.

TABLE II

Tax Levy in Bernalillo County in 1970

Category	
Total General Levy	$29,995,551.62
City	11,523,107.90
County	3,083,384.14
State	4,999,751.38
Schools	10,378,008.62
Special Levies	7,706,351.08
Total Levy	37,701,902.70
School Tax in City of Albuquerque	8,184,622.34
Assessed Valuation at 33% of Appraisal	
City	$496,302,275
County	612,263,030
School District No. 12	641,272,049
Per-Capita Property Tax	$118
For Schools	33.82
Ratio of School Tax to Total Tax	22.9%

TABLE III

Expenditures in School District No. 12

Category	1959-60	1966-67	1971-72
Administration	$527,323	$698,387	$1,291,100
Instruction	10,588,599	26,689,075	37,312,952
Direct Charge	1,717,102	1,015,644	5,327,000
Capital Outlay		679,500	387,700
Other	4,501,794	4,179,907	9,336,540
Total Operational	$17,334,818	$33,262,513	$53,655,292
Special Projects			
Building Fund		1,050,720	12,644,183
Debt Service	2,342,562	5,485,000	5,895,445
Federal		5,394,575	3,375,244
Total	19,677,380	45,192,808	75,570,164
Operational and			
Debt Service	$19,677,380	$38,657,088	$59,550,737
Per-Pupil Cost			
Operational	$325	$433	$632
Total	370	504	703
Including ESEA			743

TABLE IV

Receipts of School District No. 12

Operational Source	1959-60	1966-67	1970-71
Local: Total	$1,265,225	$2,736,967	$8,205,271
Property Tax	1,073,200	1,918,947	6,811,271
Miscellaneous	189,025	818,020	1,394,000
State	13,543,514	27,380,149	41,415,699
Federal	732,119	2,420,397	3,401,295
Total Operational	$15,540,858	32,537,513	53,022,265
Cash Balance	4,110,570	625,000	1,488,035
Resources	19,651,418	33,262,531	54,510,300
Non-Operational			
Local:			
Debt Service	2,342,562	5,394,575	5,834,475
Building Fund		5,400,000	292,494
Other		50,000	
Federal ESEA			3,260,225
Cash Balance		250,720	12,663,708
Building Fund		85,000	12,226,889
Debt Service			321,800
Federal Budget		750,000	115,019
Operational Fund and			
Debt Service	$17,833,420	$37,932,088	$58,856,740

TABLE V

General Statistics Relating to District No. 12

Item	1959-60	1966	Oct. 4, 1971
No. of Schools		100	109
Total Enrollment	55,750	76,696	84,956
Staff	2,280	3,059	3,643
Classroom Teachers	2,164	2,772	3,097
Pupil-Teacher Ratio	25.7	27.6	27.4
Pupil-Staff Ratio	24.4	24.4	23.3
Teacher Salaries			
Minimum	$4,400	$5,200	$6,100
Maximum	7,950	10,766	12,648
Bonds Outstanding	$10,177,146	$15,635,000	$22,170,000
Annual Interest	318,887	459,573	925,444
Sinking Fund	2,792,090	4,935,000	4,970,000

6.   Scottsdale, Arizona

A Rapidly Growing Community

Scottsdale, Arizona, was chosen for a brief analysis, not because of any transfer of private pupils to the public schools, but because it is an unusually affluent community with little industry and because its school system has perhaps grown more rapidly than any other in the United States. As late as 1950, its population was only 2,032; in 1960, 10,026; in 1970, 67,026.

We should note, however, that its school districts (Elementary No. 48 and High School No. 212) include a portion of Phoenix, which had a population of 105,000 in 1960 and 582,000 in 1970. In 1950, the Scottsdale school system enrolled 2,114 pupils; 6,857 in 1955-56; 15,259 in 1960-61; 24,739 in 1965-66; and 28,409 in 1970. In 1971, however, this declined to 28,323. Property assessments in the city were $48,324,029 in 1960 and $89,230,470 in the District. In 1970-71, these had increased to $103,143,617 and $167,126,869 respectively.

Needless to say, in order to absorb more than 26,000 pupils a system which expanded by 1,300% in 20 years would necessarily be forced to invest large sums in educational plant, especially in a community like Scottsdale, where only the best would be acceptable. There were 29 bond issues, totalling $37,197,000, all approved between 1950 and 1970. For this investment, Scottsdale boasted four magnificent high schools with an enrollment of 8,943 and 19 elementaries with 19,400 pupils in May, 1971. Only two of the schools antedate 1955.

The salaries of teachers in Scottsdale have been rising steadily over the years and we believe they are now at least comparable to the national norm. The minimum rose from $6,070 in 1969-70 to $6,650 in 1971-72; and the maximum from $14,234 to $15,594. Pupil-teacher ratio, based on total enrollment, stood at 27.7 in 1970-71. Based on ADA, it would have been about 25.

The Tax-Base

It should be noted that school districts as affluent as Scottsdale receive virtually no subsidy from the federal government; and that State allocations are minimal. There is however, a substantial County School Fund, which derives from a variety of sources. Nevertheless, the real estate tax has been and continues to be the principal source of revenue. In 1960, this supplied $4,572,625, or 89%, of a budget totalling $5,124,535; in 1965, in spite of increasing State aid, it furnished $8,311,233, or 64.4%, of $12,909,156. In 1970-71, the State supplied $6,330,000, or 24%; $5,882,442, or 23% came from the County; and $12,489,078, or 49.1% from the local property tax. Thus, 73% of school revenues came from local sources.

Our attention here focuses upon a single issue: at what cost to the local taxpayers can such a community educate a school enrollment which increased by 1,110 per cent in 15 years in the finest educational plant that present-day techniques can devise?

The answer is found in Table II, III, and IV. In 1956-57, the Scottsdale school tax totalled $1,187,923, which, at 49.7 mills on an assessment set at 18% of appraisal, called for a levy of $268 on a $30,000 home. This grew to $345 in 1961-62, $393 in 1967-68, and $419 in 1971-72. As any one versed in property taxation will recognize, these sums are less than those exacted in a number of old American cities.

Per-pupil costs have, of course, increased: for operation, these were $301 in 1959-60, $432 in 1964-65, and $731 in 1970-71, compared to a national norm of $375, $532, and $858. Even when we add the extraordinarily heavy expense for new construction, costs totalled only $419, $546, and $841 for these years. In 1959-60, debt service added $74, or 25%, to per-pupil costs; in 1965-66, $114, or 29%. Then, however, as enrollment levelled off, the need for new construction diminished; and in 1970-71, the debt service required only $110, or 15% of the total budget.

It would seem, therefore, that public school costs are determined only to a minor degree by the necessity for expansion; and that heavy property taxation is caused primarily by a large ratio of exempt property. It seems also that the highest expenditures are necessary in old, decaying, and shrinking cities, where very old facilities must be replaced and where social or racial problems of great magnitude confront the educators and the community. Under such circumstances, it is difficult to retain competent personnel and they must be paid the highest salaries; and many peripheral and expensive programs must be undertaken. This is the reason why per-pupil costs in New York, Detroit, Philadelphia, and Milwaukee are extremely high; and why cities like Albuquerque and Scottsdale can construct new and even opulent plants and educate rapidly growing enrollments at far less than the national average.

At all events, it is incontrovertible that the absorption or non-absorption of parochial and other private enrollees plays so small a role in the overall educational costs of cities like Scottsdale that it can simply be ignored.

TABLE I

Scottsdale School Enrollment

Year	Scottsdale Population	Phoenix Population	Scottsdale District Enrollment
1940		65,000	
1950-51	2,032	105,000	2,114
1955-56			6,857
1960-61	10,026	439,000	15,289
1965-66			24,739
1969-70			28,515
1970-71	67,025	582,000	28,409
1971-72	80,000[a]	602,000[a]	28,343

TABLE II

Assessments and Taxation in the School District

Year	In Scottsdale	In District	School Tax	On $30,000 House
1955-56		$17,754,988		
1956-57		23,841,518	$1,187,923	$268
1960-61		73,974,516	4,572,625	334
1961-62	$48,324,049	89,230,470	6,183,671	374
1965-66	72,864,228	130,270,111	8,311,233	345
1967-68	82,440,045	143,848,897	11,410,572	430
1970-71	93,802,802	157,817,000	12,489,078	393
1971-72	103,143,617	167,126,869	13,070,045	419

a.   Estimated.

TABLE III

Expenditures in the School Districts

Item	1959-60	1964-65	1970-71
Administration	$191,834	$385,740	$1,572,124
Instruction	2,759,124	$7,902,596	14,210,408
Capital Outlay	608,615	497,327	1,070,953
Other	734,362	1,946,271	3,914,537
Operation	$4,293,935	$10,731,934	$20,768,022
Debt Service	830,600	2,177,222	3,113,500
Total	$5,124,535	$12,909,156	$23,881,522
Per-Pupil Cost			
Operational	$301	$432	$731
Total	419	546	841
National Norm	375	532	858
No. of Classroom Teachers			1,024
Pupil-Teacher Ratio			27.7

Salary:	1969-70	1970-71	1971-72
Minimum	$6,070	$6,350	$6,650
Maximum	14,234	14,891	15,594
Average	10,152	10,620	11,122

TABLE IV

Revenues of the Scottsdale School System, 1970-71

Source	El. No. 48	H.S. No. 212	Total	%
Cash Balance	$288,040	$137,483	$425,523	
Co. School Fund	3,923,128	1,959,316	5,882,448	23.1
Other Co. Aid	65,158	37,216	102,370	
State Aid	3,247,162	2,845,185	6,092,347	24.0
Federal Aid	50,000	175,000	225,000	
Miscellaneous	111,000	86,000	197,000	
Total Non-Tax	$7,684,488	$5,240,200	$12,924,688	
Local Tax			12,489,078	49.1
Total			$25,413,766	
Bonds Issued 1950-1970			37,197,000	
Outstanding 6-30-'71			20,072,000	

7. Boise, Idaho

Boise, Idaho, was chosen for analysis precisely because it differs from our great cities and most of those covered in this survey, yet presents a significant aspect of American life. It is virtually an all-white community with a 1970 population of 73,330.[a] Enrollment in its Independent School District—which extended beyond the city limits [b]— was 19,034 in 1960-61, 20,528 in 1965-66, and 22,600 in 1970-71, the increase being due to a higher secondary registration. Until 1969-70, Catholic enrollment, which comprised about 7 or 8% of the total, virtually kept pace with the public. Boise, therefore, reflects the experience of a well-ordered and prosperous community where the educational plant required little expansion either because of transfers or a growing population. The evolution of the tax rates, especially in respect to school costs, should therefore be highly significant.

The Public Schools and Their Financing

The Boise school system had 29 elementary, six junior, and three senior high schools. On June 30, 1970, they were insured for $30 million and carried a bonded debt of $11,262,000, including an unspent issue of $5 million approved in 1968. The oldest building, erected in 1905, was still well kept; the entire plant is constantly being updated and embellished with improvements. The newest school was completed in 1965; another will be ready for use in 1973.

---

a.   This was 34,481 in 1960, the increase being due almost entirely to annexations. The population of Ada County was 93,450 in 1960 and 109,373 in 1970.
b.   In 1969-70, assessments on city real estate were $77,908,805, while those in the school district were $101,270,002.

In 1960-61, the Boise millage was 13.6006, of which 4.7 was for schools; in 1970, it was 16.533, of which 7.464 was for this purpose, an increase of nearly 60%. Since the taxable assessment was theoretically 16.3% of true appraisal, the ad valorem tax on a $20,000 house increased from $443 to $539, of which $153 and $243 respectively was the school levy. Since little new school construction has been necessary except for replacement or modernization, the outstanding debt is low. Furthermore, since teacher salaries in 1970-71 ranged only from $6,200 to $10,726,[a] it is not surprising that per-pupil costs have been kept and remain lower than in most communities: $352.05 in 1961-62; $465.70 in 1965-66; and $699.80 under the budget for 1970-71, including all capital outlay, debt service, and federal programs.

In Idaho, as elsewhere, the state has been increasing its contributions to educational costs. In the Boise District, the state supplied 28% of the revenues, totalling $6,471,536 in 1961-62; in 1965-66, 34.6% of revenues totalling $9,185,063. For 1970-71, when expenditures rose to $15,392,412, the state contributed $5,232,515, or 34%.

The property tax, however, has increased even more rapidly: from $3,234,065 in 1960-61 to $8,583,259 in 1970-71. This means that the per-capita school levy rose in ten years from $42.60 to $101—an increase of 137%.

Subsidiary Programs

The Boise Independent School District received $233,665 under various ESEA programs in 1969-70. And, since the Catholic schools enrolled 7% of all pupils, they probably received at least $16,000.[b] According to information supplied by the State Superintendent of Public Instruction and covering 1969-70, federal contributions in the state were $1,211,344 to the lunch program and $3,685,642 under ESEA—a total of $4,896,986. Since public school enrollment was 182,333 and Catholic about 4,400 in 1970-71, about $125,000 of this probably went to the latter.

Mr. Hicks, in the Office of the State Superintendent, declared that there was no shared-time program in operation in the state and no released time except in the areas of Pocatello and Idaho Falls, where regular provision for religious instruction during class hours was in general use for the benefit of Mormon and Catholic pupils. Textbooks, purchased with public

---

a.   We learned that the Boise Board of Education received forty or fifty applications for every vacancy.
b.   Other private schools in Boise did not participate in such programs.

funds, could be loaned to parochial schools at the discretion of local school boards. An enabling act, passed by the legislature in 1970, designed to make bus service available for parochial pupils, was declared unconstitutional by the State Supreme Court on September 2, 1971.

Protestant Parochials

The Bible Missionary Church operated a school with a modern plant serving 60 pupils in 1971. Mr. Larry Roberts, principal, stated that children of all faiths were welcome; that there were three uncertified teachers, whose salaries averaged about $2,500; that tuition was $15 a month; and that deficits were covered by church subsidies and donations from individuals. He added that enrollment and facilities would be expanded for the following year. Per-pupil costs were about $200.

The Boise Valley Elementary School, a Seventh-Day Adventist institution, was housed in an impressive structure; there were four teachers, 85-90 pupils, a fine gymnasium, and four classrooms. Tuition was $35 a month; salaries averaged about $7,000, in addition to allowances for transportation and housing. The Conference paid 20% of teacher salaries and benefits, and the local church, which made up any remaining deficit, had also financed the building with the help of a 20% subsidy from the central body. Per-pupil costs were estimated at $360.

The Catholic Schools

Enrollment in the Catholic schools increased from 1,420 in 1961 to 1,659 in 1965. For several years, they remained at the same level, but declined to 1,465 in 1970-71. We should note also that in 1961 there were 38 religious and 9 lay teachers; in 1971, these numbered 27 and 32 respectively.

The four elementary parish schools compared favorably in equipment with the public; and Bishop Kelly High School, built in 1964-65, had an enrollment of 534 in 1969, but only 470 in 1971. In his office there, we interviewed the Reverend John Francis Donohue, diocesan Director of Catholic Education, who stated that tuition at Kelly was $200 for Catholics and $300 for the 20 non-Catholics enrolled; that a voluntary confessional service was provided; that there were two daily Masses, at which attendance was voluntary; but that all students were required to participate in this ritual at least once a month. He added that the five Boise parishes subsidized the high school with $68,000 annually for operation; and that the original debt of $1.3 million had been reduced to $600,000.

The staff included four priests, ten sisters, and seventeen laymen; per-pupil cost, in addition to amortization of debt, was between $300 and $350. He stated that every student must take one class in religion daily: as freshmen, in the Old Testament; as sophomores, in the New; as juniors, in the Church and its sacraments; and as seniors, in the laws of Christian marriage.

Father Donohue stated that in the parish schools, tuition was about $15 a month and that the parishes made up any deficits; and he emphasized that many children paid no tuition whatever and that no child was ever turned away for lack of money.

Father Donohue explained that there were 62 parishes and 52,000 Catholics in the state, of whom between 15,000 and 17,000 were of school age. When congratulated on the maintenance of Catholic enrollment in Boise, he hastened to point out that in the diocese as a whole education was being further curtailed by the closing of ten more schools in June, 1971. In September, Kelly would be the only remaining Catholic high school. Whereas in 1966-67, 40% of all Catholic youth—6,000—were in Church schools, that number would fall to 3,000 in 1971-72;[a] and there would remain only twelve schools to serve 62 parishes.

Asked whether there was any hope for parochiaid, Father Donohue frankly doubted that this could be possible in a state where Catholics constituted only 7% of the population and where the powerful Church of Jesus Christ of Latter-Day Saints was opposed to it.

However, there would still be fourteen Seventh-Day Adventist, five Lutheran, and two Christian parochials, together with one Friends' and one Bible Missionary school, with a total enrollment of 1,568 in 1971. It seemed possible, in Idaho as in San Bernardino, that in a few years the majority of parochial pupils might be in Protestant schools.

Transfers from Parochial to Public Schools

Since the private schools of Boise seemed to be in relatively strong positions, few transfers were anticipated from them during 1971-73. However, Mr. D. H. Beary, Assistant Administrator of the Boise School District, declared emphatically that should all private schools close at once, their pupils could be absorbed with no difficulty whatever and with only minor expense.

---

a.   In 1940, the diocese, which is coterminous with the state, enrolled 2,556; in 1950, 2,294; in 1955, 3,106; in 1961, 5,822; in 1966, 6,004; in 1970, 4,374.

Since there were 981 classroom teachers with an ADA of 20,000 in September, 1970, the PTR was only slightly above 21, whereas the maximum permitted on the elementary level was 26 and on the secondary, 30. Even if, therefore, 1,500 transfers should occur at once, each teacher would simply accept one or two additional pupils; and this would not necessitate a single new classroom or any increase in teaching staff.

Further, any growth in public school enrollment would automatically bring additional federal subsidies and a state allocation of at least $250 for every pupil.

We should note also that a fourth high school, designed for 2,000, was soon to be completed. To pay for this and for various improvements and additions, a bond issue, voted overwhelmingly in 1968, provided more than $5 million, of which $2 million was being spent for 95 new classrooms in existing schools and $3 million for the new facility. With the completion of this program, the system would be equipped to handle 4,000 additional students. Meanwhile, the enrollment, which was 21,499 in 1967-68, increased by only 614, to 22,113, in 1970-71.

No possible transfer of pupils from the private to the public schools could, therefore, cause any dislocation or difficulty, or any noticeable increase in the tax rates.

Equally or even more significant for us was the fact that with few or no transfers in the past and with little increase in enrollment, the cost of education in Boise—and this in spite of moderate salaries—has risen in the same proportion as in the nation at large. We can, therefore, only conclude that the cost of education everywhere has been advancing at about the same tempo, whether school districts have grown slowly or rapidly, or have declined, or have or have not absorbed any substantial numbers of private school pupils.

TABLE I

Population and School Enrollment

Year	Pop. in Boise	Pop. in Sch. Dis.	Pub. Sch. Enrollment	Catholic Enrollment	Pub. Sch. ADA
1960-61	34,481	76,000	19,034	1,420	17,954
1965-66	NA	80,000	20,528	1,659	19,431
1969-70	73,330	85,000	22,113	1,628	20,810
1970-71	(74,000)	85,000	22,600	1,465	

TABLE II

Taxation in the Boise School District

Item	1960-61	1969-70	1970-71
District Assessment	$68,810,029	$101,270,000	
Bonded Debt	5,916,000	11,262,000	
Boise Assessment	35,263,451	77,980,805	
City Millage	13.6006	16.5330	
School Millage	4.700	7.4640	
District Tax[a]	$9,358,160	$16,752,889	
Per Capita	$123	$197	
District Sch. Tax	3,234,065	7,558,793	$8,583,253
Per Capita	$42.60	$88.90	$101.00
Increase			137%

a. The totals in this line are not precise since the City millages vary slightly from those in other parts of the School District.

TABLE III

Financial Data: Boise School District

Item	1961-62	1965-66	1970-71
No. of Schools	29	34	38
Insured Value	$22,493,597	$25,934,725	$30,388,406
Revenue: Total	6,471,536	9,185,063	15,392,412
Federal	231,577	532,257	401,201
State	1,813,346	3,128,444	5,232,515
County	657,251	741,588	810,625
Local Taxes	3,377,155	4,129,233	8,583,253
Other	392,207	653,540	364,818
Expenditures: Total	7,600,861	10,191,451	15,392,421
Administration	130,236	284,787	403,630
Instruction	4,277,705	6,039,713	10,013,005
Capital Outlay	1,411,776	1,161,786	369,848
Debt Service	427,422	611,125	1,100,682
Other	1,353,722	2,094,041	2,870,256
Sites, Remodeling, Etc.			645,000
Teacher Salaries:			
Low			$6,200
High			10,726
Per-Pupil Cost[a]	$352.05	$465.70	$699.80

a.   This includes not only current operation, but also capital outlay, federally-aided programs, and debt service.

Public and Catholic School Enrollments

Fargo, another prosperous city and the largest in North Dakota, was, like Boise, chosen for analysis because here also Catholic schools experienced a steady growth from 1960 to 1965, declined only slightly during the following years, and transferred only a small portion of their enrollment to the public schools. In 1960-61, when the population was 49,572, enrollment in the Catholic schools was 2,348 and in the public 8,148; in 1965-66, these totals were 2,201 and 9,866; in 1970, when the population was 52,697, the enrollments were 1,991 and 10,776 respectively.

In the state as a whole, however, and again as in Idaho, the story is very different. In 1965, Catholic schools enrolled 18,459 pupils; in 1970-71, only 11,712.[a] In the Fargo diocese, enrollment dropped from 9,254 to 4,761. At the latter date, among 117 parishes, there were only 15 which still operated schools. Since no released-time programs were in operation in the Fargo diocese, a number of catechetical centers had been established where 5,973 Catholic youth received religious instruction in 1970-71 from 127 teachers.

In 1964, there were 72 religious and 24 lay teachers in the Fargo Catholic schools; in 1970-71, these numbered 41 and 37 respectively.

Between 1960-61 and 1965-66, there was an increase in public school enrollment of 1,448, or 17%, which resulted from the higher birth-rate of the Fifties and a higher secondary enrollment. During the following five years, it rose by only 910, of whom 438 were Catholic transfers. There is

a.   According to a study prepared by the Reverend Thomas E. Kramer and published by the Educational Committee of the North Dakota Catholic Conference in 1971, the totals were 18,108 and 11,478 respectively.

no doubt that total enrollment will decline substantially during the Seventies.

The Crowded Schools

Mr. H.C. Gulbransen, Assistant Superintendent of the Fargo Schools, stated that the two senior and two junior highs were crowded and that almost all of the thirteen elementaries were filled to capacity, especially those near the outskirts of town. Mr. Lester Stutlein, County Superintendent of Schools, testified that they could not absorb the private enrollment with their present facilities. He added that the closing of Catholic schools in smaller towns, such as Langley, had caused serious problems. He observed that school levies had risen so drastically in Fargo that voters were in no mood to vote higher taxes for the expansion of the educational plant; and he added that a recent bonding proposal had been rejected.

Financial Statistics

Our quest in Fargo, as in Boise, was simply to discover what may happen in regard to school costs and property taxes in a community where public schools have expanded very little.

We found that the number of teachers had increased from 362 to 510 during the Sixties, while the enrollment increased by 2,309. The pupil-teacher ratio, which was 23 in 1960-61, fell to 21 in 1970. Meanwhile, the average salary increased from $6,130 to a generous $9,906; the city millage for schools rose from 58.79 to 135.47; and the city school levy from $2,360,798 to $5,189,125—an increase of 120%. The 1970-71 budget, including debt service, called for an expenditure of $9,179,567, with an overall per-pupil cost of $851. Operational cost alone rose from $714 in 1969-70 to $793 in 1971.

The County Auditor, Rhoda Lee, supplied additional financial data. While the total property tax increased from $6,464,021 to $9,648,552 between 1961 and 1971, the levy for schools—including that imposed by the County—rose from $3,286,143 to $6,013,440. The ratio going to schools increased from 51% in 1960-61 to 62% in 1970. In 1961, the local property tax supplied $403 for each pupil; in 1965-66, $450; in 1970-71, no less than $559.

There was a bond issue of $1,900,000 in 1959; another of $2,150,000 in 1963; and a third of $3,200,000 in 1966—on which $5,500,000 was still due in 1971 and required a payment of $625,518.

Federal Programs

The only federal aid shown in the budget for 1969-71 was $125,500 for vocational education and two NDEA programs. We do not know the extent of ESEA funding, which was kept in a separate budget; but we do not think it could have been extensive.

The Catholic Schools

St. Mary's, the oldest, is located near the Cathedral in the center of the city; it was still adequate, and the same can be said of St. Anthony of Padua. Nativity and Holy Spirit have superior plants, ample playgrounds, and large parking areas. The latter two are located in affluent areas and reflect the opulence of their clientele. These four had a combined enrollment of 1,833 in 1964, but declined to 1,395 in 1971.

The pride of the diocese, however, is Shanley High, a large and modern facility with a capacity of at least 800 students. Enrollment was 625 in 1964, but fell to 549 in 1971. Mr Harold A. Troesen, Educational Administrator of the diocese, stated that after the closing of St. James in Grand Forks, there was only one other Catholic high school in the diocese. Built in 1955, and free of debt, Shanley was supported by subsidies from five area parishes. Tuition was $312, of which the student paid from $173 to $213.50, the remainder coming from the parish to which he belonged. Salaries for the 7 lay teachers, who received health insurance also, ranged from $3,600 to $7,950; sisters were paid 2,250 and brothers $4,500 for ten months' work, in addition to board and lodging. There was no tenure or retirement program.

Per-pupil costs averaged about $250 on the elementary level and were around $400 at Shanley.[a] St. Mary's and St. Anthony's had a diagnostician every school day under an ESEA program; all Catholic schools borrowed resource materials; and their pupils participated in summer programs and received help to improve reading skills under Title I of ESEA. Schools received between $1.00 and $2.00 per pupil under Title II. However, there were no textbooks and there was no bus service at public expense for parochial pupils in Fargo. A law permitting this had been

---

a. The *Supplement to the Nonpublic Education Report*, p. 2, states that in North Dakota, the average per-pupil cost in all Catholic schools, exclusive of debt service, was $241 in 1970-71. This report was published by the Fargo diocese in 1971.

enacted, but it had severe restrictions. A released-time bill passed by the legislature provided for one hour of religious instruction weekly, which became mandatory whenever parents requested it; however, it had not been implemented in this area.

Shared time, stated Mr. Troesen, was permissible for individual students, but only four of them were taking advantage of it in 1970-71.

All Catholic schools devoted one class daily to religious instruction. One half of all elementary Catholic children were in Church schools; on the secondary level, the ratio was about 40%.

Summary

Our Fargo investigation served, therefore, once again to establish that in a comparatively affluent community which experienced only moderate school expansion or population growth, educational costs nevertheless could rise spectacularly. In ten years, the property tax for schools more than doubled. Although the district built few schools and accepted very few transfers from the private sector, per-pupil costs, nevertheless, rose to $851 compared to $648 in Helena and $703 in Albuquerque.

TABLE I

Statistics Fargo Schools

Item	1960-61	1965-66	1969-70	1970-71
Enrollment	8,148	9,866	10,727	10,776
No. Teachers	362	455	510	510
PTR	22.4	21.7		21.1
Av. Salary	$6,130	$6,880		$9,906
City Sch. Millage	58.79	71.14	117.57	135.47
City School Tax	$2,360,798	$3,261,339	$5,280,015	$5,189,929
Operational Budget			7,647,648	8,544,018
Debt Service			635,579	625,518
Total Budget			8,283,167	9,179,567
Cost Per Pupil				
Operational			$714	$793
Total			767	851

TABLE II

Revenues of Fargo Schools in 1969-70

State Aid: Total		$3,609,737
Transportation	$7,300	
Apportionment for 14,599 children	225,000	
Foundation Program:		
6,804 Elementary at $216	1,469,664	
3,140 Secondary at $316	994,752	
Special Education	60,000	
Personal Property Tax Replacement	853,021	
Federal: Vocational Aid and NDEA		128,500
Local Levy: Total		5,583,988
General	4,764,401	
For Debt Service	635,579	
Prior Year's Taxes		75,000
Other		109,000
Total	$9,009,717	$9,506,225

TABLE III

Property Taxes in Fargo

Item	1961	1965	1970-71
Valuation	$41,481,233	$44,042,718	$38,304,599
Total Tax	6,464,021	8,226,602	9,684,552
Millage: Total	155.82	182.64	252.83
County Sch.	19.00	21.00	21.10
Sch. General	52.51	72.66	119.98
Debt., Schls.	7.71	8.70	16.01
Total School	79.22	102.36	159.09
Per-Capita Tax: Total	$129.00	$160.00	$183.00
For Schools	66.00	90.00	114.00
Total Tax for Schls.	3,286,143	4,508,213	6,013,440
% of Entire Tax	51	45.7	62
Increase			83%
Per-Pupil Cost to Taxpayers	$403	$457	$559

64

Duluth, Minnesota

Ethnic and Economic Background

Duluth was chosen for analysis because of its cosmopolitan heritage and because it has remained a virtually static community for 50 years. Situated at the western tip of Lake Superior, it has an excellent port. In 1880, it counted only 3,483 souls; but during the ensuing decade, the smelters, steel mills, and transportation industry attracted a flood of Swedes, Norwegians, Germans, Poles, Italians, French, and others, who increased its population to 33,115 in 1890, 78,466 in 1910, and 98,917 in 1920. In 1970, the census counted 99,761 persons in the city. In 1910, only 19% had American parents; and 30,652 were foreign born. Among the denominations, the Roman Catholic became the largest which, in due course, established 19 parishes. There were also thousands of Protestants among the immigrants, whose descendants now worship in more than a hundred diverse sanctuaries.

The early settlers constructed their city along the waterfront, back of which the sharply rising hills provide a spectacular view of the magnificent harbor and surrounding terrain. Such industries as coal, steel, shipping, and railroads, however, required for the most part only common labor; and the community failed to develop that variety of native enterprise which produces and distributes opulence widely among the people, most of whom still lived in old, small, and second-rate housing in 1971, when the city presented a drab, even a depressing, appearance. Except for a few arteries, most of the streets were in deplorable condition: the broken paving in residential areas made driving almost a hazard.

The Catholic Establishment

The great Catholic complex was in obvious decline. The magnificent Holy Rosary Cathedral at 2801 E. 4th indeed dominates the surrounding area; and there were still 18 parish churches, which once operated sixteen schools and enrolled 3,804 pupils. These continued at approximately the same level for a decade, but were reduced drastically following 1965. One by one, St. Clements, St. Margaret-Mary, St. Peter, Sts. Peter and Paul, Sacred Heart, and Stanbrook Hall closed their doors.

In Duluth, as elsewhere, lay teachers have been replacing the religious. In 1930, there were 75 and in 1940 92 sisters, but no laymen. In 1950, there were 119 religious and 5 lay instructors. In 1964, these numbered 112 and 33; and in 1965, 125 and 45 respectively. In 1970-71, they totalled 57 and 54.

Cathedral High School, built in 1962-64 and located at 1215 Rice Lake Road, was by all odds the Catholic educational showplace of the city. Situated on a hill, immense and opulent, it overlooks the City and Lake Superior; it has several classroom buildings, an auditorium, and other facilities; it has also extensive acreage, and is equipped for various kinds of athletics. Designed for an enrollment of more than a thousand, it must have cost several million dollars. Even so, it has failed to attract a sufficient enrollment; in 1969 it had 904 pupils, but only 754 in 1970-71. In 1965, Catholic secondary schools had 1,057 students.

Public and Private Enrollment

The only other private school in Duluth was operated by the Seventh-Day Adventists: it had 26 pupils in 1970-71.

Table I traces the comparative development of public and Catholic enrollment. The ratio in the latter rose from 10.4% in 1930 to 16.4% in 1955; but then declined to 14.9% in 1961 and 14.4% in 1965. In 1970-71, it plunged to 7.8%. While Catholic enrollment dropped by 1,800, the public expanded by 2,800, of whom 1,198 were registered at the Area Institute of Technology, a number almost identical to the overall increase in school attendance.

City Taxation and Financing the Public Schools

Table II shows that the millage increased from 260.59 in 1960-61 to 413.68 in 1970-71, on assessments which rose from $50,708,113 to

$56,668,184. Levies increased from $13,206,599 to $23,296,776; and the per-capita tax for schools from $60 to $107.

Although millage increased by 153.09 points, or 58% in ten years, the property tax still fell lightly on the owner of a modest home. With a market value of $12,000, its Fair and True Appraisal would be $2,400, and the homestead valuation $1,000. At full rates, the tax would be $413.68. However, from this we deduct 31.85 debt mills, plus the Homestead and Taconite Relief of $133.64, which results in a net levy of $260.68. On a $30,000 home, however—since the Taconite allowance may not exceed $250—the tax was $1,152.52.

The Board of Education had its offices in the oldest school building in Duluth, constructed in 1884. Here we obtained a mass of information with the generous cooperation of Mr. Herbert Forsberg, Assistant Superintendent of Business Services. In 1960-61, salary schedules ranged from $3,100 to $7,350; in 1965-66, from $3,475 to $9,450; in 1970, from $4,400 to $15,000. Statistics dealing with revenues, expenditures, and per-pupil costs are summarized in Table III. Between 1960-61 and 1970-71, total disbursements increased from $9,502,071 to $23,405,313—including capital outlay, textbooks, Vo-Tech, debt amortization, federal programs, self-supporting business, and various community services which did not even exist at the beginning of the decade. Under this extreme computation, per-pupil costs rose from $460 to $960. However, total costs to local and State taxpayers rose only from $433 to $752, including capital outlay and debt service, which totalled more than $2.5 million in 1970-71. The operational cost was $397 in 1960-61; and a modest $740 in 1970-71.

According to *Basic Facts* of 1970, published by the Independent School District, the per-pupil cost for operation only and excluding federal funds, rose from $381.06 in 1962-63 to $449.59 in 1965-66 and to $563.93 in 1968-69.

These modest increases—less than the general rate of inflation—were the more remarkable since the Duluth schools have enjoyed generous public support: since 1960-61, they have been greatly expanded and improved, a splendid vocational institute has been constructed, a magnificent new high was ready for occupancy in the fall of 1971, almost 1,800 parochial pupils were absorbed, enrollment was increased from 21,747 to 24,418, the teaching staff expanded from 823 to 1,116, the pupil-teacher ratio reduced from 26.3 to 23.7, and elementary classes lowered in size from 29.36 to 24.37 while the secondary fell from 23.4 to 20.11.

The school plant consists of 30 elementaries, 6 junior, and 4 senior high schools, together with the Institute of Technology, designed to serve 1,200 day students and 3,000 older adults in evening classes. Although the entire enrollment increase consists of Vo-Tech day students and parochial transfers, three bond issues totalling $11,450,000 were approved since 1963. With these funds, Vo-Tech was completed in 1968 and the New Central High School on Central Entrance stood ready for full use in the fall of 1971. There have been many other improvements, including 82 new elementary classrooms. Altogether accommodations have been provided for 4,500 additional pupils.

Federal and Other Programs

Mr. Elmer Bernard, Administrator in charge of grants, supplied detailed information concerning federal subsidies, which, totalling $2,428,997 in 1969-70, were used for a variety of purposes, such as Headstart and Follow Through, $579,000; Model Cities, $550,000; the Vocational Institute, $200,000; and several minor programs, $167,000. Under ESEA, $584,297 was distributed, of which $4,357 under Title II went to parochial schools and $38,400 under Title I was used for the benefit of 160 Catholic pupils—an average of $240 each. Catholic schools, which benefitted also by the federal lunch program in the same manner as the public, received more than $15,000 for free meals.

There was no shared- or released-time program in operation in Duluth.

The Catholic Schools

Interviewed at the diocesan education center, Sister Marilyn, Director of Catholic Schools, stated that there remained only 7 elementary schools under her jurisdiction in the city, of which 3 had 8 and 4 had 6 grades. Sisters, all of whom are degreed or certificatable, received salaries of $1,750 a year, in addition to lodging, health insurance, and some other fringe benefits. The diocese had no retirement plan for anyone; but sisters paid 45% of their salaries into their mother houses to care for those too old to work.

There were no teaching brothers in the diocese; priests received starting salaries of $3,600, in addition to fringes. Salaries for lay teachers ranged from $3,850 to $6,200, and were theoretically 80% of the scale paid in public schools.

Catholic elementaries were financed by tuition of $75 for the first, $50 for the second, and $25 for the third child from the same family. Average per-pupil costs were $200; deficits were covered by the operating parish churches. Costs were expected to rise to $250 in 1971-72.

During 1970-71, the diocese bussed 7th and 8th graders from four elementary schools at a cost of $43 each; but in 1971-72, under the terms of a newly enacted law, the state was expected to underwrite this service entirely.

At Cathedral High, tuition was a straight $300. Assessments were no longer being levied against the parishes for operational costs; instead, the United Catholic Appeal raised $97,000 in 1970-71. Since the operating budget alone was $426,000, there remained a deficit of $100,000. Many projects were undertaken to raise this money; $21,000 was collected during a 21.9-mile Development Walk. Breakfasts, bake sales, bingo, a Las Vegas Night, a St. Patrick's Dance, a Ginger Bread House (where aprons, dresses, etc., are sold) were pressed into service. But, as of May 17, 1971, the diocese still faced a deficit of $35,000 for Cathedral High.

Beyond all this, the cost of debt service remained on the $1,250,000 mortgage still outstanding. Each parish was assessed about $6,000 or $8,000 a year to meet this obligation. Operational per-pupil costs were $486; including amortization, about $650. Should all teachers be paid the salaries prevalent in public schools; should they be provided with the same fringe benefits and retirement income; and should the school offer the same programs available in public education, costs would probably approach those in elite secular private institutions.

We could only marvel at the dedication of Sister Marilyn. "On that Development Walk," she said with a grin, "people gave me $366, which I put into the fund for the Cathedral High School."

"What you need," we observed, "is a Woman's Lib. Movement."

"Well," she smiled, "we do work for a pittance."

Summary

Duluth, so lacking in the outward flush of prosperity, has nevertheless, met its educational challenge with colors flying. It has updated its plant, made vast additions, created new opportunities, and absorbed nearly one-half of the total private enrollment. All this has been achieved at minimal cost; and any future exigency could certainly be met without difficulty. There was nothing to indicate that the public schools have anything of a financial nature to fear in the future; and if every Catholic school should close suddenly, it would scarcely create a ripple in the general life of the community and their students would be welcomed with open arms into a system blessed with ample space and the best facilities. Should Cathedral High close and be acquired by the Board of Education, there would be surplus room in the public system for a generation to come.[a]

---

a.   From the recitation of Sister Marilyn we reached the conclusion that Cathedral High was in serious financial difficulty; that we were correct in this, has since been confirmed. In a release dated Nov. 9, 1971, the *Religious News Service* stated that in 1972-73, the institution will open its academic year as an ecumenical high school, a development resulting from the problems it has failed to solve. The operation of the school will be

TABLE I

Enrollment in the Duluth Schools

Year	Population	Enrollment	Public	%	Catholic	%
1930	101,718	23,718	21,242	86.9	2,476	10.4
1940	101,065	20,469	18,010	88.0	2,459	12.0
1950	104,511	19,394	16,215	89.9	3,179	12.1
1955		23,408	19,604	83.6	3,804	16.4
1961	106,884	25,391	21,619	85.0	3,787	14.9
1965		25,751	22,034	86.6	3,717	14.4
1970	99,761	26,471	24,418	92.2	2,053	7.8

TABLE II

Property Taxation in Duluth

Item	1960-61	1965-66	1970-71
Assessment	$50,718,113	$48,403,356	$56,668,184
Total Tax	13,206,599	16,304,678	23,296,776
Millage	260.59	321.267	413.68
For Schools	127.104	146.877	190.39
School Tax	$6,446,475	$7,387,022	$10,722,071
Per-Capita Tax	$124	$157	$233
For Schools	60	71	107

turned over to an 8-member board of trustees; all religions will be studied, or presented, under the leadership of rabbis, ministers, priests, and sisters. Students from all faiths and various socio-economic backgrounds will be enrolled. Catholics will retain ownership of the land and will service the debt; but the trustees will operate the school and determine its curriculum. The tuition will be increased by $140 to $440—precisely the sum expected for each student under the provisions of the new parochiaid law enacted by the State legislature in 1971 and now being challenged in the courts.

Whether all this will enable Cathedral to survive as a Catholic property and to amortize its debt remains to be seen.

TABLE III

Financial Data: Duluth Public Schools[a]

Revenues	1960-61	1965-66	1970-71
Local Tax	$6,042,445	$7,252,335	$10,355,790
County	177,268	121,694	250,642
State Apportionment	224,780		251,620
State Income Tax	219,880		217,450
State Foundation	2,689,221	5,277,271	7,225,463
Cost, Per Pupil to Taxpayers	$433	$574	$752
Federal	33,269	1,323,272	2,972,775
Lunches	307,553		172,473
Other	470,842	843,479	1,126,236
Grant	21,204		
Total	$10,165,257	$14,818,051	$22,572,449
Disbursments			
Administration	181,441		470,130
Instruction	5,800,001	15,825,283[b]	12,689,304
Textbooks			1,095,595
Plant Operation	1,045,777		1,854,496
Maintenance	411,473		518,690
Auxiliary	479,809		11,014
Fixed Charges	644,231		1,435,087
Transportation	124,969		226,273
Capital Outlay	314,877	381,306	2,506,083
Debt Service	485,509	886,889	1,045,697
Health Service			151,174
Food Service		534,760	592,618
Community Service			796,901
Other	13,962	31,204	121,251
Total	$9,502,049	$17,659,442	$23,514,313[c]
Expenditures Per Pupil			
For Operation	$397	$717	$740
Total	440	801	963

a. In 1960-61, this was known as the Duluth School District; in 1965-66, it became the Independent School District No. 3; in 1970-71, it was changed to District No. 704.

b. This sum includes all items shown under 1960-61 down to Capital Outlay.

c. It is to be noted that this budget includes the cost of new buildings, equipment, debt service, the new Vo-Tech, federal programs, textbooks, self-supporting lunches, community services, etc., etc.

10.   Green Bay, Wisconsin

A Prosperous Catholic Citadel

Green Bay, the oldest city in Wisconsin, and another virtually all-white community, was chosen for analysis because of the decisive manner in which it has solved its educational problem. A thriving commercial center with an excellent port, it is the capital of a lush agricultural region. A variety of flourishing enterprises in grain, fish, dairying, and manufacture have brought wealth to its people. Its population was 31,017 in 1920, 46,235 in 1940, 52,735 in 1950, and 62,888 in 1960. Then came its greatest expansion—to 87,239 in 1970.

Even when Green Bay was only half its present size, it already had 16 Catholic parishes. In 1961-64 they operated 13 elementary and 2 secondary schools with an enrollment exceeding that in the public schools of the city. Although there were 20 Lutheran and a variety of other Protestant congregations in 1971, these represented only a secondary element in the life of Green Bay.[a] Nevertheless, its ethos has not been crippled by the demands of the Church: for, although its laymen have provided generously for its schools, they have also cooperated with the community as a whole in the creation of a good temporal life.

How, then, has this prosperous, rapidly growing, and predominantly Catholic community supported its public and its private schools?

---

a.   In 1970, there were two Lutheran schools with 335 pupils and one SDA school with 36.

Educational Enrollments

Table I traces the evolution of school enrollments in Green Bay. In 1930, there were 9 Catholic schools with 2,998 pupils; in 1955, 12, with 7,526; in 1964-65, 16 with 11,169. Then, however, in spite of a great increase in school-age population, a decline set in: the enrollment fell to 8,641 in 1969 and to 6,895 in 1970-71.

We should explain that in July, 1965, the Green Bay School District expanded by annexing 2 high schools and 8 elementaries with 3,971 pupils. For 1960-61 and 1964-65, therefore, we show the enrollments in both areas in Table I. Since all Catholic schools were located within what constituted the previous district, their enrollments were not altered after the expansion. Inside the former area, they constituted 53.4% of the total in 1960-61 and 50.6% in 1964-65. During the ten years following 1960-61, total attendance in the whole area increased from 20,044 to 29,827; and in the public sector, from 12,828 to 22,912. Most significant, however, are the statistics from 1965 to 1971: while enrollment in the public schools rose by 8,019 over 14,893, that in Catholic schools fell from 11,169 to 6,895. The Catholic ratio in the whole area was 45.5% in 1960-61; 42.9% in 1964-65; 37.9% in 1965-66, 29% in 1969-70; and 23.1% in 1970-71. It will be substantially lower in 1972.

In 1965-66, however, the whole school population began to level off: during the following five years, while the population increased by at least 10,000, the public schools gained 5,234 pupils and the Catholic lost 3,746, for a net increase of 1,356. Between 1969-70 and 1970-71, there was an actual net loss of 29.

The Catholic Educational Complex

Since most of the Catholic schools were built after 1930 and 8 of them, including the splendid Premontre High, are of post WW II vintage, they are, by and large, well equipped and in excellent condition. Holy Martyrs and Resurrection were built since 1965. The old St. Willebrord and St. Patrick's, built in 1915, were the only ones which had been retired in 1971. The others were modern in every respect and comparable to their fine public counterparts. Since all but two were more than ten years old, they were, presumably, only slightly burdened with debt; and since, at their peak, they enrolled more than 11,000, they must have had a large proportion of vacant seats. Attendance in several had fallen in 1971 to half of capacity: St. Agnes and St. Joseph had a combined enrollment of 2,510 in 1964, but only 1,185 in 1970.

This drastic reversal seems strange indeed when we realize that between 1940 and 1961, while the population of the city was increasing by 40%, enrollment in the Catholic schools grew by more than 200%. Since, during those years Catholic laymen were pouring untold millions into their schools, the question naturally arises: why do they now refuse to utilize the institutions for which they paid so dearly?

It is true that the loss of religious instructors may have created a problem: in 1930, with a pupil-teacher ratio of 46, there were 65 sisters and no lay staff members at all. In 1940, there were 115 sisters, 4 laymen, and 3,565 pupils. In 1961, there were 212 sisters and 73 lay teachers with a pupil-teacher ratio of 33. In 1971, there were 141 sisters and 151 lay instructors, with a ratio of slightly more than 23 to 1. However, it is difficult to believe that the cost of 75 lay teachers over an equal number of religious could equal the expense of building a dozen large and sumptuous schools. In fact, the total salaries for 150 laymen could be met by an annual contribution of $50 from each of the Catholic families in the city.

Operational costs had, of course, risen in 1970-71; Sister Madonna, interviewed at the Catholic Education Center, stated that these were about $270 on the elementary and $500 on the high school level for operation alone. Since tuition was only $30 a year for the first child, $25 for the second, and $20 for the third from the same family, it is hard to see how this could have been a serious deterrent. The thirteen parishes still operating elementary schools in 1971 maintained them by subsidies; and all sixteen were assessed for the support of Premontre and St. Joseph's Academy.

Sister Madonna, who did not forsee any additional closings in the immediate future, stated that teaching sisters were to receive $2,500 in 1971-72. Each fall the Packers play a "Bishop's Charity Game"—which is always sold out in advance and nets the Catholic schools a very handsome sum.

The Public Schools

Since a growth of 40% during the Sixties is unusual and since the ratio of public school enrollment rose from 54% to 77% during the decade, the statistics in Table II are significant. We find here that the property tax between 1961 and 1970 increased from $8,057,300 to $26,250,750; the per-capita levy from $128 to $299 (or 134%) and that for schools alone from $63 to $170—or 169%. However, we should note again that at least three-fourths of this must be charged to general inflation; and where a rapid growth in population has occurred, additional allowance must be made for necessary capital expenditures. It is also pertinent to point out that the largest increase—20%—came between 1969 and 1970, when school enrollment increased by only 717, or 3.5%.

Table III shows that the school property tax increased from $7,715,839 to $13,958,502 between 1967 and 1971; and that salaries, during this period, almost doubled—from $7,230,007 to $14,153,889. The operational budget alone increased from $4,041,679 in 1961 to $18,213,374 in 1971, with—it must be remembered—an enrollment that grew from 9,328 to 22,912.[a] Per-pupil costs, therefore, which increased from $433 to $796,were still less than those in the nation as a whole.

In 1961-62, there were 408 teachers for 9,328 pupils; in 1964-65, 512 for 10,922; in 1970-71, 1,102 for 22,912. Pupil-teacher ratios therefore fell from 23.3 to 20.8—one of the lowest we have observed.

Classrooms, however, were still at a premium in Green Bay in 1970-71. Mr. Edwin B. Olds, Superintendent of Schools, stated that the Joint School District had found it necessary to employ various expedients to care for the influx into its 7 secondary and 25 elementary schools. Forty-eight Sunday school rooms were rented in 7 Protestant churches; and 21 relocatable classrooms were being utilized until facilities nearing completion became available.

Existing structures had an insurable value of $41,076,386 in 1971. In 1961, the outstanding debt was $11,553,000; in 1968, this had risen to $17,967,183; but the permissible limit was $66,038,700.

Since school bonds and debt service are included in the general city budget, they do not appear in the financial reports of the schools. It was obvious, however, that a tremendous program of expansion was under way. In 1968, $8,943,426.09 was received and $3,110,675.06 was expended for remodeling, additions, new construction, and the acquisition of sites. This left $5,832,751.03 for the continuation of expansion and improvements.

Property Taxation

In Green Bay, valuations on property are placed theoretically at 100% of 1960 market prices with allowances for depreciation and obsolescence. A house which sold for $20,000 in 1960 might, therefore, now be appraised at $15,000. The 1970 millage of 46.536 would therefore result in a

---

a.　　This increase was due in part to the absorption of Catholic pupils,in part to population growth, and in part to expansion of the school district. In 1965, the District was extended to include several peripheral areas which had developed during recent years.

levy of $698. If the house were new with a present market value of $30,000 (about $20,000 in 1960) the tax would be $930.72.

Federal Programs

Neither the revenues nor the expenditures shown in Table III include any of the federal programs. For information concerning these, we were indebted to Mr. John Sewell, in charge of ESEA programs. Under four titles of this act, $476,125 was received and distributed during 1970-71, of which at least 25% was expended for the benefit of parochial students or schools. We learned that the Lady of Charity school, operated for emotionally disturbed girls, received benefits for its 70 pupils amounting to many thousands of dollars.

Mr. Edwin Olds, Superintendent of the Green Bay School District, proved a rich source of information.

Were the public schools filled to capacity?

They had been for five years. The District was using 21 relocatable classrooms and renting as many as 40 rooms in church buildings. In 1971-72, however, only two of the latter would be necessary.

How had the challenge of a rapidly growing population and thousands of transfers from private schools been met?

Since 1965-66, four new schools with a capacity of 4,000 had been built and many additions had been made to others.

What of the future?

In 1971-72, one new elementary school with 20 classrooms would be opened. On the planning board, there was a high school for the south side which would be ready in 1976. Sites had been obtained and plans completed for several other schools up to 1990.

Did all elementary schools have kindergartens?

Since all public but none of the parochial schools were so equipped, all Catholic pupils spent their first year in the public system.

Was there any released- or shared-time program?

None in Green Bay.

Was bussing available for parochial pupils at public expense?

Yes, just the same as for those in public schools.

Had it been difficult to obtain funds for the public schools in a community so heavily Catholic?

The Green Bay Board of Education had no power to raise funds on its own—it was fiscally dependent on the City Council. The Board made plans for the School District and presented them to the Council for its consideration, which had full bonding authority. After the Council takes affirmative action, there is a 30-day interval in which petitions may be filed to force a referendum—but there had never been one.

It is unnecessary to go to the people for approval of a bond issue?

Correct.

How is the Board of Education constituted?

Its members are appointed by the mayor and confirmed by the Council.

How are the members of the Council elected?

There is an aldermanic system with 28 members elected from wards. The majority were Roman Catholics and a two-thirds majority was necessary for the approval of a bond issue.

What has been their attitude toward the public and parochial schools?

Enlightened and generous; the public schools have never been refused anything necessary for their best development.

How were the Catholic schools doing? Sister Madonna seemed optimistic.

Their enrollment has been falling steadily. Their elementary schools have been advertising that they will accept pupils of any faith—for tuition. Premontre is in trouble—its enrollment is falling by a hundred a year.

Has the transfer of thousands of pupils from the parochial schools caused any friction or misunderstanding?

None whatever!

Would the Green Bay public schools be filled to capacity for the foreseeable future?

Yes.

How would the crisis be met if several Catholic schools were to close without previous notice?

The Board of Education has already decided that if a parochial school closes entirely, negotiations will at once begin to take over the building, either through purchase or on a long-term lease, and it would then be operated as an integral part of the public school system. A resolution has already passed the Council providing that money be made available if and when such an event occurs.

What would happen if every Catholic school should close on very short notice?

In that case, a Master Plan already in existence would go into effect. A bond issue would be floated and would be used to lease or buy parochial schools and build new facilities as necessary.

What would be the effect of this on the property tax?

The State would supply much of the cost. The tax on the average home would propably go up about a hundred dollars.

What would be the savings to Catholic parents?

Several million dollars for operation alone; and their churches might get millions for buildings they would no longer be using.

The Decline of the Catholic Schools

It is quite certain that more than half of the people in the Green Bay School District, which has a population of about 115,000, are Roman Catholics;[a] they must number at least 12,000 families, with perhaps 15,000 school-age children. Since Seventh-Day Adventists often triple-tithe, is it too much to ask of Catholics that they contribute a single tenth to their Church? If they did so, its income in the Green Bay area would be $12,000,000; and if only half of this were used for its schools, there would be $400 for every pupil.

So why, we wonder, cannot the Catholic schools survive? Have their laymen—recently so lavish in their generosity—gone on strike? Or, if they are giving as they did for twenty years after 1944, what is the Church doing with the money?

---

a.   The *Official Catholic Directory* of 1971 states that in the entire diocese there are 315,142 Catholics in a population of 726,552; and their proportion is considerably higher in the city and its immediate environs than in the surrounding countryside and smaller towns.

TABLE I

Public and Catholic School Enrollment

Year	Total	City-District	Catholic	Catholic Ratio
1930	9,314	6,316[a]	2,998	32.2%
1940	11,515	7,950[a]	3,565	31.0%
1955	15,260	7,734[a]	4,526	49.3%
1960-61	20,044	9,328	10,716	53.4%
1960-61	23,544	(12,828)[b]	10,816	45.4%
1964-65	22,041	10,922	11,169	50.6%
1964-65	26,062	(14,893)[b]	11,169	42.9%
1965-66	28,451	17,678	10,773	37.9%
1969-70	29,836	21,195	8,641	29.0%
1970-71	29,807	22,912	6,895	23.1%

TABLE II

Millages and Taxes in Green Bay

Item	1961	1965	1967	1971
Assessment	$334,547,300	$464,178,175	$545,753,925	$564,262,025
Tax	8,057,645	14,197,185	21,628,708	26,250,750
Per Capita	$128	$189	$250	$299
Millage	23.380	30.580	39.660	46.536
School Millage	11.489	17.059	23.256	26.311
School Tax	$3,959,434	$7,818,910	$12,702,550	$14,840,675
Per Capita	$63	$104	$147	$169

a. Estimated

b. On July 1, 1965, the Joint Green Bay School District No. 2 was expanded by annexing two high schools with 1,500 pupils and eight elementaries with 2,471–a total of 3,971. In parentheses for 1960-61 and 1964-65, we show the appropriate total enrollments of all schools which constituted the enlarged District after July, 1965, which thereafter included at least 18,000 more people than before and at least 30,000 more than there are within the Green Bay City limits. All Catholic schools included in the total are within the area of the pre-1965 District. In 1960-61 and 1964-65, Catholic enrollment comprised more than half the school pupils within Green Bay.

TABLE III

The Budgets of the Green Bay School District[a]

Revenues	1961	1965[b]	1967	1971
Local Tax	$2,641,265	$4,360,957	$7,715,839	$13,958,502
Intermediate			149,800	193,550
State Aid	528,376	864,500	1,857,911	3,559,855
Federal			71,413	47,181
Lunch Sales	103,643	175,949	2,994	15,902
Transfers	201,499	283,962	67,507	
Clearing Accts.			285,757	438,384
Carryovers	88,481	46,806	102,089	
Totals	$3,563,264	$5,732,174	$10,253,310	$18,213,374
Expenditures				
Administration	$110,764	$144,703	$189,583	$365,435
Instruction	2,871,428	4,215,591	7,230,007	14,193,889
Transporation	66,443	118,381	360,630	709,779
Operation	487,626	625,542	849,929	1,304,880
Maintenance	226,719	244,589	270,115	533,406
Fixed Charges	207,444	261,531	249,402	771,409
Debt Service	28,021	37,730	8,959	29,569
Capital Outlay	43,234	84,107	259,159	186,195
Carryover			461,157	118,812
Totals	$4,041,679	$5,732,174	$9,878,941	$18,213,374
Cost Per Pupil	$433	$463	$549	$790

a.   It should be noted that these revenues do not include ESEA and other federally-funded programs.

b.   Statistics for 1965 do not include schools annexed that year.

A City Unique for Analysis

Of all the cities we have surveyed, Dubuque, in certain respects, stands alone; and we found no other so fruitful for our understanding of the immense drama that is now taking place on the American scene and especially within the Catholic community, lay and religious.

Dubuque is a city with a background more heavily Catholic than any other we have encountered. We believe that it must be fully 85% of that faith. As late as 1960-61, 60.5% of its youth were in Catholic schools, whose enrollment increased by more than 2,000 to 11,022 in 1966-67. All of the 11 Catholic parishes still operated schools in 1971; and the magnificent Wahlert High is the pride of the diocese.[a] Even in 1971, there had never been any tuition in the elementaries. And yet, about 1966-67, Catholic parents began transferring their children to the cramped, understaffed and generally obsolete and inadequate public schools. What is more, they voted generous bond issues to expand and improve them; and they accepted increased taxation to support their current expenses.

In 1961-62, Catholic enrollment nationally comprised about 12% of the total; this fell to about 7.5% in September, 1971. But in Dubuque, the ratio fell from more than 60% to about 35%; and it continues to decline.

Since the non-Catholic community of Dubuque is small, we must recognize that what has taken place is peculiarly a Catholic phenomenon.

Virtually all-white Dubuque, the oldest municipality in Iowa, had a population of 13,000 in 1860; 39,141 in 1920; 49,670 in 1950; and 62,853 in 1960, after which it declined to 61,351 in 1970.

Even more than Duluth or Butte, the central section of Dubuque presents a depressing spectacle. Business structures are dilapidated, homes are small and aged, many stores are vacant. And this seems strange, for, situated on the west bank of the Mississippi, it is the natural outlet for one

---

a.   Four of the elementary Catholic schools in Dubuque were among the ten largest in Iowa; and Wahlert is by far the largest private school in the state. Visitation Academy for girls was closed in 1970.

of the most fertile agricultural regions in America. It would seem that, with progressive leadership, it could have become a wealthy metropolis, an opulent center for trade, shipping, and manufacture. Beyond the bluffs which rise sharply above the lowlands along the great river, there are, indeed, newer developments and better residential areas. But the principal portion of the city still lies on the lower level, as it did at the turn of the century.

Although Iowa as a whole is heavily Protestant or religiously uncommitted, it contains two or three pockets which are overwhelmingly Catholic; of these, Dubuque may constitute the most outstanding example. There were no non-Catholic private schools, and only 33 non-Catholic churches, most of which were very small.

The city itself is a sufficiently extraordinary phenomenon, but the rich agricultural area to the west is even more intriguing. For here, during more than a century preceding 1960, there had never been any public school at all. Then at last, this area also organized a public school district, which enrolled several thousand pupils in 1971, including several towns and villages.[a]

Upon arrival in Dubuque, the newcomer contemplates with wonder the ubiquitous and enormous churches. There is St. Raphael's Cathedral, with its adjacent, antiquated school at 231 Bluff Street. At the edge of the business district is St. Patrick's, which, with its school and rectory, fills almost an entire block.

Only two blocks distant stands the German St. Mary's, which has the tallest steeple in town and which also covers a whole square. The buildings are very old, the school is inadequate, and there is no playground: its enrollment was 807 in 1961 and 517 in 1971.

A few blocks away we found the huge Holy Ghost Church with its adjacent school which served 1,152 pupils in 1965 and 1,008 in 1971.

Holy Trinity and Sacred Heart are also situated in the lowlands. Collumbkille, Nativity, and St. Anthony are located on the upper level and have more modern schools. Resurrection is an almost new facility at the edge of town. St. Joseph's, which has a circular sanctuary, and a large, beautiful school with 605 pupils, is the Catholic elementary showplace. To this was attached a large sign which proclaimed:

---

a.   In 1955, the school millage in Dyersville was .780, and in New Vienna, 3.496. At the same time, it was 24.985 in Dubuque.

BEST FRIEND
of the Iowa Taxpayers
Non-Public Schools of Dubuque County
Save the Taxpayers $8,000,000 Annually

Wahlert High School, built about 1958 and designed for an enrollment of 2,500, is another of those magnificent facilities calculated to retain Catholic pupils on the secondary level. It had more than 2,200 boys in 1966-67. Since then it has become co-educational by absorbing those formerly enrolled at Visitation Academy. Nevertheless, even with this addition, attendance fell to 2,000 in 1970-71.

The visitor soon discovers that sanctuaries, schools, and rectories constitute only a fraction of the Church complex: great religious buildings confront him on every hand. Its educational and administrative offices are located in a large structure at 1229 Loretta. Even more impressive are the Aquinas Institute of Theology; Loras College; Clark College; the Mercy Medical Center and Xavier Hospital; the Mellary Abbey; the Center for Catholic Charities; and various convents, including the magnificent former St. Bernard's Seminary, now used as the Mother House for the Sisters of Presentation and located near Wahlert High School. In its historic development, Dubuque has indeed been the Catholic City of God.

Since the public facilities in Dubuque are minimal; since the cost of public schools has always been the largest element in local taxation; and since less than 40% of all pupils attended them in 1960-61, it would seem that a low rate of property taxation should have prevailed.

This, however, was not the case: for property levies have always been heavy and in 1970 its general school millage was 69.516—approximately double the State average.[a]

The reason for this must be sought in the fact that for generations the great majority of the citizens gave a very large portion of their labor to the Church, which converted its revenue into awe-inspiring forms of tax-exempt property. A much smaller ratio, therefore, remained for the construction of housing or the expansion of business enterprise. Multi-million-dollar cathedrals, churches, priories, seminaries, convents, retreat houses, etc., contribute nothing to the economy or to the operation of the city. On the other hand, the small properties of the producers had to be taxed at an exorbitant rate.

---

a.   *Data on Public Schools* Part 4, 1969-70, p. 25, published by the State Superintendent of Public Instruction, shows that in the 476 school districts of the State, the school tax millage averaged between 35 and 38.

Nor was this all: since the Church seemed to offer the most attractive careers available, the more capable young men entered the priesthood or a vocation, and thus drained from the secular community those spirits who might otherwise have embarked in trade or manufacture—occupations which would have increased their own personal wealth and the taxable property of the community. At the same time, the most devoted young women, took their vows of chastity, obedience, and poverty to serve God and the Church forever: the community was therefore deprived of its best potential mothers, while the Church grew rich and the secular city was suspended in poverty and deprivation.

The School District and Taxation

In 1945, the Dubuque School District consisted of the 11 square miles which were coterminous with the city itself. Between 1946 and 1960, both were gradually extended to an area of 33 square miles; and about 1958-59, the Dubuque Community (as well as the Western Dubuque Community) School District was established. Between 1961 and 1966, the former reached its present limits of 245 square miles. In 1961, the taxable value of the city was $71,556,963 and of the School District $74,542,353; in 1970-71, these totals had increased to $94,065,204 and $125,474,728.[a] Millage increased from 73.485 to 145.764; and the total tax from $4,791,383 to $13,711,320. The school millage rose from 25.524 to 74.842[b] and the levy from $1,944,538 to $7,040,028.

Let us see how this has affected the small homeowner. Since assessed valuations are 27% of current market, a $20,000 house in 1960-61 would pay $397, of which $139 would be for schools. In 1970-71, the comparable levies were $787 and $404. On a $30,000 house, the tax, without computing the homestead credit of about 10%, would be $1,181.

In view of the paucity of public facilities, these taxes are onerous enough. The library, for example, is no better than one would expect in a town of four or five thousand. The ancient city-county building should have been replaced long ago, but bonds for this purpose have been rejected. Since social life has always revolved primarily around the Church, little provision has been made for parks or other forms of public recreation.

---

a. The Western Dubuque Community School District, which did not even exist in 1955, had an assessable property base of $35,846,498 in 1969-70, and collected $1,665,280.90 in school taxes on a rate of 46.456 mills.

b. This included, for the first time in 1970, 1.5 mills for a college.

A few years ago, Dr. Garland H. Wessell, a dynamic personality, became Superintendent of the Dubuque Community School District; and he has met the immense challenge with extraordinary vigor and success. When he took the helm, only 41% of the area pupils were in public schools; in 1970-71, the ratio had been increased to 61.1%.

Table II tells the story of public-private education in Dubuque. In 1960, Catholic schools enrolled 8,963 pupils while the public had only 5,852. Both systems grew at a parallel rate until 1966-67, when the former peaked at 11,166 and the public schools enrolled 8,645. Then began a dramatic reversal: in 1969-70, public school enrollment attained 11,630 and, for the first time, exceeded the private, which dropped to 9,671. In 1970-71, this development accelerated: the public rose to 12,900, the private fell to 8,200. For 1971-72, these totals were expected to be 13,600 and 7,500 respectively.

Dr. Wessell and his assistants supplied voluminous data concerning enrollment, finances, and expansion. He stated that until 1970 several Protestant churches belonging to the National Council operated a program for released time but that this had now been terminated; and that there never had been any such arrangement for Roman Catholics.

Dr. Wessell went into considerable detail concerning the elaborate shared-time programs operating for the benefit of Catholic pupils. Time spent by them in public schools was treated as a partial equivalency of enrollment; for example, if two pupils each spent half a day in a public school, this constituted one full-time equivalency, and the public schools received State funds according to that ratio. In 1970-71, there were 2,262 shared-time students with 1,060 full-time equivalencies.

There was no provision for supplying textbooks to private school pupils at public expense.

Concerning transportation, Dr. Wessell explained that there was no direct reimbursement from the state. However, the Dubuque Community District operated 51 busses on regular routes and carried 4,478 pupils in 1970-71. Elementary children had to live 2 miles and secondary students 3 miles from school to be eligible for this service. Parochial pupils were taken to a public school if their first class of the day was there; and they were taken home if their last was there.

Teachers in Iowa have no publicly funded retirement program except that which applies to all government employees.

The PTR was 25.2 on the elementary and slightly higher on the secondary level. All teachers must be highly qualified. In 1960-61, salaries ranged from $4,000 to $7,500; in 1970-71, from $6,875 to $13,063, plus fringe benefits worth several hundred dollars.

Asked whether there were still communities in Iowa without public schools, Dr. Wessell stated that a large area west of Dubuque had no such school until about 1960; however, the Western Dubuque Community District, which began with 700 pupils, had 3,000 in 1970-71. In Ryan, for example, the Catholic Church had closed both its elementary and secondary school; but in Dyersville there was still no public school.

Asked how the public schools had been able to increase their enrollment from 5,800 to 13,000 in a few years in a static community, Dr. Wessell explained that between 1951 and 1965, not a single new classroom had been added nor a penny voted for capital improvements. It was 1964 before a bond issue of $1,900,000 was voted for repairs and modernization. But in 1967, another for $6,500,000 was overwhelmingly approved for expansion. At the same time, the schools were given an automatic levy of 2.5 mills for ten years—good for $3,100,000 for additional construction. Additions to the high school and several elementaries had already been completed; and two new grade schools with a capacity of 1,000 had been built. Since 1967, 282 classrooms, including 20 portables, had been added. Furthermore, the new Hampstead High School, with a capacity of 2,200, would open in the fall of 1971, and would increase the possible secondary enrollment in the public schools to more than 6,000. Finally, Visitation Academy with 20 classrooms had been leased for three years to serve Catholic pupils enrolled in shared-time classes.

The school plant was valued at $27 million and outstanding bonds totalled $8 million. There were fourteen elementary, two junior, and now two senior high schools. Since the District had several million dollars of funds specifically earmarked for new construction, several of the old schools were shortly to be replaced with modern facilities.

Would enrollment continue to increase and would the flood of Catholic transfers continue?

Dr. Wessell believed that the Catholic schools would continue to shrink; that Wahlert High alone was losing at least a hundred students a year; and that at least 700 more Catholic pupils would enter the public schools in the fall of 1971. However, it was his opinion that without transfers, enrollment would decline.[a]

Asked what would happen should all the Catholic schools close at once, he declared that the public schools could and would absorb any number who applied for admission. Whatever might be necessary would be

---

a.   A study published by the Iowa State Superintendent of Public Instruction shows that enrollment in the State will drop by more than 15% (from 749,889 to 621,492) in 6 years because of the declining birth-rate (*Data on Iowa Schools*, Part I, p. 29).

done. Some of the Catholic schools might be leased or purchased until they could be replaced with new construction. Everything would be determined by the will and actions of the Catholic laymen who sent their children to the public schools and then voted bond issues to build new ones and to maintain them.

Had there been any difficulty so far in absorbing several thousand Catholic pupils? and had there been any friction over religion in the public schools?

"None whatever!"

School Finances

The financial development of the Dubuque Community School District is reflected in Table III. We should note that in 1960-61 and even in 1965-66, there was no outstanding debt because no bonds had been voted since 1951. With no construction until the later Sixties, the overall per-pupil cost was $393 in 1960-61 and $464 in 1965-66. Then, however, because of the great expansion and general inflation, this rose to $891 in 1969-70 and to $1,013 in the budget for 1970-71.[a] For operation alone, it was $856 in 1969-70 and $911 in 1970-71.

Federal Programs

From Mrs. Hutchison, Director of ESEA Title I programs, we learned that in 1970-71 the District had 944 identifiably disadvantaged children, of whom 425 were in Catholic schools; and that about $100,000 of the $221,804 total was expended on programs for their benefit.

Mr. Cletus H. Koppen, who supervises the distribution of all ESEA funds except those under Title I, stated that about $80,000 or a little more was distributed during the year under Title II and VI, of which about one-third went to parochial schools.

Since pupils in public schools received hot-lunch subsidies totalling $126,995 in 1970-71, we computed the Catholic share of this in Dubuque at about $55,000.

The Catholic Schools

Interviewed at the Catholic Diocesan Education Office, Sister Margaret

---

a.   *A Comparative Table of Per-Pupil Costs*, published by the State, places this at $1,005.41 for 1970-71 and the projected 1971-72 enrollment at 13,462.

King of the Order of Presentation stated that no tuition at all was charged in the elementary schools; that pupils paid only a book rental of $14 or $15 a year. At Wahlert, it was $150 for freshmen, $185 for sophomores, and $215 for juniors and seniors. Sisters received $1,900 in 1970-71, but were to get $2,400 in 1971-72.[a] Each parish church subsidized its own school and paid an assessment for the operation of Wahlert.

Sister Margaret provided a release, according to which the diocesan enrollment in 1966-67 was 41,878 and 33,189 in 1969-70; and that there were 1,219 religious and 619 lay teachers at the earlier date and 920 religious and 656 lay instructors in 1969-70.

And so we found in Dubuque—as in Green Bay—a plant which not long before had been filled to capacity but which was now gradually being abandoned by the patrons who had financed it. And this was true not only of the old elementaries, but even of the magnificent new Wahlert, where attendance was already 500 or 600 below capacity.

What then lies in store for education in this overwhelmingly Catholic city which, in 1966-67, began to reject its sectarian schools and vote generous bond issues for the public? We can scarcely believe that the principal cause is or has been financial: for there is no tuition whatever in the elementary schools; nor is that charged in the high school sufficient to constitute a serious deterrent.

Proponents of parochiaid declare that this would give parents a freedom of choice. However, we might suggest that the experiences of the two Dubuque Community School districts reveal that at least in this instance Catholic parents have exercised this freedom in a most deliberate manner. They have elected to send their children to, and spend their money for, the public instead of their own sectarian schools, even when they did not previously pay one penny for public education. We believe that a new generation of Catholic laity is turning progressively from sectarian to secular education because of a strong desire to enter the mainstream of American life. Why they waited so long, or why a drastic turning point was reached, about 1965-67, is a question of intense interest and fundamental importance.

Maquoketa and West Delaware

Leaving Dubuque on Highway 20, a short drive brings the traveller to Dyersville, a town of about 3,000, where we saw several hundred children

---

a.   In 1940, there were 171 sisters and 8 lay teachers in the Dubuque Catholic schools; in 1970-71, there were 145 religious and 163 lay instructors.

playing in the streets around St. Xavier's school and Basilica. At the edge of town, there is a modern facility resembling a modern public high school.

At the office of the new consolidated school operated by the Maquoketa Valley District in Delhi, we interviewed Mr. John M. Thomas, Superintendent, who explained that the new structure in Dyersville was a Catholic school; that the town has never had a public school; that for years there was only one Protestant family there, who sent their children out of town; that the new high school has a heavy debt, serviced by means of assessments against several parishes. According to the *Official Catholic Directory*, the Dyersville elementary school had 811 pupils and the new high school 274 in 1961; but in 1970-71, the former had 588 and the latter 550.

Mr. Thomas explained that his district embraces 190 square miles and has 1,000 elementary and 400 high school pupils. Within the area, there now remains only one parochial school—in Earlsville, with 120 pupils. There had been no difficulty whatever in absorbing 150 Catholic pupils, nor would there be if the Earlsville parish were to discontinue its school. The per-pupil cost in the Maquoketa District in 1970-71 was $944 on the secondary and $627 on the elementary level, with an overall average of $723, which includes bus service but does not cover amortization of debt.

In Manchester, seat of Delaware County, we interviewed Mr. William Raisch, Superintendent of the West Delaware Community School District, which includes Ryan, Masonville, Dundee, Greeley, and, of course, Manchester itself.

He stated that a new elementary, a junior high, and a senior high had recently been completed. The District has 2,560 pupils, of whom 1,235 attended the secondary schools in the city (many were bussed in). The Catholic high school in Ryan was closed in 1965 and the elementary in 1968,[a] after which the buildings were torn down. The public school there was reduced from 6 to 4 grades and all those above that level were bussed into Manchester, where St. Mary's, with 219 pupils,[b] had closed its 7th and 8th grades, and was the only parochial school remaining in the whole West Delaware Community School District.

In 1960-61, the school millage was 38.788; in 1965-66, 49.093; in 1967-68, 58.012, and in 1970-71, 61.515, with a total millage of 109, compared to 146 in Dubuque. This rate was maintained while almost the entire school plant was being replaced and nearly half its enrollment bussed over considerable distances.

---

a.   These schools had an enrollment of 261 in 1961 and 253 in 1965.
b.   This school had 363 pupils in 1961 and 384 in 1965.

TABLE I

Property Taxes in Dubuque

Year	1960	1965	1970	1970-71
Assessment	$71,566,963	$84,034,980	$93,883,452	$94,065,204
Tax Collected	4,791,380	7,124,137	11,353,640	13,711,320
Per Capita	$76	$157	$186	$221
Millage: Total	73.485	84.665	128.454	145.764
For Schools	25.524	31.182	58.881	74.842
School Tax	$1,944,538	$3,100,710	$5,527,830	$7,040,028
Per Capita	$31	$50	$90	$115

TABLE II

Public and Catholic School Enrollment

Year	Total	Public	Catholic	% Cath.
1920	7,818	4,065	3,735	48.0
1940	8,778	4,489	4,289	48.8
1960-61	14,815	5,852	8,963	60.5
1964-65	17,426	7,148	10,278	59.0
1966-67	19,811	8,645	11,022	56.4
1969-70	21,201	11,630	9,671	45.1
1970-71	21,108	12,900	8,208	38.9
1971-72	21,100	13,600	7,500	35.5

90

TABLE III

Financial Data: Dubuque Community Schools

Revenues	1960-61	1965-66	1969-70	1970-71
Assessment	$74,542,353	$96,633,635	$122,915,261	$125,474,728
Local Taxes	1,921,519	2,771,006	7,266,739	8,921,466
State Aid	181,900	364,925	2,433,111	3,086,959
ESEA Funds			145,000	185,000
Lunch Aid			125,000	126,995
Other	179,262	185,785	85,000	185,000
Total	$2,282,681	$3,321,716	$10,054,850	$12,505,420
Expenditures				
Administration	53,025	93,450	305,115	357,660
Instruction	1,473,620	2,376,967	5,993,041	7,129,080
Attendance			84,488	91,480
Health	61,990	87,917	327,545	394,585
Fixed Charges	105,394	170,500	762,126	1,033,244
Oper. & Main.	348,495	487,132	1,173,810	1,422,650
Community		10,750	168,439	164,625
Capital Outlay	53,750	95,000	512,740	371,194
Debt Service			30,000	100,000
Federal			186,690	289,532
Carryover			409,981	496,950
General Fund	$2,096,274	$3,321,716	$9,953,975	$11,851,000
Site Fund	9,329	25,000		
Schoolhouse	164,864	311,623	**430,002**	1,217,134
Courses Fund	30,135			
All Funds	$2,300,602	$3,658,339	$10,383,977	$13,068,134
Cost Per Pupil				
Operational	$359	$411	$854	$911
Total	393	464	895	1,013

Kansas City, Kansas, was chosen for analysis because it is an old mid-western city of medium size, with large Catholic and Negro minorities. Since it is typical of many others throughout the United States, its experience should be significant.

Within its older boundary, the city has remained static for many years: in 1930, its population was 120,857; in 1940, 121,450; and in 1960, 121,901. However, during the Sixties, it annexed surrounding areas which increased its count to 168,682. In 1960, there were 28,182 Negroes; in 1970, they numbered 34,400 in the expanded city, or 20.4% of the total.

Most of the city, especially the inner area, is very old; the narrow streets, the little lots, and small houses reflect little evidence of affluence. It is only in the northwest area and in the newer suburbs that larger houses and more spacious homesites are to be found.

It was not possible to make a complete analysis because the school district was unified and enlarged in 1967 and previous statistics were not comparable; no detailed reports were available from the Board of Education; and, finally, the material obtained from the State Superintendent of Public Instruction in Topeka did not cover all the data usually sought in this investigation.

Enrollments

Catholic schools in Kansas City, which enrolled 926 in 1896, grew rapidly after 1910. In 1920, there were 16, with an enrollment of 3,638; in 1930, there were 19, with 4,437, who then comprised about 20% of the total city enrollment.

Table I gives public and private registrations from 1960-61 to 1970-71. The large increase of 1966-67 over 1960-61 resulted from the formation of the Unified District No. 500, which was expanded to include the recently annexed areas of Kansas City. Since Catholic enrollment for each year includes an area roughly equal to the public school district, the statistics are comparable.

Within the limits of the older city, enrollment totalled 27,809 in 1961, of whom 6,464, or 23.2%, were in the parochials. In 1966-67, when District No. 500 attained an enrollment of 33,665, the Catholic pupils totalled 6,536, or 16.3%. Then began a very significant development: in 1968, the public sector increased to 35,048, but the Catholic declined to 5,641 and comprised only 13.9% of the total. Then public enrollment also began to decline, gradually but continuously, to 34,223 in October, 1971. Meantime, Catholic attendance fell to 4,601, or 11.8% of the total.

The most important facts reflected in Table I are (1) that while public enrollment declined by 825 or 2.4% between 1968 and 1971, the Catholic fell by 1,937, or 29%; (2) that total enrollment fell by 2,762, or 6.9%; and (3) that the public schools reduced their enrollment significantly even while absorbing almost 2,000 parochials.

Note particularly that the kindergarten enrollments declined from 3,170 in 1967 to 2,652 in 1971. This means that, because of the falling birth rate, total enrollment must drop during the Seventies by at least 5,000 below that of 1971, which was itself well below that of 1968.

Taxation and Public School Finances

Table II traces the development of property taxation, which increased from $99 per capita in 1960 to $138 in 1964 and to $217 in 1970; however, of this, only $39, $52, and $79 was levied in support of the local schools. On a $20,000 house, the tax was a modest $470.50 in 1970, of which $176.50 went for education.

The information in Table III was supplied by the State Superintendent of Public Instruction. We note that Kansas City has had and still has an extremely low per-pupil operational cost. In 1960, this was $280; in 1967, $442; and in 1970, $507—compared to a national norm of $375, $628, and $858 respectively. Even when debt service is included, the total for 1970 was only $542.

We note that the PTR has been declining slowly over the years in Kansas City from 26 in 1960 to 25.44 in 1967 and to 25.1 in 1970.

During a tour of the city we found that the public schools, by and large, were modern and equipped with adequate playgrounds. It is evident that the taxpayers have not been niggardly with them.

During interviews at the Administration offices of the Board of Education, we learned:

(1) That a bond issue of $24.5 million was approved in 1970, which would be used to construct one junior and two senior highs and two elementaries, and to complete five other projects. There were 61 schools, including one vocational institute, in 1971: fifty elementaries, eight junior and five senior high schools in the District.

(2) There was no shared- or released-time program in operation.

(3) The state reimbursed the District with $32 of the $36 which it cost to transport each of 10,800 pupils in 1970-71, who were required to live at least 2.5 miles from school to qualify for this service. Parochial pupils were served only on regular routes.

(4) The salaries for degreed teachers ranged from $6,500 to $9,500; those with MAs and 33 years of service could receive a maximum of $11,200. All teachers were certified; every five years they had to accumulate 9 additional hours of academic credit.

(5) About half the schools had lunch programs with subsidies from the USDA.

The Catholic Schools

At the Catholic diocesan center, we interviewed Mr. Patrick M. Cigich, Assistant Superintendent of Schools in the Archidiocese, who stated:

(1) There was a subsidized lunch program in only 2 of the Kansas City Catholic schools.

(2) All parochial pupils qualified for bus service in the same manner as those in the public schools.

(3) There were no free textbooks for pupils in private schools.

(4) There was no shared- or released-time program.

(5) No schools had been built in the diocese for a number of years; and only one in Kansas City for a long time.

(6) At St. Patrick's Elementary the tuition was $65 a year for each child; at St. Joseph's, $40 for the first from a single family and $15 for each additional child; at St. Ann's and the Cure of Ars, $50 for the first, $70 for two, and $100 for three or more; and at St. John Evangelist, $10 for the first, $15 for two, and $20 for three children. At Ward High School, tuition was $300.

(7) In the 14 elementary schools in Wyandotte County (roughly coterminous with the School District No. 500), there were 223 pupils with

Spanish surnames and 233 who were Negro,[a] a ratio of 5%.

(8) In 1964, the elementary schools of the diocese enrolled 20,000; in 1971, 13,000.

(9) Sisters in Kansas City received $2,200 plus fringe benefits in 1970-71; lay teachers about $300 to $400 less than those in public schools. There was a retirement program for lay teachers in the high schools only. There was Blue Cross and Blue Shield coverage for everyone.

(10) Only two elementaries participated in Title I programs of ESEA; however all Catholic schools received benefits under Title II ranging from $1.25 to $2.50 per pupil.

Summary and Conclusions

In 1964, there were 19 Catholic schools in the city; of these, 14 were still in operation in 1970-71. The age of the system can be realized from the fact that there were 12 in 1910, 16 in 1920, and 19 in 1930. Those which have been closed are, for the most part, very old, located on cramped sites, and, according to modern standards, quite inadequate. Most of those still in operation in 1971 will need replacement within a few years.

Thus we found that while some of the newer Catholic schools in out-lying areas have held their own, most of those in the Inner City had lost enrollment or closed entirely. The Cathedral of St. Peter school at 409 N. 15th Street, had 550 pupils in 1965, but only 181 in October, 1971; St. Anthony declined from 198 to 135; St. Benedict from 271 to 99, and then closed in June, 1971. Even the new Bishop Miege in Johnson County, which had 1,070 in 1965, enrolled only 850 in 1970-71.

Our analysis of Kansas City demonstrates conclusively that in a static city, the public schools can, without increasing enrollment, absorb a large influx of pupils from a parochial system.

Assuming that present trends will continue, more of the old parochials in Kansas City will cease operations during the Seventies; but this will not occasion any increase in public school enrollment. We believe that the better parochials will, in the newer areas, continue to serve a declining clientele; however, since the public schools are undergoing a tremendous program of improvement and replacement, it is certain that they could, without the slightest difficulty, absorb every private pupil who might wish to transfer.

---

a. In the public schools, the ratio is about 25% in Kansas City.

TABLE I

School Enrollment in Kansas City, Kansas

School Enrollment

Year	Population	Public	Catholic	% Cath.	Kindergarten
1950	129,553				
1960-61	121,901	21,345	6,464	23.2	
1965	123,521				
1966-67[a]	165,000	33,665[b]	6,536	16.3	3,170
1968	166,000	35,048	5,641	13.9	2,988
1969	166,500	34,683			2,854
1970-71	166,682	34,387	4,752	12.1	2,679
1971-72		34,223	4,601	11.8	2,652

TABLE II

Assessments and Taxation in Kansas City

Item	1960	1964	1970
Assessment	$96,121,037	130,547,139	$184,288,043
Millage: Total	12.5218	13.0806	19.60421
School	4.9942	4.9181	7.35554
Total Tax	$12,043,966	$17,075,476	$36,220,448
School Tax	4,856,000	6,420,320	13,255,294
Total Per Capita	$99	$138	$217
Per Capita Sch.	39	52	79
Tax on $20,000 House	300.50	313.93	470.50
For Schools	119.80	118.00	176.53

a. In 1966, Kansas City annexed Quindaro, Wyandotte, and Shawnee and thereby increased its population to 166,682 in 1970.

b. The Unified School District was established in 1967, which thereafter embraced approximately the same area as the expanded Kansas City.

TABLE III^a

General Statistics Concerning Schools

Item	1960	1967-68	1969-70
Enrollment			33,348
Teachers			1,369
ADA	21,345	31,382	
PTR	26.0	25.44	25.1
Operational Cost	$5,986,800	$13,964,950	$16,899,787
Av. Per-Pupil	$280	$442	$507
Including Debt Service			542

---

a. The statistics in this table supplied by the State Superintendent of
Public Instruction, and are not identical to those in Table I, supplied by
the Board of Education in Kansas City.

An analysis of St. Paul was inevitable because it has been the North Central American capital of Roman Catholicism—ironically enough, surrounded by great numbers of Scandinavian Lutherans, who possibly constitute a majority in the sister-city, Minneapolis.

Between 1880 and 1920, great numbers of German, Irish, French, Polish, Bohemian, and other Catholics came to St. Paul[a] and established their schools and churches, in many of which worship and education continued for decades in their foreign tongues. In 1886, there were 6 church schools with 2,115 pupils; in 1905,18 with 7,217; in 1920, 21 with 8,943; and in 1964, 52 with 33,318. Then a rapid decline set in; by 1968, the enrollment was 24,649 and in 1970-71, it had dropped to 20,811. In September, 1971, at least three more were to be closed with an additional loss of about 2,000 pupils.

Parochiaid, and Parochial Decline

When Catholic authorities began proclaiming that, without subsidies, their schools would continue to shrink or cease operations entirely, they also mounted a persistent campaign in Minnesota to obtain parochiaid from the state. On May 14, 1971, after protracted and acrimonious debate, the Senate passed a bill (already approved in the House and advocated by the governor) to provide $21 million in tax credits and

---

a.   In 1910, of 214,744 people, there were only 61,594 with native-born parents; in 1920, there were still only 77,378 out of 234,698 in this category.

98

tuition refunds for parents whose children attend private schools. Mr. Ernest Lindstrom, Majority Floor Leader of the House, denounced the law as unconstitutional. In the summer and fall of 1971, two suits, supported by various organizations, were filed to invalidate it.

That more than a dozen of the old Catholic schools in St. Paul should have been closed during the Sixties is not too difficult to understand: they were obsolete, inadequate, and in deteriorating areas. But this does not explain why St. Joseph's Academy, near the great Cathedral, which had 720 students in 1965-66, fell to 350 in 1969-70, and ceased operations in June, 1971. Even more extraordinary is the case of Hill; completed in 1959 and designed for 1,200 boys, its enrollment fell to 729 in 1970 and it closed its doors in 1971. When another magnificent high school, the Brady, was completed in 1964-65, with a capacity enrollment of about 2,000, the hierarchy must have been confident that expansion would continue indefinitely. Its student body, however, which was 1,130 in 1968, fell to 948 in 1970-71.

Private and Public Schools

The public schools of St. Paul had been in straightened circumstances for decades, which is not surprising, since the thousands of parents with children in parochials had little motivation to vote public school bond issues. We found, furthermore, that the Catholic schools have been far more affluent than their public counterparts: in 1968, the official assessments on the former were $7,488,010, while those on the latter totalled only $4,309,800.[a] This means that a value of at least $75 million was placed on the parochials while the public schools were rated at only $43 million.[b] It is interesting to compare these statistics with those in Minneapolis, where the public schools represented an investment of $94,500,000, while all private schools combined totalled only $16 million, of which $6,500,000 was invested in Catholic facilities. We should note, however, that in spite of the higher ratio of pupils in public schools in Minneapolis, the overall millage and tax there were lower than in St. Paul.

Table I traces the development of public and private school enrollment in St. Paul. Table II does the same for the state. Perhaps the most significant fact emerging from these statistics is that the ratio of Catholic pupils in the City increased from 23% in 1920 to 42.6% in 1964 and then

---

a.   Assessments are theoretically about 10 or 11% of true value.
b.   The 1970 *Financial Report* of the St. Paul School District placed the value of all school property at that date at $53,585,280.76. There had, of course, been considerable expansion between 1968 and 1970.

declined to 29.2% in 1970. We note that while private education statewide was far less prevalent than in St. Paul, a roughly parallel development occurred. In 1910, only 4.5% of total enrollment was in church-related or other private schools; but this ratio rose to 14.2% in 1955 and to 25.2% in 1965—after which it declined rapidly to 11.8% in 1970.

The Research Department of the Catholic Education Center at 251 Summit Avenue in St. Paul issued a document on March 1, 1971, stating that in 1963-64 the diocese had 179 schools with an enrollment of 80,206; but that, in 1970, there were only 143 with 60,486 pupils. In a plea to the State legislature for parochiaid, Reverend John R. Gilbert, Superintendent of Education in the St. Paul diocese, asked this question: "Why should others support schools which are losing their own support from within?"[a] To this he replied that "Church members of 1970 are contributing far more to...the schools than ever before..."—a statement which certainly needs close scrutiny. And was he referring to actual dollars or to a proportion of income?

In 1964-65, there were 600 religious and 388 lay teachers in the St. Paul Catholic schools; in 1970-71, these numbered 372 and 494 respectively. According to the *Education Statistics*,[b] the average pay for lay teachers was about $6,500 in 1970—at most, $4,000 more than the salary and maintenance for a sister or a brother; and, since the number of the former increased by only 106, their total of increased emoluments could not have exceeded $425,000, which was offset by the reduction of 228 religious, whose cost would have been at least $575,000. The net savings, therefore, should have been not less than $150,000. And we must remember that in 1970-71 the Catholic schools of St. Paul alone received well over a million dollars in federal benefits above those granted in 1964. It is therefore difficult to see how an enrollment of 20,000 in 1970 could have entailed heavier expenditures than one of 33,318 in 1964-65.

Nor is this all: between 1952 and 1965, Catholic laymen continued to pour vast sums into the construction of new schools. Our Lady of Peace, Hill, St. Bernard, Archbishop Murray, and Brady—for secondary students—were all built during these years, at a cost of at least $12 or $15 million. On the elementary level, St. Thomas the Apostle, St. Odilia, St. Peter Claver, St. Pascal Baylon, St. Gregory, Transfiguration, Guadalupe, Nativity, St. Jerome, Immaculate Heart of Mary, Maternity of the Blessed Virgin, and Corpus Christi were completed at a cost which probably

a. "A Philosopy of Education," reprinted in the *Nonpublic Education Report*, published by the Fargo diocese.
b. Published by the Research Department of the St. Paul Catholic Education Center.

exceeded $20 million. At least $2.5 million a year, therefore, probably went into construction alone between 1952 and 1965. If this was possible during that period without any serious negative reaction, why is it now necessary to close magnificent schools presumably free from debt? And why must so large a portion of a system which served more than 33,000 in 1964 now stand idle?

It is certainly pertinent to note that while the hierarchy emphasized the tax-savings of their schools to the public, they have never stressed the huge economies which public schools offer their own laymen: would it be correct to assume that the latter have made their own calculations and decisions in this matter?

Dr. Louis A. Haak, Jr., Supervisor of Administrative Research for the Board of Education, stated that, in spite of thousands of transfers, and although it is not required by law, the average class in the public system had been reduced from 29 to 24 during recent years. Since he is active in a parish school, his assurance that the public system has been able to absorb thousands of parochial pupils without any difficulty was particularly significant. Simply by increasing the average class size to thirty, about 12,000 new students could be accepted. He stated that State Foundation Aid ranged from $142 to $390 per pupil, depending on need and local effort; and that should a crisis arise in St. Paul, such contributions might approach the maximum.[a] Dr. Haak also pointed out that between 1970 and 1971—in spite of several hundred transfers from private schools—the public enrollment actually dropped from 50,558 to 49,962.[b]

We toured the city inspecting private and public schools; and were fully confirmed in our previous impression that the former are far more opulent and more abundantly equipped with playgrounds and other facilities. Sometimes we noted a huge church with its magnificent school just around the corner from an old and inferior public facility. There is certainly nothing in the public domain superior to Brady, Lady of Peace, Murray, or even Hill. Yet we noted that St. Rose of Lima, at 1284 Eldridge, with its new and beautiful circular church, has a modern school, which enrolled 549 pupils in 1969, but is now closed. Immaculate Heart of Mary and St. Luke—with a combined enrollment of 1,991 in 1964 and 1,567 in 1970— have magnificent new schools, located only a few blocks from each other. Many of the buildings carried signs, of which the following was typical:

---

a.   State Foundation Aid was $173 in 1967 and $207 in 1970 in St. Paul.
b.   This is total enrollment or Average Number Belonging, which was almost 3,000 more than ADA.

THE TAXPAYER'S BEST FRIEND
St. Mark's School Saves
the Taxpayers $740,000
Saves $671 per pupil; Buildings Worth
$2,008,116.00

We can testify that this valuation was conservative.

What has it cost the City taxpayers to absorb some 12,000 or 13,000 transfers in a few years?

Between 1960-61 and 1970-71, millage increased from 172.52 to 348.2; the total property levy rose from $40,716,978 to $91,854,100; and that for schools from $12,100,972 to $38,915,100—an increase of more than $10 million in the last year alone. The per-capita levy for public schools increased from $39 to $126—more than 220%.

This, of course, was due to various causes and roughly paralleled the experience of other Minnesota communities which had few or no transfers from parochials. The fact is that public school enrollment increased much more rapidly between 1960 and 1965—when there were no transfers—than it did during the following five years. At least two-thirds of the increase can be charged against general inflation; since 1960-61, the average salary of teachers rose from $6,400 to $10,200. Because the pupil-teacher ratio was reduced from 30 to 24, it became necessary to increase the staff from 1,682 to 2,650. Other significant factors contributing to rising costs have been (1) the need for increased facilities and new buildings to replace those many decades old; and (2) the demand for new and improved services never provided by the parochials. For years, it was virtually impossible to obtain funds to improve or expand the public system: one bond issue of $8,779,000 in 1950 and another for $11 million in 1953 were the only ones voted until 1959, when an issue of $23 million was approved to be expended over a period of years. It was nine more years before another (for $10,000,000) was approved. In 1964, debt service cost $1,397,599; in 1970-71, the outstanding debt was $42,064,000,[a] and the cost of amortization had risen to $3,604,032.55.

Table IV summarizes revenues and expenditures in the Independent School District No. 625.[b] We find that general receipts between 1960-61

a. This means that the public schools had been neglected so long and so recently improved that the City was in debt for more than 80% of its educational plant.

b. The Board of Education has offices on the upper floors of the City-County Building in the center of the City.

and 1970-71 increased from $17,644,798 to $48,904,602; and per-pupil operating cost from $387 to $967. The overall cost rose from $432 to $1,093—the increase being more than $140 during the last year alone—which resulted largely from expanding personnel and higher salaries. This is the highest operating cost we have encountered.

In spite of all this, the property tax for the ordinary home owner was not as onerous as one might expect: and this was because of the complicated manner in which assessments are computed. A home valued at $18,000 carries a Fair and True Appraisal of $6,000, which is assessed at 40%, or $2,400: but the homestead exemption reduces this to $1,800, which, at 350 mills, entails a tax of $630. However, there is, in addition, a 35% Homestead Credit or Taconite Relief, which reduces the net levy to about $450. On a $30,000 house, the tax is about $800—still considerably less than in Duluth and in a number of other cities such as Milwaukee.

The Public School Plant

In 1970-71, the St. Paul school plant consisted of 64 elementaries, 18 secondaries, and the splendid new Vocational Institute. All were fully utilized; there were even 37 portable classrooms. Many of the buildings, however, were old, one dating back to 1874[a] and 14 from the 1880s. The bonds voted in 1950, 1953, and 1959 were used for various additions and improvements to existing buildings; for the construction of 16 elementary and 5 high schools; and, most of all, to erect the Vocational Institute, completed in 1966, at a cost of about $8 million. In the meantime, enrollment increased from 34,726 in 1950 to 50,588 in 1971. Over a period of 17 years, about $45,000,000 has been expended.

Looking across the freeway from a window in the Holiday Inn, one can observe the large rectangular building which houses the Vo-Tech, which enrolled 2,600 full-time high school graduates and served several thousand adults in evening classes. Mr. Gerhard Nelson, Coordinator of this remarkable enterprise, gave us a tour of the large facility, explaining that it now involves an investment—including equipment—of more than $15 million. There are, he stated, 31 vocational schools in the State, which prepare tens of thousands of graduates for positions in business and industry. They are parts of public schools systems, but do not prepare for college entry and are wholly separate from conventional academic programs.

---

a.   This was being razed and replaced by a new building in 1971-72.

Channelled through the State Superintendent of Public Instruction and District No. 625, the federal government supplied $1,847,297.01 for capital expenditures in 1969-70, and a total of $2,335,079.41 for ten ESEA programs. Since the public schools enrolled 70% and the Catholic 30% of their combined enrollment, we concluded that of this sum at least $700,000 was expended for projects and programs benefitting parochial schools and pupils.

The State Superintendent of Public Instruction issued a report in 1969-70 showing that $845,076.52 of federal money was expended in St. Paul for lunches in the public schools; and, since the parochials received comparable subsidies for this purpose from the same source, but independently, we computed the Catholic share at not less than $350,000. The Catholic schools of St. Paul, therefore, enjoyed federal benefits costing the taxpayers well over $1 million in 1969-70, or about $50 for every pupil enrolled.

We interviewed Mr. Leonard F. Urbaniak, Business Administrator and Coordinator of Government Programs at the Catholic Bureau of Education, which is housed in what was once the vast mansion of the railroad tycoon, J. D. Hill, at 240 Summit Avenue. He stated that under Title II of ESEA, Catholic schools received about $1.25 for every pupil, or $25,000 in 1970-71; and that there were 4,000 identifiable Catholic "disadvantaged" children in the city,[a] for each of whom an average of $145 was expended under Title I, a total of $580,000. There was also some aid under other ESEA titles. He stated further that the U.S. Department of Agriculture supplied 15,000 Catholic pupils daily with free lunches worth about 45 or 50 cents each: a total value of $1,500,000 in the diocese, which enjoyed direct or indirect federal subsidies totalling some $4 million in 1970-71.

Mr. Urbaniak stated that there are about 200 Negro pupils among 60,000 in the diocese.[b] All of them were previously in the St. Peter Claver School, but are now distributed among four parishes to comply with federal regulations.

Catholic pupils had been receiving some bus service at public expense in smaller communities, but so far none in St. Paul or Minneapolis. A law

---

a. In the whole diocese, there were about 12,000, for whom about $1,750,000 was expended under Title I of ESEA alone in 1969-70.
b. In the St. Paul public schools, Negro enrollment in 1968 was 2,907 out of 50,222, or 5.8%.

providing shared time was enacted in 1969, and about 800 Catholic pupils were taking advantage of this. Released time during school hours was also permitted: 500 in St. Paul and 2,000 in the diocese were participating in this program.

Mr. Urbaniak concluded by saying that Hill, St. Joseph, and St. Therese were closing in June, 1971; and that several other schools were on the verge of doing so, but were withholding any further announcements until they could be definite.

Dr. Dale E. Henry, Associate Director of Catholic Education, stated that sisters received salaries of about $1,500, in addition to maintenance; that tuition in elementary schools ranged from $60 a year downward; and that about 8% of all pupils paid none at all.

A New Program of Expansion

After 1959, as already noted, nine years passed without the approval of a single bond issue. Then, in 1968, after absorbing thousands of Catholic transfers, the public schools were voted $10 million, to which the federal government added a grant of $1 million, for a new program of expansion and replacement to provide for several thousand additional pupils. By September, 1972, one junior and one senior high were scheduled for completion; three old elementaries were to be replaced; and various additions and improvements were being made to other schools.

Summary

The falling birth rate had already come into full operation in St. Paul in 1971. Although the Catholic schools enrolled 12,507 fewer pupils than six years earlier, the public had added only 5,084, of whom more than 2,500 were registered at the Vocational Technical Institute, which did not even exist in 1965. Although the population remained virtually unchanged, there were 9,000 fewer births between 1959 and 1967 than between 1951 and 1959: which accounts for the fact that total enrollment dropped from 78,822 in 1964 to 69,462 in 1971. It is also certain that it will continue to decline, at least until 1979.

If all Catholic Schools should close at once, a large portion of the transfers could be absorbed simply by increasing the size of classes; the city could lease or purchase some of the better parochial facilities, especially Hill, Brady, Murray and Lady of Peace. Taxes would no doubt increase somewhat; but federal subsidies and State Foundation Aid would cover much of the cost. There is no doubt that the community would then grant the schools any reasonable request, for it would be united in a common cause. Finally, and perhaps most important of all, Catholic parents would be relieved of the necessity of paying something like $8 or $10 million a year for the support of a competing educational system; and they would be able to wield definite influence in the operation of the schools attended by their children.

And would it be unreasonable to suggest that perhaps an even greater blessing would be the commingling of the entire youth of the city in the great melting pot known as the public school?

T A B L E I

Catholic and Public School Enrollment in St. Paul

S c h o o l E n r o l l m e n t

Year	Population	Total	Public	Catholic	% Catholic
1886	133,156			2,115	
1910	214,744			7,217	
1920	234,698	38,910[a]	29,967	8,943	23.0
1930	271,606	53,557	39,617	13,940	26.2
1940	287,736	51,723	37,728	13,995	27.1
1950	311,349	53,214	34,726	18,488	34.7
1961	313,411	73,945	42,762	31,183	42.4
1964	310,000	78,822	45,504	33,318	42.6
1968[b]	309,000	73,891	49,242	24,649	32.9
1970-71	308,686	73,399	50,588	20,811	29.2
1971-72	308,000	69,962	50,962	19,000[c]	27.6

a. In addition to numbers given in this column, there were some private non-Catholic schools which enrolled 2,574 in 1965 and 2,280 in 1970, almost all of which were in Lutheran schools except for 595 in the St. Paul-Summit school in 1965 and 636 in 1970.

b. It should be noted that Vo-Tech, which did not exist in 1964, enrolled about 2,000 in 1968 and 2,500 in 1971. Had this not been established, total enrollment would have fallen by 11,520 between 1964 and 1971, instead of by 9,980.

c. This assumes that Catholic enrollment in Oct., 1971, fell by 1,800 under that of 1970-71.

TABLE II

Public and Private Enrollment in Minnesota

Year	Population	Public Sch. Enrollment	Private Enrollment	Total Enrollment	% In Non-public
1910	2,075,708	440,083	21,000	461,083	4.5
1920	2,404,125	503,597	45,374	548,971	8.3
1932	2,585,000	558,148	64,300	622,448	10.4
1955	3,174,000	597,000	98,570	695,570	14.2
1965	3,555,000	552,000	186,000	738,000	25.2
1970	3,767,975	928,030[a]	124,934	1,052,964	11.8

TABLE III

Millages and Taxes in St. Paul

Item	1960-61	1964-65	1970-71
Taxable Assessment	$236,013,089	$246,281,845	$260,972,668
Total Millage	172.52	239.79	348.20
For Schools	51.2731	81.98	149.20
Total Tax	$40,716,978	$59,049,366	$91,854,100
For Schools	12,100,972	20,195,124	38,915,100
Per Capita Tax	$130	$190	$294
For Schools	39	65	126

a. We can only account for the enormous increase of 1970 over 1965 by the following factors: the great number of transfers from private schools; the development of kindergarten and summer schools; the increase in secondary registrations; and the tremendous expansion of vocational institutes, which added their full- and part-time students to the total enrollment of public schools.

TABLE IV

Financial Data in the St. Paul Schools

Revenues	1960	1965	1969-70	1970-71
Local Taxes	$10,960,004	$18,422,082	$25,029,589	$34,667,602
State Aid	5,319,629	7,198,498	9,884,500	10,387,000[a]
Sales Tax Aid			1,374,850	1,375,000
Federal Aid	125,272	235,516	280,000	250,000
Tuition	64,482	83,873	398,000	499,000
Special Taxes	379,810	509,906	507,500	403,000
Miscellaneous			53,400	63,000
Com. Service	143,584	216,132		
Carryover	255,034	431,521	1,226,400	1,280,000
Total	$17,247,814	$27,097,540	$38,754,239	$48,904,602

Expenditures				
Administration	411,099	594,574	943,742	1,502,355
Instruction	11,335,520	16,951,894	29,774,982	35,792,247
Operation	1,648,949	2,554,454	3,430,456	4,074,425
Maintenance	573,344	1,070,040	1,487,640	3,160,170
Health	465,834	702,571	1,111,296	1,514,916
Fixed Charges	1,594,935	2,576,062	335,922	209,466
Transportation	95,409	139,899	513,365	718,307
Community Serv	419,707	578,900	1,100,792	1,709,716
City Services			224,000	224,000
Total	$16,544,798	$25,168,396	$38,754,239	$48,905,602
Debt Service		3,429,055	5,146,335	6,422,942
Grand Total		$28,598,451	$43,900,574	$55,328,544
Cost Per Pupil				
Operational	$391	$541	$787	$967
Overall		615	867	1,093

---

a.   This includes federal aid channelled through the State.

The visitor to Milwaukee is impressed by the multiplicity of tall steeples and shimmering domes; and he cannot but marvel at the enormous dedication and sacrifice that must have gone into their construction. The telephone book lists nearly 600 Protestant and miscellaneous churches in the metropolitan area, of which 220 are Lutheran. Even so, the Catholic Church comprises the dominant faith.

Not to analyze Milwaukee would have been unthinkable; for its history epitomizes the essence of Catholic growth and development in America. Of the 35 Catholic parishes in the city in 1892, 14 were German, 10 Polish, 2 Bohemian, 1 Slovenian, 1 Irish, and the others unclassified. The 1971 *Official Catholic Directory* gives 83 parishes within the city alone, which operated 78 schools as late as 1965. But in 1971-72 enrollment dropped by 23,000 and the number of schools had been reduced to 59.

In 1840, Milwaukee was a village of 1,700 souls. But a flood of immigrants following the Civil War pushed the population to 71,440 in 1870, 204,468 in 1890, 372,857 in 1910, and 457,147 in 1920. Even then, only 130,845, or 28.6% of its people, had native parentage. By and large, until well after WW I, Milwaukee was a predominantly German-Polish city. However, by 1930, when the population had risen to 578,249, the foreign born numbered only 109,383.

School Enrollments

As the birth rate soared at the close of WW II, the total number of school-age children increased from 119,368 in 1950 to 147,328 in 1955, 188,386 in 1961, and peaked at 206,997 in 1966. Meanwhile, public school registrations expanded from 66,544 in 1950 to 129,648 in 1969 and to 130,617 in 1970.

During the last hundred years, Milwaukee witnessed a tremendous growth and then a rather sudden decline in its Catholic schools. In 1892, as shown in Table I, they enrolled 9,991; in 1910, 19,029; in 1930, 30,442; in 1950, 34,800; in 1964, they reached their peak of 52,097. In 1965, they fell to 51,021; in 1966, to 47,913; in 1968, to 44,321; in 1970-71, to 31,504; and in the fall of 1971, to 28,701. Throughout the Fifties, they educated half as many as attended the public schools and continued nearly at this level well into the Sixties. In 1950, the Catholic ratio of school enrollment was 33.8%; in 1961, 32.4%; in 1968, 24%; in October, 1971, 17.2%.

The Roman Catholic is not the only strong parochial system in Wisconsin; for both the Missouri and the Wisconsin Lutheran Synods operate a considerable number of schools. In September, 1956, the former had 22 with 4,500 pupils and the latter 25 with 3,300 in the County, of whom 6,537 were in the City. In 1961, this number had risen to 8,663; in 1966, it was 8,659; in October, 1971, the total had declined slightly to 7,392. In September, 1968, the Martin Luther High School, built at a cost of $2.3 million and designed for 1,000 students, was dedicated by the Missouri Synod. The Wisconsin Synod opened two new schools in 1968 in the Milwaukee area.

There were also a few other private schools which enrolled 419 pupils in 1966 and 649 in 1971.

Property Taxation

Since there are so many magnificent churches and so much other exempt property in Milwaukee, it should not be surprising that, in spite of the large parochial systems, taxes have always been heavy.[a] The total assessments as well as the millages and levies for various purposes for 1955, 1961, 1965, and 1970 are shown in Table II. Between those years, the property levy rose from $82,271,015 to $245,042,245, while the population remained relatively static. The per-capita tax tripled from $115 to $345; and that on a $30,000 house rose from $785 to $1,450.[b]

---

a.   In Sept., 1971, the Associated Press released a feature article stating that the middle class in Milwaukee is the most heavily taxed group in the United States (cf. Arizona *Republic*, Sept. 24, 1971). Added to the heavy property tax, there is a sales and use tax of 4% and a personal income tax of 5.2% at $5,000 and 10% at $14,000.

b.   In the County as a whole, however, the millage in 1970 was only 35.82, compared to 48.33 in the City. In the suburb of Franklin, it was only 15.03—less than one-third of the Milwaukee rate.

School Revenues and Expenditures

In Table III and IV, we summarize public school revenues and expenditures. Since enrollment increased from 66,544 in 1950 to 129,648 in 1968, a tremendous program of construction became necessary; the number of school buildings increased from 97 in 1950 to 147 in 1965-66; and the teaching staff from 2,468 to 4,730. Between 1955 and 1970, nearly $150 million was expended for capital improvements. The bonded debt, which was $17,883,000 in 1956, rose to $48,160,583 in 1970; and the inventory of school property from $75,056,065 to $210,975,355.

Certainly, no such achievement could be accomplished without sacrifice. In 1956, the City tax provided $18,241,418 for the schools; in 1961, $29,769,742; in 1966, $48,125,042; and in 1970, $77,177,750. In 1971, the school budget called for a property tax of $91,236,413. Between 1956 and 1970, the operational cost rose from $25,083,297 to $93,839,827; and for 1971-72, this was pegged at $113,942,411. In spite of the fact that State Aid rose from zero to $25,881,695, the local property tax supplied an ever-increasing ratio of total support: in 1956, it was 58%; in 1970, 75.3%; and in 1971-72, 80.1%.

These totals do not include capital outlays, which are handled in a separate budget. Nor do they include interest on bonds, since these are serviced directly from the City budget. Federal programs, which involved expenditures of $2,374,362 in 1966 and $5,770,755 in 1970, are treated as independent entities.

According to the official statistics supplied by the Board of Education, the per-pupil cost of schooling rose from $329.85 in 1956 to $746.58 in 1970. According to our own computations, when capital outlays and federal programs are included, the totals for these years were $393.15 and $833.33. In 1971-72, the operational cost rose to $876 and the overall to $1,013.

The Racial Composition

In 1930, when the population of the city was 578,249, it had only 9,442 Negroes; in 1960, the comparable totals were 741,324 and 62,453; and in 1970, 717,000 and 105,000.

Nor have the Milwaukee schools suffered any substantial loss of enrollment because of a white exodus; and the absorption of parochial transfers, being unrelated to racial tensions, has proceeded in a manner similar to that occurring on the national scene, where Catholic enrollment dropped by about 30% between 1965 and 1971. The experience of a major, predominantly white, city like Milwaukee, therefore, where the decline was 45%, should be highly interesting and informative.

Nevertheless, there is a racial factor in the public and the Catholic schools. Both took a racial census in 1970; and the results, as shown in Table VII, are illuminating. In the latter, the elementary Negro enrollment was only 487 among 19,438, or 2.51%; on the secondary level, they numbered 197, or 4.71%, among 4,182. The public schools, in contrast, enrolled 34,355, who comprised 26% of their pupils. Had blacks constituted the same percentage in all schools, their ratio would have been just under 20%.

Catholic School Statistics

The number of Catholic schools increased from 23 in 1892 to 66 in 1930, 82 in 1946, and 98 in 1965; during the next five years, 23 of these were discontinued. Even more significant are statistics concerning their staff: in 1910, this totalled 405, of whom 402 were religious—almost all sisters. In 1930, in a staff of 760, there was only one lay teacher. Thereafter, such personnel increased, slowly at first, but with ever-increasing tempo: in 1940, the ratio was 832 to 30; in 1950, 1,094 to 49; in 1955, 1,006 to 195; in 1961, 1,076 to 438; in 1965, 1,063 to 562; and in 1970, lay teachers constituted 54.1% of the force: 688 among 1,274.

Class-sizes in Catholic schools are no less significant; and, since Milwaukee constitutes a practical microcosm of its entire American complex, we consulted old directories for specific data. In 1892, the pupil-teacher ratio was an incredible 66.2; in 1900, this had fallen to 47.4; in 1930, to 40; in 1955, 35.7; in 1964, 35.3; with sharply reduced enrollment, it fell to 24.8 in 1970-71.[a]

The Reverend Leslie A. Dernieder, Deputy Superintendent of the Milwaukee Catholic Schools, stated that in 1970-71 teaching priests received $2,400, in addition to transportation, housing, meals, health insurance, and provision for retirement. Sisters received $2,750, plus health insurance, lodging, meals, and limited transportation; but they provided for their own retirement through their orders. Lay teachers averaged $7,500 on the elementary and $9,000 on the secondary level.[b] They also received health insurance and were eligible for retirement benefits which ranged from $105 to $180 a month, in addition to Social Security.

---

a.   Some parochial teachers may have been part-time. In the public schools PTR dropped from 29.9 in 1945-46 to 23.3 in 1969-70.
b.   Public school teachers received salaries averaging $4,700 in 1955-56 and $10,095 in 1969-70.

Reverend Dernieder stated also that tuition in elementary schools, which ranged from zero to $100 in 1970, averaged about $65.00; and that per-pupil costs, 75% of which were met through parish subsidies, averaged $259. In the thirteen secondaries, of which 4 were diocesan and 8 private, tuition ranged from $350 to $700; since this did not cover total costs, each school was forced to raise somewhere between $75 and $200 per pupil from other sources.

Special Programs

Officials at the Board of Education declared, and Reverend Dernieder confirmed, that there was no released-or shared-time program in operation in Milwaukee; nor did the state or the Board of Education provide textbooks for church-related institutions. Catholic schools do, of course, participate in the state-federal lunch program, as do the public; and, since the latter received $365,104.79 in 1969-70 to subsidize it, we estimated that the former were given $150,000 in 1965 and possibly $85,000 in 1970 for this purpose.

Sister Carolita, in charge of federal programs, stated that until recently 8 schools had qualified for programs under Title I of ESEA; but that, since 1970, all of these, except St. Stanislaus, had been removed from Church control. In the coming year, she stated, less than 200 pupils would be qualifying for such aid.

She added that in 1969-70 Holy Angels was given $17,000 under a Title II program for help in reading; and an average of $1.25 to $1.50 per-pupil was received for library and audio-visual aids.

Bussing, however, which is heavily funded in Wisconsin, serves public and private pupils alike. Mr. Richard F. Wenzel, Director of Student Transportation, explained in detail how this operates and what it costs. In 1970-71, 16,000 pupils were transported, of whom 2,000 were in private schools. The total cost was $1,735,500, for which the Board of Education received approximately $725,000 as reimbursement from the state. For 1971-72, the total budget for this service would be $2,238,500.

To carry 2,000 Catholic and Lutheran pupils, the Board spent $199,681 in 1970-71, for which the state returned a reimbursement of $34,895. Thus, $164,786 was collected from the local taxpayers to transport parochial children in Milwaukee.[a]

---

a.   The Seventh-Day Adventist school refused to accept this service.

What, then, has happened to the Catholic schools? Between 1930 and 1955, they were growing much faster than the public. At the former date, their enrollment equalled 35.9% of the public: in 1950 and 1955, this ratio exceeded 53%. Then, however, began a continuous decline: to 45.2% in 1964, 41.1% in 1965, 38% in 1966, 31.8% in 1968, 24% in 1970, and 21.5% in 1971.

In his book, *Freedom in Education,* Father Virgil Blum makes an impassioned plea for freedom of choice; and cites the Francis Jordan High of Milwaukee as a case in point. When it began operation in 1959, parents waited an entire day and night to register their children at the school. At 5 P.M. the previous day enough were already in line to complete the enrollment. The disappointed parents, therefore, according to Father Blum, had no freedom of choice. In 1965, the Francis Jordan had 501 pupils; in 1968, it closed its doors—for lack of them. The parents had exercised their freedom of choice by transferring their children to the public schools.

Even more extraordinary is the case of Madonna High, completed in 1965 at a reputed cost of $4.5 million. With a capacity of 1,000, its enrollment never exceeded 268; this fell to 255 in 1970, when its deficit reached $104,696.[a]

Since Catholic educators dedicated ten new schools in Milwaukee between 1961 and 1968, they must not have foreseen what was in store. Before 1970, 15 schools closed; and, what is even more unusual, ten others were "separated"; i.e., they were removed entirely from Church control. A feature article in the Milwaukee *Journal* of May 2, 1971, entitled "What Ails Our Catholic Schools?" describes these extraordinary events in detail.

And what are these "Separated Schools"? Located in the Inner City, they have, according to Father Dernieder, ceased to communicate with the diocese and have become, to all intents and purposes—even while professing Catholicity—essentially secular institutions.

According to an article in the Milwaukee *Sentinel* of May 31, 1967, "a group of about fifty Catholic laymen . . . proposed that all schools in the ten-county archdiocese be owned and operated by a board of trustees, the majority of whom would be elected by church members. . . ." The existing board of education, they complained, "is appointed by and is merely advisory to Monsignor Edward J. Goebel, Superintendent of Schools." They proposed that an independent corporation be established, which would own and control the facilities; Catholic tenets would be

---

a.　Cf. Milwaukee *Journal,* Feb. 26 and May 2, 1971.

taught, but a lay board would make all contracts for teachers and buildings, determine curricula and policies, and publish complete financial reports, comparable to those available from the public schools. Although this proposal was received with little enthusiasm by the diocesan authorities, it has borne fruit in a system of community schools. Msgr. Goebel has also resigned.

That simmering dissatisfaction has existed among the Catholic laity for years was reflected in the fact that elementary schools were losing enrollment long before they began charging substantial or, in fact, any tuition at all. Nor is it recorded that the laymen objected to subsidizing their schools through parish contributions even after a considerable proportion of the teaching staff became laymen. In 1964-65, when enrollment reached its peak, there were already 499 lay teachers among a total of 1,505: since these increased only from 562 to 688 between 1965 and 1970, the additional cost involved could not have been a decisive or even a substantial factor. This was at least partially confirmed by Father Arthur Baertlin of St. Catherine's, located in a good, middle-class neighborhood, when he declared that of the 1,000 families in his parish, less than 200 sent their children to the parish school; and that disputes over its cost and operation are "causing polarization in the church."[a]

At the public Department of Education, we met its Director of Accounting, Mr. Ray J. Lewandowski, one of Father Baertlin's parishioners, who is a loyal Catholic with a broad educational perspective. He stated that tuition at St. Catherine's had been $60 for three or more children of the same family until 1968-69, but that it had now been raised to $125 for every child. However, even this was not the cause, but the result, of withdrawals: parents had for years been transferring their children to the public schools and, having done so, were unwilling to contribute heavily to maintain the church school, which, he declared, had a capacity of 600 but a present enrollment of only 200.

Why, we wondered, have Catholic laymen been transferring their children to the public schools?

"The most important reason is the quality of education—the public schools are much superior. They have better teachers, more courses, and more complete facilities."

Had the Catholic schools been deteriorating?

"Decidedly. Years ago, they had sisters with degrees and religious dedication who gave the kids a good education, both basic and religious. Now, they have hired inexperienced and uncertificated lay people who are

---

a.   Milwaukee *Journal,* June 6, 1971.

neither dedicated nor competent. I told my pastor that I wouldn't let my children into his school any longer."

Were there other important reasons?

"I would place rising tuition next; third, too much agitation for civil rights; fourth, lack of accountability; fifth, absence of lay control or influence; and, sixth, general disillusionment with the Church."

How important was accountability?

"On second thought, I would place this ahead of high tuition as a reason for withdrawing children from Catholic schools."

What should be included under "accountability"?

"We have no control over the money we contribute to the parish. What is worse is the fact that those who manage church and school finances are not competent to handle the funds. For example, when they were already beginning to lose pupils, they built Madonna High at a cost of nearly $5 million, and now it stands empty. Those who spend our money should be accountable for its use."

How much do Catholics in general contribute to their church?

"The pastor used to get up in the pulpit and tell the people how much they had to give, and they gave it. Those days are over. Now, I'd say only a few give as much as 5 or 6% of their earnings and lots of them, even those who go to Mass every Sunday, probably don't give more than 1%."

Will you explain about civil rights agitation: what do most Catholic laymen think of Father Groppi?

"He's a troublemaker! And when people found that their hard-earned money was being used to support his kind of activity, they just refused to give any more money to the Church."

Why doesn't the archbishop censure Groppi?

"The Bishop just sits there and says nothing."

You spoke of general disillusionment: is there a great deal of ferment in the Church?

"Yes, a tremendous amount. Some people are upset because Latin has been replaced with English. The old conservatives feel that nothing is certain anymore. Others are in rebellion over other things."

What about lay control of schools?

"There never has been any in the Catholic schools, and they will never again have general support from laymen without it."

What are these Separated Schools of which I have read?

"We have several pilot schools in the ghetto which have been removed from Church control entirely and are operated by a laymen's corporation. The Church was closing them for lack of revenue anyway. They are called Community Schools and they have removed every religious symbol. We hope to get federal money to help finance them."

116

What about religious instruction in them?

"As to that, I do not know."

What religious instruction is the Church giving pupils who attend the public schools?

"It doesn't amount to anything. They pretend to have classes in religion after school or on Saturday, but they talk about everything except religion."

Parochiaid in Wisconsin

In Wisconsin, as in many other states, a terrific battle over parochiaid has for some time been in progress. In late October, 1971, the Assembly on a tie vote defeated a bill to provide parents of pupils in private schools with state income tax credits of $38 for grade school children and $69 for those in high schools. In the course of bitter debate, Rep. Kenneth Merkel, himself a Catholic with children in parochial school, declared that the CEF should not be seeking public funds when Catholics themselves are refusing to support their own schools.[a] Rep. Anthony Earl declared that the problem was not one of dollars, but of spirit; and he declared that "we will be asked time and again to add more dollars." Dennis Conta, another Catholic Assemblyman, declared that the Church schools are very badly administered, that even with parochiaid they would continue without public supervision, and that many of their teachers are uncertified. Rep. Herbert Showalter stated that "Catholic schools will flourish. . .so much more if the state will keep its grubby, greasy little fingers out of them." Rep. James Azim, another Catholic parent, voted against the bill even though his constituency was overwhelmingly Catholic.

The Future of the Public School Plant

We have noted the great generosity with which Milwaukee taxpayers, in spite of the heavy cost to them and in spite of the large proportion with children in parochials, have provided capital outlay for the public schools: none have ever been required to hold double sessions. Following this tradition, on April 7, 1971, they approved a bond issue of $60 million, which, added to $16 million from the regular construction fund, will provide additions to 25 existing schools and for the building of at least a dozen others.

---

a.   Cf. Milwaukee *Sentinel,* Sept. 22, 1971.

It is therefore certain that no matter what demands may be made upon public education, its facilities will be ample to meet every responsibility. We should point out that between 1950 and 1965, when the population of Milwaukee increased from 637,000 to about 725,000, or 14%, the public school enrollment rose from 66,544 to 124,122, or 89%; and did so without any serious difficulty. Between 1965 and 1971, attendance in Catholic schools dropped by 22,320, yet public school enrollment increased by only 6,025. Between 1970 and 1971, for the first time in 24 years, public enrollment actually declined: from 130,617 to 130,147; and this in spite of the heavy influx from the Catholic schools.

To determine what future elementary and secondary enrollment will be, we need only consult the records for kindergarten registrations and the census of school-age children. In 1947-48, kindergarten attendance totalled 10,845; in 1951-52, 12,083; and in 1955-56, 16,454. In 1960-61, however, it fell to 14,409, and in 1968-69 to 11,744. Elementary enrollment, which was 94,602 in 1967-68, declined to 85,676 in 1971. The school census reached 188,386 in 1961 and 206,997 in 1966, but fell to 201,125 in 1968 and to 193,827 in June, 1971: a loss, in five years, of more than 13,000.

The lower birth rate reduced total enrollment for the first time in 1968, when it was 180,645, compared to 182,294 in 1967. Thereafter, the rate of decline increased rapidly, to 170,468 in 1970, and 167,125 in 1971. It is therefore not a matter of speculation, but a certainty, that by 1978-79, total enrollment must fall to about 135,000.

If every private school in Milwaukee should close during the next six or seven years, enrollment in the public sector would be only 5,000 higher than in 1970. Should all Catholic schools close while other privates continue at their present level, public enrollment would be less than in 1970.

Should Catholic enrollment decline to 15,000 and other private schools continue at 1965-70 levels, public school attendance will drop from its peak of 130,617 in 1970 to about 112,000.

Everything indicates, therefore, that as the new program of public school construction and expansion reaches completion in 1977, it will not only have ample facilities to care for all who apply, but will possess a considerably larger plant than necessary. It will, therefore, be able to reduce class sizes still further, supply additional programs, and give more individual attention to every pupil.

TABLE I

School Enrollment in Milwaukee[a]

Year	Total	Public	Catholic	%	Lutheran	Other
1892			9,981			
1900			13,815			
1910			19,029			
1920			22,378			
1930	118,305	84,280	30,442	25.7		3,183[b]
1940	111,066	78,183	30,585	28.4		2,318[b]
1950	102,664	66,544	34,800	33.8		
1955	129,548	80,087	42,756	33.0	6,537	1,178
1961	166,225	105,738	51,532	32.4	8,663	1,161
1964	178,139	115,158	52,097	28.8		9,573[b]
1965	183,432	124,122	51,021	27.9		9,324[b]
1966	184,274	126,279	47,913	26.0	8,659	419
1968	180,645	129,648	44,321	24.0		8,923[b]
1970	170,458	130,617	31,540	18.5	7,822	781
1971	167,125	130,147	28,701	17.2	7,392	649

a. All data from the *Annual Report* issued each year by the Board of Education, except Catholic enrollments, which are from the official Catholic directories. The slight discrepancies in totals are perhaps due to the fact that totals were taken during different months of the year.
b. These totals include Lutheran enrollments and are estimates.

TABLE II

The Property Tax in Milwaukee

Item	1955	1961	1965	1970
Valuations[a]	$3,029,534	$3,763,672	$4,014,665	$5,027,261
Total Millage	26.10	42.68	39.46	48.33
Gen. & Sch.	17.85	24.75	29.06	36.16
Total Levy	$82,871,015	$129.016,241	$160,632,666	$245,042,254
General	54,085,077	48,296,037	116,678,898	85,756,042
School		42,563,153		96,010,004
Per Capita	$115	$174	$225	$345
On $30,000 House	785	1,280	1,185	1,450

TABLE III

The 1971 Revenues and Expenditures of Public Schools

Revenues		Expenditures	
Tax Levy	$91,236,431	Administration	$4,992,495
State Aids	19,399,337	Instruction	79,840,742
County Aid	1,204,700	Attendance	958,826
In Lieu Taxes	2,021,000	Transportation	2,390,000
Tuition, Fees	761,500	Operation	9,474,865
Lunches	3,360,000	Maintenance	5,296,738
Miscellaneous	591,181	Fixed Charges	5,850,222
Surplus	4,990,804	Food Services	4,447,257
Operating Balance	3,204,684	Activities	691,266
Current Revenues	$126,769,637	*Total Operational*	$113,942,411
Sale of Bonds	4,832,266	Special Funds	10,236,200
Total Receipts	$131,601,903	Community Service	596,789
		Capital Outlay	6,826,503
		Total Expenditure	$131,601,903

Cost Per Pupil: Operational $876

Including Federal Programs and Debt Service   1,013

---

a.   Valuations in thousands, representing theoretical full cash value.

TABLE IV

Revenues and Expenditures (Continued)

Revenues	1961	1966	1970
City Tax	$29,769,742	$48,125,042	$77,177,750
State Aid	4,572,175	6,217,554	25,881,696
County	899,950	1,154,300	1,205,400
Shared Taxes	865,687	1,279,150	1,844,547
In Lieu Taxes	125,337	122,833	108,039
Tuition	299,324	300,037	663,944
Lunches: Sales	1,091,289	2,018,305	2,701,749
Federal Aid	332,015	1,445,105	838,198
Other and NDEA	365,785	417,518	528,261
Total	$38,321,403	$61,079,844	$110,949,584
Non-Revenue	1,010,423	2,538,702	8,563,593
Federal		946,644	5,602,144
Other		1,592,058	2,961,449
Total Receipts	$39,331,826	$63,618,546	$119,513,177
Expenditures			
General	38,738,619	56,587,433	93,839,827
Recreation	457,256	580,899	952,912
Capital Outlay	10,914,307	12,211,606	8,538,310
Federal Loss		1,427,718	119,371
Grand Total	$50,110,182	$70,807,656	$103,450,421
For Federal Programs		2,374,362	5,470,755
Total		$73,182,018	$108,921,176
Bonded Debt	43,816,000	58,302,100	48,160,583
Value of Property	125,413,384	176,000,789	210,975,345
Cost Per Pupil			
Operational	$396.95	$484.92	$746.58
Total	472.73	572.77	833.33

TABLE V

Instructional Information

Year	Teachers	Buildings	ADM	PTR	Av. Salary
1945-46	2,360	95	70,078	29.9	
1950-51	2,468	97	68,800	27.9	
1955-56	3,278	122	88,920	27.1	$4,700
1960-61	3,915	141	97,174	24.8	6,021
1965-66	4,730	147	114,644	24.3	7,140
1969-70	5,316	156	123,699	23.3	10,095

TABLE VI[a]

Financial Data Concerning Catholic Schools in 1970-71

Tuition	Range	Average
Elementary	$ 00.00 to $100	$65.00
Parish and Diocesan		
Secondary	$350.00 to $700	$475.00
Private High School	$500.00 to $750.00	$600.00
Per-Pupil Cost		
Elementary		$295.00[b]
Secondary		$500.00[c]

Emoluments of Teachers		
Priests	$2,400	Plus a variety of fringe benefits
Sisters	$2,750	
Lay:	$7,500	
Average Elementary	$9,000	Plus health insurance and retirement from $105 to $180 per month, in addition to SS.

---

a. All information supplied by Reverend Leslie A. Dernieder, Deputy Superintendent of Milwaukee Catholic Schools

b. Parishes pay 75% of cost in the form of subsidies.

c. Must raise from $75 to $200 per pupil through drives and from investments.

TABLE VII

Racial Composition of Milwaukee Schools in 1970-71

The Public[a]			%
Enrollment		132,349	
White		93,023	70.5
Negro		34,355	26.0
Indian		726	.5
Oriental		349	.3
Spanish-American		3,898	2.7

The Catholic[b] Elementary		%	High School	%
Enrollment	19,438		4,182	
White	18,438	94.86	3,817	91.27
Negro	487	2.51	197	4.71
Oriental	24	.12	14	.33
Indian	59	.30	23	.55
Sp. American	430	2.21	131	3.13

a.   Article in Milwaukee *Sentinel* of April 30, 1971.
b.   Data supplied by the Milwaukee Catholic Office of Education; not all, but representative schools, reported for this survey.

On April 2, 1971, The Most Reverend Charles A. Buswell, Bishop of the Pueblo diocese, published a statement filling an entire page in the Pueblo *Chieftain* in which he announced that the two Catholic high schools and ten elementaries in the city would close the following June.[a] Since this was the largest Catholic educational system in which so drastic a step had occurred, it became national news.

The Bishop described the development of Catholic education in the city, its long history, and the great devotion and sacrifice which had maintained it. However, he pointed out that less than one-fourth of the local Catholic youth were in Church schools; that enrollment had been declining; that there had been a heavy loss of religious; that "building debts [had] hit the parishes and the diocese. He admitted there "was also some disenchantment with the Catholic schools on the part of many in the Church." He explained that this diocese, the Archdiocese of Denver, and the Colorado Catholic Conference, had expended thousands of dollars and that great personal effort and sacrifice had been made to inform the citizens and the legislature of their plight. In spite of all this, the children's Tuition Aid Bill had failed of enactment by the legislature.

Further, the Bishop knew "of no realistic reason to expect any significant financial assistance from either the Federal Government or the State Government in the next five or six years . . . . While we will continue to explore every avenue of financial assistance which might help in non-public education, I must realistically conclude that little if any financial assistance is likely to come in the next few years."

The great problem in the Pueblo diocese and its parishes was impending bankruptcy: $125,000 was due on Roncalli; the two high schools had

---

a.   This followed the rejection by the state legislature of a bill that would have provided $200 of parochiaid for each Catholic pupil.

operating deficits of $87,034; the sixteen parishes had run in the red during the year by $194,615; and there were other operational deficits of $173,076. In short, unless the parishes could produce additional revenues of $616,000, expenses could not be met.

Since the laymen had met all demands for a hundred years, we can only conclude that the disenchantment of which the Bishop spoke must indeed have been wide and deep; and that it caused his People of God to close their purses ever more tightly after 1965.

The closing of the Pueblo schools has received considerable press coverage. An article under the byline of Ken Hudson, published in the Pueblo *Clarion-Ledger* Sept. 16, 1971, sounded the tocsin of alarm; for here we read that "Public school teachers and students had felt the impact immediately, with as many as 47 and 48 children in some classes. . . ." But "Pueblo's property owners won't feel the effect in their pocketbooks for a year and a half. . . ." According to the Reverend Joseph J. Behr, Superintendent of the Catholic schools, "that 18-month delay in letting the citizens feel the full effects of church school closing is part of a national public school public relations attempt to convince the people that the nation's five million parochial school children can be absorbed easily and inexpensively. . . ." An article in the *National Catholic Reporter,* of October 29, 1971, was entitled "From the Ashes Rises New Hope."

In the following pages, we offer the results of our own intensive investigation of taxes, school finances, educational facilities, teaching personnel, per-pupil costs, pupil-teacher ratios, and enrollments in the Pueblo schools. The Administration Building of the Board of Education is housed in an old redstone mansion located at 102 W. Orman Avenue, where we interviewed various key personnel, among whom Miss Virginia Spitzer, Secretary-Treasurer of the Board, proved a rich source of information.

Pueblo Schools and Population

Pueblo, home of the Colorado State Mental Hospital and largely dependent on the steel industry for its economy, is the third largest city in the State; following 1910, when its population was 41,747, it enjoyed a steady growth, which reached 63,685 in 1950. During the next decade it increased almost 50%, after which it experienced a gradual growth to 96,746 in 1970.

Although more than half its citizens are Catholic, the Church never enrolled more than 4,036 pupils in all its schools and they comprised only 13.1% of the District enrollment in 1964. Table I shows that in 1910, less than 5% of the youth were in parochial schools; however, both the number and the ratio of those so enrolled increased, especially after 1945, and reached a total of 3,552 and a percentage of 12.8 in 1961. After 1964, attendance fell, at first gradually, then more rapidly, declining to 2,701 and a ratio of 9% in 1970. In the whole diocese, which enrolled 7,705 pupils in 1965, there remained in October, 1971, 14 schools with 2,018 pupils. That the Church never approached its ideal of full religious education is shown by the fact that even in 1965, more than 24,000 of the Catholic youth were in the public schools.

Between 1961 and 1964, enrollment in both public and Catholic schools increased: the former from 24,232 to 26,601; and the latter by 484, or 13.6%. Although the population continued to grow, the falling birth rate became operative after 1965, when public enrollment reached 27,475. Between 1968 and 1970, the public schools absorbed 898 Catholic pupils; but registrations increased by less than a hundred and were 272 less than in 1965.

Ken Hudson states that in 1971 alone the public schools were forced to absorb 2,713 Catholic pupils; however, Miss Spitzer stated that the actual transfers totalled no more than 2,200; and the official records show that enrollment between October, 1970, and October, 1971, increased by only 401. At the same time, by leasing two Catholic schools, the public increased their capacity by 1,600.

Pueblo has a large minority of Chicanos; in October, 1971, its public schools enrolled 40 orientals, 30 American Indians, 601 Negroes, 11,039 with Spanish surnames, and 16,892 others. Thus, more than 40% of the school enrollment was Hispanic.

Taxation and Financing

After 1965, two former districts were combined into School District No. 60, which extends beyond the city limits. District No. 70, which does not concern us in this study, comprises the remainder of the County. However, since there were no parochial schools in the latter area, the comparison in Table I is comprehensive.

The combined assessments in Districts 1/60 and 20/60 increased from $139,836,662 in 1959 to $158,397,012 in 1965; the millages rose from about 39 to about 49; and the revenue from $6,143,765 to $8,049,042. The per-capita property tax for schools rose from $67 to $85, which was indeed modest, since this reflected an operating increase in per-pupil cost only from $348 to $432, which was well under the national norm of $375 in 1960 and $532 in 1965.

An unprecedented development occurred following 1965; while the assessments increased slightly to $166,090,615 in 1969 in the now unified

School District No. 60, the millage actually declined from 48.969 to 45.475; the total property tax for schools from $8,049,042 to $7,551,971; and the per-capita levy from $85 to $79; and this in spite of the fact that class sizes were reduced, teachers' salaries increased about 20%, and many improvements and additions completed in the school plant.

For fifteen years not a single bond issue had been voted: then, one of $8,361,000 was approved in 1965, which made possible a program of modernization, replacement, and relocation of school facilities, which received a great impetus in June, 1970, when the voters approved an additional bond issue of $16,000,000. Of this, $4.5 million was allocated for the remodelling of Central High, $7 million to construct the new Centennial High, $1 million for the new Fountain Elementary, and various sums for other additions and improvements.

Since new teachers were added in 1970 and their salary schedules again increased; and since the amortization of the new debt would add to the cost of education, the school millage was increased to 61.160 on an assessment which expanded from $166,090,615 to $177,136,200. As a result, the tax rose by more than $3 million to $10,833,650; and to $112 per capita. As shown in Table IV, the per-pupil operational cost rose from $348 to $679 between 1960 and 1970; and the overall cost from $399 to $796—which, all things considered, was quite reasonable.

It should be understood that all this happened before it was known that Catholic schools would close; and had no relevance whatever to that development. As the new program of construction is completed and the debt liquidated, capital costs will decline and Pueblo will have a school plant of which it can be justly proud: 4 modern senior and 6 junior highs, together with 30 elementaries, completely equipped with everything necessary to serve 30,000 students.

When the schoolmen obtained a 1970 millage of more than 61 on this sharply increased assessment, they actually received more than was strictly necessary; and Mr. Emil Paripovich, in charge of special personnel, stated that for 1971-72, the school millage would be reduced by .47—in spite of the previously unexpected heavy influx of parochial pupils.

It seems, therefore, that the dire predictions concerning heavy tax increases have no basis in fact.

Pupil-Teacher Ratios

Table III shows that the Pueblo schools have a comparatively low PTR, which was reduced from 27.6 in 1960-61 to 23.2 10 years later. It should be noted also that this was based upon full enrollment: if computed, as it normally is, by ADA, it would be considerably lower. We note, furthermore, that the lowest ratio ever was attained **after** the Catholic schools closed. It is therefore indeed difficult to understand why any class would consist of 47 or 48 pupils. Thus, from whatever angle viewed, the public schools are not only well equipped for their work, but have been and are doing it at nominal cost.

The Tax on Real Estate

Since the assessments are 30% of appraisal in Pueblo, the owner of a $20,000 house paid a total tax of $463.50 in 1959, $505.00 in 1965, and $613 in 1970; of which $252, $294, and $370 respectively was for education. Anyone conversant with tax-rates in other parts of the nation will note that these sums are modest indeed and that the citizens of Pueblo have quality schools at reasonable cost.

We might add that the recently completed and magnificent McClelland Library at 100 East Abriendo Avenue, for which a levy of 1.5 mills has been imposed, is another monument of cultural achievement.

Subsidiary Programs

In various interviews we learned:

(1) From Mr. Brian Macartney, in charge of transportation, that the public schools owned five busses and contracted with private companies for the operation of ten others; in 1970-71, 628 pupils were served, but in 1971-72, this number had been increased to 2,200 and was available to anyone who lived at least 1.5 miles from the nearest school; and would cost the system $100,000. He stated also that there never had been any publicly funded transportation for private school pupils;

(2) From Miss Spitzer that neither the state nor the Board of Education supplies free textbooks to anyone;

(3) That there never has been any released- or shared-time program in operation in Pueblo;

(4) From Miss Betty Harney, in charge of lunch programs, that 32 of 42 schools participated in them; and that in September, 1971, 9,874 meals were served daily. In 1970-71, a total of 1,135,940 meals were served, of which more than half were free or nearly so. The subsidies totalled $519,311, of which $156,500 was furnished by the Board of Education and $362,811.33 by the federal government. In the 1971-72 budget, the Board had allocated $250,300 for lunches. Miss Harney did not know to what extent the parochials had participated in federal subsidies in this regard, but assumed that it was proportional to enrollment;

(5) From John Garnett, in charge of other federal subsidies, that 21 of 41 schools qualified for Title I ESEA programs in 1971-72; and that between 2,500 and 3,000 pupils might be eligible. However, since sufficient funds were not available, only 1,800 in an unduplicated count were actually being served—at a cost of $450,000. In 1970-71, students involved totalled 1,554, of whom 192 were in 6 parochial schools; since the total allocation was $359,706, or an average of $232, an estimated $50,544 was used for pupils in Catholic schools.

From all federal programs, including NDEA and EPDA, the public schools would therefore receive approximately $1 million in the 1971-72 school year.

State and Local Contributions

In Pueblo, property taxation has been and continues to be the principal source of revenue. In 1960, the federal government supplied $213,475, the State about $2 million, and local sources some $6 million—about 75%; in 1970-71, the State equalization had grown to $8,056,929; nevertheless, local sources still supplied $10,522,948, which was 56% of the operational budget of $18,751,182. It is therefore doubly remarkable that the Pueblo schools have been able to absorb more than 4,000 parochial pupils over a 5- or 6-year period and still maintain the low tax-rates and pupil-teacher ratios shown in our tables.

At the Diocesan Office

At the education offices located over the sanctuary of the St. Anthony of Padua Church at 225 Clark Street, we interviewed Mrs. Fern Latino, Administrative Secretary of the Catholic schools. She stated that with the exception of the two high schools and one elementary under lease, only marginal uses have been found for a dozen buildings which were fully utilized as recently as 1968. Attempts are under way to use them on the parish level as community centers, for religious education, or in youth programs. Some are free of debt, but the Cathedral School at Sacred Heart, built in 1960, still carried an encumbrance of $154,000; and there were debts on some of the others.

Asked what is being done religiously for Catholic youth now enrolled in the public schools, Mrs. Latino stated that classes are being conducted after school, on Saturdays, and over the weekends; and that a very effective youth program had been established by teams of teachers which serve one parish and sometimes more than one.

She said that at least 65% of the population of Pueblo is Catholic; that

129

the same proportion obtains among the Chicanos; and that some of the latter may now be found in Protestant denominations.

She stated that tuition at Roncalli High was $280 in 1970-71 and that per-pupil cost was about $650; that the tuition in the elementaries had averaged about $100 for the children of a single family; that per-pupil cost averaged $250; that sisters were paid $2,080, plus health insurance; that lay teachers were paid 90% of the salaries prevalent in public schools; and that in 1970-71, more than 60% of the instructors were lay.

She could see no likelihood that Catholic day schools would resume.

Asked what had become of the religious formerly teaching in the Pueblo schools, she stated that while a few remained to do parish work, most of them had been assigned to other positions by their orders.

The Catholic Educational Plant

During a tour of the city, in which we inspected many public and all Catholic schools, we found that most of the latter were old, inadequate, and far inferior to those in the public domain. Should parochial education be re-established on a large scale, most of these old facilities would have to be replaced at staggering cost. The only completely modern facility was Roncalli High; but this was never able to enroll even half of its capacity; and, as Bishop Buswell pointed out, not even the interest on its debt had been paid during the last year.

In Pueblo as elsewhere the evidence seemed to indicate that the malaise of the Catholic schools was falling enrollment, which, we believe, must have reflected a general rejection of them by the laity.

The Impact of Catholic Closures

At the Board of Education, we inquired minutely as to what steps had been taken to receive the sudden influx of parochial pupils. First of all, Seton High, a rather old facility, was leased for $45,000 a year, but with no option to buy; then the splendid new Roncalli, equal to anything in the public sector, was leased for three years at $125,000 annually (the exact amount due on the mortgage) with option to purchase in 1974 with an additional payment of $1,088,000. Stripped of religious symbols, Seton enrolled 714 7th and 8th graders in October, 1971; and Roncalli became a "middle school" for 5th and 6th, and 7th graders, with an enrollment of 748. The capacity of the two schools is about 1,600.[a]

---

a.   In their last year of operation under Catholic control, the two schools enrolled a total of 734 pupils.

The teaching staff had been increased by 28 over that of the preceding year; of these, however, 5 were engaged in new special programs, federally funded, which did not affect the Pueblo budget. Of the remaining 23, only 18 were necessary because of the parochial transfers, which caused a net increase of 401 in enrollment. The principal cost, therefore, consisted of salaries for 18 new teachers (about $175,000) and an additional sum for leases. Since other operational charges are about 25%, total new expenditures would be about $440,000.

Since 2,200 transfers were effected, the per-pupil cost averaged $200; actually, it may have been even less, for many pupils simply entered small classes without necessitating any additional teachers.

But this is only one side of the coin. Since the State Equalization totalled $8,056,929 in 1970-71, or $291 per pupil, the Pueblo schools will receive approximately $640,000 in 1971-72 from this source alone to cover the cost of educating the new arrivals. Nor is this all: the State legislature set up a Contingency Fund of $588,000 to help in just such emergencies; from this, the Pueblo system received $293,767.96.

Summary

The Pueblo schools can therefore well afford to reduce their property millage: for they will receive about $933,000 from the state to offset expenditures of about $440,000.

Nor should we forget the financial benefits to Catholic parents. To maintain a school system with 3,000 elementary and 1,000 high school pupils would cost them at least $1,250,000 annually.

And so we find that the Pueblo public schools have absorbed 4,000 parochial pupils without the slightest difficulty; they had more per-pupil facilities after the transfers than ever before; the plant was undergoing a tremendous and continuing expansion; and all this had been and was being accomplished at substantial savings, not only for Catholic parents, but also for the non-Catholic taxpayers of the city as well.

TABLE I

Public and Private School Enrollment

Year	Population	Public	Catholic	%Cath.	In Whole Diocese
1910	41,747		365		
1920	43,050		1,274		
1930	50,096		1,128		
1940	52,162		896		
1950	63,685		1,661		
1955			2,602		
1961	91,181	24,232	3,552	12.8	6,945
1964		26,601	4,036	13.1	7,594
1965		27,475	3,652	11.7	7,705
1968		27,116	3,599	11.6	
1970	96,746	27,203	2,701	9.0	5,253
1971-72		27,604	None	00.0	2,018

TABLE II

Taxation in Pueblo

Assessments	1965	1969	1970
County	$183,727,160	$194,547,210	$208,570,480
City	107,514,457	116,969,713	126,781,716
Sch. Dis. 1/60	62,044,641	166,090,615	177,136,200
Sch. Dis. 20/60	96,352,371		
Millages: Total	84.169	84.725	102.210
Co. School	12.875		
Sch. Districts	36.094	45.475	61.160
Total Tax	$12,101,890	$13,651,440	$17,873,374
School Tax	8,049,042	7,552,971	10,833,650
Per Capita: Total	$129	$144	$185
For Schools	85	79	112

TABLE III

General Statistics

Item	1960-61	1965-66	1969-70	1970-71
No. of Schools	36	38	39	42
Enrollment	24,232	27,475	27,116	27,604
Kn.	2,236	2,311	2,093	
El.	12,455	13,216	12,497	
Jr. H.	5,798	6,183	6,332	
Sr. H.	3,743	5,765	6,194	
Staff	1,125	1,165	1,277	1,323
Teachers	878	1,061	1,143	1,191
Ratios:				
Pupil-Staff	21.6	23.6	21.6	20.9
Pupil-Teacher	27.6	25.9	23.8	23.2
Per-Pupil Cost	$399	$472	$690	$796
Teacher Salaries:				
Minimum	$4,350	$5,100	$6,000	$6,600
Maximum	5,675	8,450	11,000	13,500

TABLE IV

Financial Data Concerning The Pueblo Schools

Revenues	1960	1965	1970-71
Local Tax	$3,092,125	$4,837,923	$5,492,462
Foundation Levy		1,033,282	3,011,315
Capital Fund			354,272
Reserve			1,975,600
County	1,664,977	1,978,423	536,103
Specific Ownership	278,875	415,598	
Non-Collectible		-392,567	-325,702
Delinquent		19,000	15,000
State Equalization	1,946,675	3,123,144	8,056,929
Miscellaneous	44,000	157,700	
Federal	213,475	175,000	319,615
Interest		67,000	149,000
Other Local	155,794	48,275	67,615
Bond Redemption Levy		1,178,590	598,943
Balances	1,011,597	1,457,676	1,570,486
Total	$8,407,518	$14,099,044	$21,821,638
Bonds Sold		8,361,000	15,015,000
Bonds Outstanding	19,290,000	11,813,000	21,880,000
Interest Due			1,658,737
Expenditures			
Administration	184,725	234,985	394,994
Instruction	5,387,953	8,021,392	12,235,363
Supplies	371,118	470,480	869,065
Attendance	9,801	9,850	6,475
Health	63,163	91,487	101,917
Transportation	26,222	28,204	71,029
Operation	871,684	1,066,765	1,469,003
Maintenance	357,343	318,386	519,015
Fixed Charges	547,998	1,251,427	1,991,896
Pensions	194,899		
Other	344,602	390,778	1,092,425
Total Operational	$8,359,509	$11,883,754	$18,751,182
Debt Interest	1,216,859	1,097,246	2,943,501
Grand Total	$9,576,368	$12,981,000	$21,694,683
Per-Pupil Cost			
Operational	$348	$432	$679
Overall	399	472	796

That we analyze Detroit was natural, even mandatory: for, after the Michigan legislature voted $22 million of parochiaid in 1970, opponents circulated petitions to force a referendum on a constitutional amendment to prohibit not only this but any similar appropriation. In spite of a bitter campaign in which parochiadists charged that the amendment, if ratified, would even deny fire protection to private schools, the people voted decisively to interdict the use of public funds for sectarian education. When Cardinal John Deardon announced that a large number of schools in the diocese would be forced to close, the news made national headlines; and it was predicted that this would precipitate an educational crisis and cause the tax-rates to zoom skyward.

We discovered that Catholic enrollment, which had been expanding for a hundred years without interruption until 1961-64, began a slight but definite decline in 1965, shrank considerably in 1966-68, and was further sharply reduced in 1969-70. Table I traces the development of public and Catholic enrollment. In 1896, there were 23 Catholic schools with 11,240 pupils; in 1910, 34 with 18,152; in 1920, 55 with 39,239; in 1946, 111 with 72,755; in 1955, 163 with 85,482. The system remained very nearly at this level for ten years, then dropped to 137 schools with 72,942 pupils in 1968, 107 with 53,982 in 1970, and 81 with 37,549 in the autumn of 1971.

The public schools enrolled 221,687 in 1946 and increased gradually to a peak of 298,027 in 1965 without absorbing any Catholic transfers. And then a new kind of phenomenon occurred: while Catholic enrollment fell by 49,294, or 56.3%, that in the public schools declined to 285,498. The latter were not, therefore, inundated by this flood of parochial pupils: on the contrary, the public schools actually declined by 13,000 between 1965 and 1971. Total enrollment fell by more than 60,000, for reasons which we shall examine in due course.

Let us note that in 1950, the Catholic ratio of school enrollment was 26.9%; in 1961, 23.2%; in 1965, 21.8%; in 1970, 15.9%. In 1971-72, it fell to 11.6%.

Public Education

Since the present writer left Detroit in 1960 after residing there for nearly thirty years, a return in 1971 was a nostalgic experience. Basic alterations were evident on every side. The population had become 45% black; a number of old hotels and apartments stood abandoned, even boarded up; one comparatively new but empty motel on Woodward Avenue stared forlornly at the passerby. Large areas along this great thoroughfare had been razed and consigned to weeds. Yet the city has a magnificent government center on downtown Jefferson and other impressive structures in the area; the classic library and art museum had been greatly enlarged. The Board of Education had moved into the 14-story Maccabees Building, which it had purchased, and every nook and corner of which was occupied by Administration.

Whatever difficulties Detroit may have had, there is no lack of apparent opulence in public education, the cost of which has increased by 450% to local taxpayers in 24 years. Table III shows what has happened to taxes: in 1946, the City collected $97,018,724, of which $25,964,246, or 26.7%, went to the schools. However, with the inexorability of fate, in Detroit, as elsewhere, taxes have been increasing continuously. In 1970, the total levy was $289,401,378, of which $137,348,457, or 47.4%, was allocated to education. The per-capita levy for schools, therefore, increased from $13.67 to $92. Since assessments are 50% of value and since the school millage rose from 8.653 to 24.015 in 24 years, the school levy on a $30,000 house increased from $130 to $360.[a]

Table IV and V show the revenues and expenditures of the Detroit common schools during the Sixties, together with their bonded debt, capital outlays, and value of plant. Revenues for the General Fund increased from $129,365,307 in 1962-63 to $235,443,778 in 1970-71. Local property tax for its support rose from $75,641,586 to $107,817,285; federal subsidies from $1,388,309 to $23,989,158; and state aid from $44,622,406 to $89,857,222. It is evident that the Detroit schools have been accorded generous treatment: for in 1955-56, $11,840,794 was expended for construction and improvements; in 1961, the amount was

---

a.   Since the County of Wayne also imposes a property tax which has ranged from 4.7 to 7.1 mills and since the total millage in 1946 was about 37, a $20,000 house at that time paid a tax of about $370; in 1970, a $30,000 home would have paid $870.

$19,535,674; in 1965-66, it was $13,265,602; and in 1969-70, $23,535,674.[a] In the meantime, the money expended for debt retirement increased from $1,207,821 to $9,379,238. As old buildings are abandoned, they are replaced by new ones; and additions are constantly under way in existing plants.

The total budget, including funds expended from bond issues, was $145,935,803 in 1961 and $269,619,201 in 1970. It should be pointed out that in spite of enormous increases in state and federal aid, the local property tax, which contributed 52.8% in 1955-56, still supplied 51.1% in 1970.

We note that there were 273 schools in 1962-63 and that this number had been increased to 348 in 1970; that the system possessed no less than 455 buildings at the latter date; that the bonded debt rose from $47,897,500 to $106,230,000; and that the value of the physical plant and equipment expanded from $248,751,763 to $429,414,797.

We need not be surprised, therefore, that the per-pupil cost of elementary and secondary education increased sharply. According to information supplied by the Board of Education and reproduced in Table VIII, this was $79.90 on the elementary level, $117.08 in junior highs, and $106.32 in senior secondaries in 1940. For special education it was $182.11. In 1970, the comparable amounts were $598.70, $761.41, $800.23, and $1,655.23, with an overall average of $779.75. According to our own computations in Table V, the per-capita cost for operation alone was $438 in 1961 and $828 in 1970; including all costs, the totals were $507 and $861, sums which are definitely less than the national norm in spite of the substantial influx from parochial schools.

Table IX and X contain information concerning the number of teachers, their average salaries, pupil-ratios, and median class-sizes. We find here that Detroit has been very generous, not only as to school buildings and equipment, but also with its teaching personnel; for the median pay of classroom teachers rose from $5,499 in 1955-56 to $8,367 in 1966, and to $12,254 in the spring of 1971. In the meantime, the overall pupil-teacher ratio dropped from 31.26 to 26; and the staff-ratio from 29.27 to 24.1. The median class size fell from 35.35 in 1955 to 26 on the elementary level; from 37.15 to 26.1 on the junior high; and from 32.39 to 27.8 in the senior secondaries. It should be noted that although these statistics reflect substantial reductions, classes in Detroit still are substantially larger than, for example, in St. Paul and other cities we have surveyed.

On the whole, therefore, we concluded that, in spite of crucial internal

---

a.   In 15 years, more than $250 million was spent on the Detroit school plant.

problems, which we shall consider, and frequent demands for more money as well as dire predictions should it not be forthcoming, the Detroit public schools are flourishing materially; and this without unduly oppressive levies on local property. Never in the past has the system had such ample funds for expansion or operation; never before were salaries so high in comparison with income in other fields of endeavor; and the elaborate continuing program of construction is replacing obsolete facilities and providing new ones at a rapid tempo. And perhaps its greatest victory and achievement is to be found in the manner in which it has absorbed an enormous influx of black pupils and is preparing them for full participation in the social and economic life of this nation. The challenge involved in absorbing parochial pupils has been and will be of comparatively slight significance.

Racial Composition and Problems

As we have noted, blacks now constitute approximately 45% of the population of Detroit; however, their public school enrollment shows a far higher ratio— a fact due in part to the higher Negro birth rate[a] but even more to the extremely low percentage of minority races in private schools. Forty years ago, Negroes constituted so small a ratio and were so completely concentrated in their own areas that all but a few schools were wholly Caucasian; but during World War II, great numbers of them came to Detroit, settled there permanently, and produced a large generation of offspring. However, even as late as 1961, there were still 73 schools without a Negro pupil; but in 1965, there were only 30 in this category. As shown in Table VI, there were 130,765 Negro children in the public schools in 1961, when they constituted 45.8% of the enrollment; in 1965, their ratio had grown to 54.8%; and in 1970, to 64%.

In 1970, the Catholic Archdiocese took a racial census of its schools and found that out of 124,537 pupils in 181 respondent schools, only 5,449 Negroes were enrolled. This means that among 54,000 pupils in Detroit only 2,400, or 4.4%, were black. Since most of these were concentrated in the discontinued schools of the Inner City, the racial disparity in those remaining will be even greater in 1971-72.

This factor has contributed heavily to the racial imbalance in the

---

a.   During the Fifties, the white birth rate was about 24 per thousand, while the Negro was 35. In 1961, the public school enrollment was 45.8% black; however, among all school enrollees, totalling some 388,000, the Negro ratio was 34.7%, while in the population as a whole it constituted 29%.

public schools. Assuming that the black ratio in Catholic schools was 4.4% in 1964-65, the white enrollment would have been 82,000. If we add to these about 5,000 white pupils in Lutheran and other private schools, there would—in the absence of all parochials—have been 161,500 Negro and 220,000 white pupils in the public system, which, in fact, had only 133,335 of the latter at that time.

It would be a mistake to minimize or underestimate the problems created for the public schools by the heavy Negro concentration in Detroit, which has resulted in severe tensions. In 1920, its population was 993,670, with only 41,613 Negroes, who increased to 128,521 in a population of 1,568,662 in 1930, still only 8.2%. In 1950, there were 300,506 Negroes in a population of 1,849,568, or 16.2%; in 1960, 482,223, among 1,670,144, or 29%; in 1970, 660,000 among 1,510,000, or 43.7%.

Under the byline of Jerry M. Flint, an article appeared in the New York *Times* on March 23, 1969, which stated: "The fear of a serious racial explosion in the Detroit school system is growing," as well as the fear "that teachers and administrators will quit the system." And this in spite of the fact that "Detroit was the first to use an integrated primer picturing Negroes and the first to decide that Negro history had been downgraded in textbooks. . . . It built new school buildings in Negro slum areas more than a decade ago and has emphasized the hiring of Negro teachers for years. The 11,000 teacher force is 40% Negro and the administrative staff is 25% Negro. . . . Among 300 principals, 30 are Negro. . . ." Nevertheless, " 'We are hell bent for disaster,' said Martin Kelish, president of the Organization of School Administrators and Supervisors, . . . 'and I'm not sure anything can be done about it.' "

The author continued: "Last week's meeting of the Detroit Board of Education was broken up by screaming teenagers. When Dr. Norman Drachler, the school superintendent, took the microphone. . . .the only response was a Negro girl shouting 'Shut up, honkie' ."

In order to meet this fearful challenge, the federal government has been pouring tens of millions into the City. An elaborate publication called *The Constant Search: The Story of Federal Aid to Detroit Schools,* does not mince words or underestimate the difficulties of a typical teacher in an Inner City school, who, the author states, "felt like driftwood, floating in a sea of faces. Suspicious faces, snarling faces, silent faces. . . . They were his students, and daily as he walked the corridors, his mind caught impressions—the gleam of a knife, scratches of obscenity on a wall, the steaming warmth from a couple leaving a clinch. . . . Students had been involved in break-ins and enterings, assaults, rolling of drunks, gang fights, arson, car thefts, carrying concealed weapons and any other crime short of murder. . . . Meanwhile, time seemed to be running out."

That schools have been able to operate at all in the face of such obstacles is indeed an indication of heroic effort and resolve. That success—greater than could have been anticipated in 1969—has crowned their work was evident in September, 1971, when the registration of some 285,500 youngsters was completed without serious incident. At great cost to itself and with infinite patience, Detroit is inducting tens of thousands of Negroes into the mainstream of American life; a task which the parochials have evaded virtually in its entirety.

Mr. Merle Hendrickson of the Department of Planning and Building explained that there had been no bussing of children to the nearest school; however, there is a rather elaborate system of transportation, which cost $2,710,233.16 in 1969-70 and which takes children from areas with overcrowded schools to others where a surplus of seats is available.[a] In 1970, 7,000 pupils were bussed; in 1970-71, the number was only 3,000. Since the population during recent years has been shifting rapidly from the Inner City and its periphery toward the middle sections, this has created a serious problem. Mr. Hendrickson displayed an immense map, on which schools with green tags had excess facilities and those with red were afflicted with shortages. There is no dearth of teaching stations: the difficulty is in their distribution. With the completion of the building program in overcrowded areas, further bussing was not contemplated.

Non-Catholic Private Schools

When Catholic spokesmen total the number of non-public pupils that may or probably will be transferred to the common schools unless massive subsidies are provided, they usually include all private schools with their own. However, we find in Table VII that while the Catholic schools in Detroit lost 42,170 pupils between 1965 and 1971, all other private schools increased their enrollment from 4,993 to 5,200.

Federal and State Subsidies

Federal subsidies to the Detroit public schools increased from $298,675 in 1955 to $23,989,188 in 1970-71. This enormous undergirding of local education was channelled through various agencies administered by an elaborate complex. A massive document entitled *A Guide to Federal Programs*, 1970-71, describes more than forty of these, organized in seven principal divisions. Under Title I of ESEA alone, $13,903,010 was expended in 22 programs, of which $6,855,662 went for the "Great Cities Project." One of its objectives was to reduce youth activity "in acts of vandalism and violence." There was even an allocation of $271,308 for the continuing education of pregnant girls, tutored in their homes or in special classes. $895,429 was allocated for the purpose of reducing class sizes in 35 selected schools of the Inner City.

For Title II of ESEA, the funding was $1,500,000; and for Title VI, $424,349. Under the Economic Opportunity Act, we find Follow Through, $292,327; Neighborhood Youth Corp, $1,278,790; Parent-Child Center, $175,000; Pre-School Child and Parent Education, $1,107,438; and several others.

Included in state subsidies of $89,857,222 in 1970-71 were funds for special programs under the State Aid Act totalling $9,317,113. Millions of additional dollars were also supplied by the state and federal government for lunches and other services and programs.

Catholic Education

Mr. Donald M. Stock, Director of Teacher Personnel, furnished detailed information concerning the salaries of religious and lay teachers; retirement plans; and other fringe benefits, as shown in Table XIII. He supplied also the data on the racial composition of Catholic schools shown in Table VI; and he gave us a prepared document, according to which, by 1975, schools in the Detroit Archdiocese will be staffed by 1,350 religious and 1,000 lay teachers and have an enrollment of about 60,000, compared to the 106,000 of 1971-72; and will have 1,000 religious and 750 lay teachers in 1980, with a projected enrollment of about 45,000: Table XII shows that this totalled 189,399 in 1961; 202,676 in 1965; and 141,452 in 1970-71.

Pupil-teacher ratios in the Catholic schools are shown in Table XI:36.6 in 1965 and 27.2 in 1971; in the whole diocese, as shown in Table XII, they were 35.9 in 1965 and 28.5 in 1970-71.

Mr. Theodore Karpowitz, in charge of State and Federal Programs, stated (1) that 1,000 Catholic children participated in ESEA Title I programs in 1970-71, funded with $360,000; (2) that the federal government provided Catholic schools with $141,120 under Title II; (3) that it spent $110,800 on a work-training program for Catholic junior high pupils; and (4) that the system received $284,000 to subsidize school lunch programs. Thus a total in excess of $1 million was expended by government agencies for the benefit of Catholic children—an average of about $20 per pupil in Detroit.

---

a.   There is no state reimbursement for this service—it is simply an element in the City school budget.

There is no subsidized bus service and there are no free textbooks for Catholic pupils in Detroit.

Mr. Karpowitz explained that Michigan law makes it mandatory for public school authorities to release a child for two hours weekly for religious instruction at the written request of a parent. However, no Catholic child in Detroit participated in this program in 1970-71; and only two parishes of the diocese—St. Alexander in Farmington and Queen of Apostles in Frazier—offered this service, of which only a few children took advantage. In order to participate, transportation had to be furnished either by the parents or the parish. Furthermore, such release could take place only in a manner that would not interfere with the class-schedules of pupils in public schools.

From 36 out of 262 Catholic schools with 142,000 pupils, 2,530 took advantage of shared-time or dual-enrollment programs with instruction in a great variety of subjects. Sometimes the public school was across the street; at others it was several blocks or even miles distant. In six instances, there was only a single pupil; other schools sent 30, 50, or even a hundred. St. Anne's High of Macomb County, sent 243 to the Fuhrman Junior High; and St. Joseph's Elementary in Monroe sent 225 to the Mason School—a mile away—to take Physical Education. Physics, Science, Languages, Music, Art, Mathematics, Auto Mechanics, Drafting, Woodworking, Electricity, Chemistry, Typing, Shorthand, Home Economics were favored subjects. In Detroit itself, however, only 6 schools and 58 pupils participated.

Sister Emeline, Assistant Superintendent of Education, was gracious and informative. She supplied material concerning the latest enrollment and the schools which had closed in June, 1971. In the whole diocese, 13 high and 51 grade schools with about 36,000 pupils ceased operations. She supplied also the estimates given in Table XIV, according to which tuition in Detroit Catholic elementaries ranged from $75 to $300; in parish highs from $250 to $400; in diocesan secondaries, from $500 to $600; and in private schools (i.e., those owned and operated by orders) from $700 to $800. She estimated per-pupil costs on the grade level at about $300; and on the secondary, from $450 to $900.

With such reduced enrollment, we asked, would the ratio of religious teaching personnel increase?

No, for it had not been possible to pick up any additional sisters.

What was being done with the sixty or more closed schools?

Thirty-one parish schools and one Archdiocesan high school were being leased to public school boards. This had been done before; and this year, all or portions of sixteen schools would be leased to the public system in Detroit alone. The city of Port Huron might buy the $1.5 million Central High School there; and the same thing might happen in other places.

What about other facilities?

Good use would be found for most of them: some for religious instruction and others for community purposes.

Had not parochial enrollment begun dropping in 1965 and were not fifty schools closed before 1971 in Detroit alone?

Sad, but true.

What were the principal reasons for this development?

The most important by far is financial—it costs too much to maintain a large private system of education.

What are the principal factors in increased costs?

The loss of sisters, increased salaries for everyone, and general inflation.

Did not parents begin withdrawing their children before substantial tuition was charged?

When they moved to the suburbs, they placed their children in the public schools either because we had none in the area or because we had no room for them.[a]

Were there other reasons?

Lack of transportation and of certain courses, facilities, or programs in our schools were other reasons.

Are some parents dissatisfied because they feel Catholic schools no longer impart a solid religious education?

No.

Do some parents object to the Catholic schools because of clerical control or lack of financial accountability?

That would be a kooky objection.

What do you see in the future for Catholic education?

"As things are going now, within five years all Catholic schools will be private; that is, they will be separated entirely from parish support or control. They will be organized in a totally different manner, possibly as corporations under lay or diocesan control and ownership. Their maintenance will come from gifts and tuition, and they will enroll children from Catholic families who can afford quality private education and who believe in it enough to support it."

Would that not be a new concept?

---

a.   It should be noted, however, that this cause is no longer operative; for, of the 64 schools closed down in June, 1971, 43 were in the suburbs.

"Not entirely, for some of our best private schools, operated by orders, are very much like that now."

But it would mean, would it not, that the great bulk of Catholic children would be in the public schools?

"Yes."

Would this result in a lower Church-retention rate of its youth?

"Time will tell."

The Public School Plant

Mr. Merle Hendrickson stated that the Board of Education had for some time rented various facilities, especially for pre-school or special programs. As the construction program develops, fewer such leases have become necessary; in June, 1971, the use of ten Protestant church buildings was terminated. In their place, nine other facilities had been leased as Pre-School Centers. The use of four Catholic Schools was continued in 1971-72 and leases were negotiated on five others to care for the overflow in certain public schools. Mr. Hendrickson stated that the rental on St. John Evangelist was $1,700 a month; on St. Stanislaus, $2,400.

The problem, however, was neither total enrollment nor the influx from private schools, but rather the mobility of the population, and the great disparity of school-age children in different areas. Some had as few as 17 per hundred families, while in others the ratio reached 67. The Inner City had lost more than half its enrollment since 1960 and in some of the outer fringes the pupil-ratio was very low. Families with young children were concentrating in the middle areas, where schools were, consequently, overcrowded. For example, the Redford, built for 2,600, enrolled 4,300 in September, 1971.

According to an article published in the Detroit *Free Press,* March 19, 1963, 14 elementary and 2 junior highs had been built, 14 others started, and 11 additions completed during the four preceding years. That this program of construction continued is evident from the fact that in 1963 there were 273 schools and in 1970 no less than 348. On May 27, 1970, the Detroit *News* announced that the Board of Education had approved the construction of new buildings and additions costing $53 million.

Mr. Hendrickson stated that twenty Inner City schools had been demolished: some being no longer required and others replaced by new facilities. Fourteen additions to existing plants were scheduled for completion between April, 1970, and July, 1972; and thirty-one other additions, improvements, or new buildings were in various planning stages in the fall of 1971. Since approximately $20 million is being spent annually for new facilities, it seems that future needs will be amply provided.

The Program of Absorption

Had the 1965-71 Catholic school decline occurred between 1960 and 1966, there would indeed have been a serious problem. Various developments, however, have coalesced to avoid all danger of any disruption in Detroit resulting from the closure of Catholic schools.

First of all, its population has been falling at the rate of nearly 20,000 a year: it was 1,849,560 in 1950, 1,670,144 in 1960, and 1,492,914 in 1970. This alone should have caused births to decline by at least 450 each year. However, since the birth rate of the Fifties was about 30 per thousand and compared to less than 20 in the Forties, school attendance, in spite of falling population, rose from 295,000 in 1946 to 385,000 in 1965.

At that point, two great forces came into play: the total population continued to decline; but, far more important, the sharply falling birth rate of the Sixties became evident in the declining kindergarten registration, shown in Table II. In 1955, 31,200 were thus enrolled; in 1960, 30,092; in 1965, 29,934; in 1967, 26,102; and in 1970, 24,511. In October, 1971, the number fell to 23,801.

Kindergarten enrollees of 1955 completed grade school in 1963 and high school in 1967. For those of 1960, the comparable dates became 1968 and 1972.

Thus, we find (1) that the declining population reduced the number of school-age children by at least 5,000 between 1960 and 1970; and that the declining birth rate caused elementary and secondary enrollment in the fall of 1971 to decline by an additional 52,000 below the level of 1964. Total enrollment in all Detroit schools fell from 380,919 in 1965 to 328,247 in 1971.

It has been argued that in cities like Philadelphia the principal motivation keeping white parents from fleeing to the suburbs has been the existence of private and predominantly white schools. What effect the closing of many parochials in Detroit will have in this respect remains to be seen. Since many of the schools closed during the last five years are located in heavily Negro areas, it is certain that they did not include many white pupils. Since Detroit Catholics still have neighborhood schools available, it is unlikely that the white exodus will increase substantially because of the 1971 closures. It is therefore obvious that the decline of Catholic enrollment has presented and now poses no problem whatever for the public schools. Even with a falling population, they absorbed 65,797 additional pupils between 1950 and 1965; and no one ever heard of any difficulty occasioned by this enormous increase.

It should also be pointed out that if all the pupils still in the parochials were to enter the common schools, their extreme racial imbalance would, to a considerable degree, be overcome and rectified. Let us consider the fact that if the private schools had continued to expand after 1964 as they did after 1940, the public schools in 1971 would have enrolled only 50,000 white pupils compared to 180,000 black.

Finally, we should evaluate the fact that since the falling birth rate will further reduce enrollment at least until 1979, the public schools will be operating with a smaller enrollment than in 1965 even if every private school in the city closes its doors.

TABLE I

Catholic and Public School Enrollment

School Enrollment

Year	Population	Public	Catholic	% Cath.
1900	285,704		10,506	
1910	465,706		18,152	
1920	993,078		39,239	
1930	1,568,662		74,142	
1940	1,623,452	236,248	70,268	22.9
1946		221,676	72,755	24.9
1950	1,849,568	232,230	81,678	26.9
1961	1,670,144	288,146	86,824	23.2
1964		294,727	85,843	22.6
1965		298,027	82,958	21.8
1968		292,097	72,942	19.9
1970	1,492,914	286,057	53,982	15.9
1971		285,498	37,549	11.6

TABLE II

Enrollment in the Detroit Public Schools

Level	1955	1960	1967	1970	1971
Kindergarten	31,200	30,092	26,102	24,511	23,801
Elementary	138,384	142,609	140,489	133,548	147,026
Junior High	53,239	57,402	62,028	66,259	46,790
Senior High	38,001	43,962	53,704	50,810	63,648
Miscellaneous	11,707	11,240	12,000	10,929	4,233
Totals	272,528	285,304	294,323	286,057	285,498

TABLE III[a]

Property Taxation in Detroit

Year	Assessment[b]	Total Levy	School Levy
1946		$97,018,724	$25,964,246
1950		130,818,515	42,528,497
1955	$5,156,732,034	171,432,276	66,057,737
1961	5,507,996,411	211,827,299	88,879,748
1965	5,196,904,960	194,367,374	85,592,510
1970	5,719,272,840	289,401,378	137,348,457

a. There is also a County levy kept in a different budget. The millage for this was 4.715 in 1945, 7.191 in 1961, and 7.0 in 1970.
b. This is the State Equalized Valuation, which is about 10% higher than the City Assessed.

TABLE IV

Financial Data Relating to the Detroit Public Schools

Revenues	1962-63	1965-66	1970-71
Property Tax	$75,641,586	$81,920,460	$107,817,285
Federal	1,388,309	18,733,403	23,989,159
State	44,622,406	61,196,532	89,857,223
County		476,914	710,979
Investments	478,733	1,402,019	3,207,388
Tuition	593,140	1,457,329	1,544,406
Lunch Sales	3,942,285	4,139,259	5,343,222
Bookstore	1,053,882	1,097,869	685,919
Other	1,635,966	2,262,143	2,288,197
Total General	$129,356,307	$172,685,928	$235,443,778
Building	32,716,588	17,702,627	21,974,795
Debt Retirement	2,192,108	3,938,599	11,470,248
Grand Total	$164,265,003	$194,327,154	$268,888,822
Bonded Debt	47,897,500	67,785,000	106,230,000
No. of Schools	273	325	348
Value of Plant	$248,751,763	$350,188,694	$429,494,797

TABLE V

Expenditures General Fund	1961	1966	1970
Instruction	$84,558,431	$109,271,081	$169,980,313
Operation	12,458,714	17,194,990	24,926,870
Maintenance	5,846,219	7,493,469	10,536,081
Administration	2,749,533	3,917,356	5,773,576
Fixed Charges	9,179,373	8,064,451	7,888,741
Other	11,607,879	23,344,791	17,579,048
Total General Fund	$126,400,149	$169,286,138	$236,684,629
Building Fund	19,535,674	13,265,602	23,555,335
Debt Retirement		4,026,377	9,379,238
Total Expenditures	$145,935,803	$186,578,116	$269,619,201
Per-Pupil Cost			
Operational	$438	$568	$828
Total	507	582	861

TABLE VI

Racial Composition of Detroit Schools

Date	Public			Catholic		
	Enrollment	Negro	%	Enrollment	Negro	%
1961	285,521	130,765	45.8			
1963	293,745	150,565	51.3			
1964	294,822	161,487	54.8			
1970	286,057	183,000	64.0	124,539	5,449	4.4

TABLE VII[a]

Detroit Parochial Enrollment

Category	1965	Oct., 1970	May, 1971	Oct., 1971
Catholic	77,719	48,816	47,446	37,549
Lutheran	3,862	3,747	3,650	3,835
SDA	287	355	348	338
Jewish	384			
Quaker	72	350	355	388
Non-Denom.	388	582	615	639
Total	82,712	53,850	52,414	42,749

TABLE VIII

Operational Per-Pupil Cost in Public Schools

Year	Elem.	Junior H.	Senior H.	Special	Average
1940	$79.90	$117.08	$106.32	$182.11	
1950	188.92	272.51	263.87	417.87	
1960	335.82	462.46	461.07	739.97	
1965	392.37	528.28	536.10	877.73	
1968	497.91	664.02	720.01	1,289.96	
1970	598.70	761.41	800.23	1,655.23	$779.75

---

a. Data supplied by Detroit Board of Education.

TABLE IX

Teacher Salaries and Pupil Ratios

Year Staff-Pupil	Classroom Teachers	Average Salary	Ratios Teacher-Pupil	Staff-Pupil
1954-55		$5,499		
1960-61		7,171		
1963-64		7,649		
Oct., 1965			31.26	29.24
Mar., 1966	10,173	8,367	29.1	27.3
Mar., 1971	9,684	12,254	26.0	24.1

TABLE X

Median Class Size in Detroit Public Schools

Year	Kng.	Elem.	Jr. High	Sr. High
1955-56	31.72	35.35	37.16	32.39
1960-61	32.01	34.48	33.59	30.89
1963-64	33.39	35.52	34.73	31.71
1970-71	26.60	26.00	26.10	27.80

TABLE XI

Staff and Staff-Pupil Ratios in Catholic Schools

Year	Staff	Religious	Lay	% Lay	Pupil-Staff Ratio
1961	2,133	1,689	444	20.5	40.7
1965	2,255	1,583	672	29.9	36.6
1971	1,983	970	1,013	51.1	27.2

150

TABLE XII

Staff and Pupil Ratios in Detroit Archdiocese

Year	Enrollment	Staff	Religious	Lay	% Lay	Pupil-Staff Ratio
1961	189,399	5,530	3,481	2,049	36.9	34.3
1965	202,676	5,642	3,512	2,130	37.7	35.9
1970-71	141,452	4,930	2,191	2,749	55.5	28.5
1971-72	106,080	3,930	1,980	1,950	49.6	27.0

TABLE XIII

Financial Data in Catholic Schools in 1970-71

Personnel	Salaries	Retirement	Health Insurance
Religious	$2,750	In Order	Yes
Lay			
Maximum	13,690		
Minimum	7,004		
Est. Av.	9,400	$200	Yes: No Tenure

TABLE XIV

1971 Tuition and Per-Pupil Costs in Catholic Schools

Type	Tutition Range	Estimated Cost
Elementary	$75-$300	$300
Parish High School	250-400	450
Diocesan High School	500-600	650
Private High School	700-800	900

Some Private Schools

(We have visited a great many non-Catholic private schools, interviewed their officials, and obtained financial data concerning their operations. In order to compare their costs, programs, purposes, and equipment with those in public and Catholic schools, we offer a brief analysis of a few such representative institutions.)

1.   The Verde Valley School

Leaving the main highway just south of Sedona, Arizona, the visitor drives over two miles of narrow, gravel road, before arriving at the Verde Valley School, situated amidst encircling colorful and spectacular mountains. The institution was founded in 1948 by the philanthropist, Hamilton Warren, who has also provided an endowment of $600,000. In 1964, it was incorporated on a non-profit basis, primarily so that gifts and legacies might be tax-deductible.

Mr. Samuel Guarnaccia, in charge of admissions, explained that Verde Valley is a four-year secondary with 120 boarding students, of whom 60 are boys and 60 are girls, housed in dormitories where two students occupy a room and two rooms share a bath. There are, in addition, 8 day students. There is a staff of 28, of whom 24 are full-time instructors; everyone, except the headmaster, does some teaching.

The "school community," consisting of students, staff, maintenance personnel, etc., totals 175, all of whom, except the 8 day students, live on the campus, eat in the dining hall, and share in the close companionship of this isolated educational enterprise in the midst of the desert.

There are ample opportunities for athletics and other extra-curricular activities: the school owns 12 riding horses; there are tennis and volley ball courts, a riding range, a running track, and soccer and baseball fields.

153

There are plenty of classrooms; a good library; and the newly constructed Brady Hall is large enough to accommodate an audience of 300 and has a stage fully equipped for dramatic presentations.

Although the school is completely secular, there is a weekly chapel service at which speakers representing a great variety of viewpoints appear and with whom students often engage in subsequent "rap sessions."

Since the pupil-teacher ratio is less than five, instruction is essentially on a tutorial basis. And the quiet isolation of this self-contained community so far removed from the noise and bustle of the great schools is certainly conducive to study, conversation, and contemplation.

There are accommodations only for 120 boarders, and the student roster is always filled. It should be noted, however, that the school seeks a 10% representation from minority groups, such as blacks, Indians, and Mexican-Americans. In order to enrol these, the institution has a generous scholarship program which costs $65,000 a year and which involves 25 students of whom 8 receive not only full scholarships, but even an additional stipend for personal needs; 17 others enjoy partial scholarships. These are boys and girls of intellectual promise from families which can contribute only marginally or not at all.

Mr. Guarnaccia stated that the plant was valued at about $1 million; that it has no debt; that the Hamilton family at one time simply paid deficits from its own resources; that, since some of the buildings are growing somewhat obsolete, a fund-drive is now under consideration; and that sometimes it has been necessary to dip into the endowment to meet current expenses. There is never any surplus.

All members of the staff receive their meals and are provided with comfortable apartments and medical insurance as part of their compensation; and, since this need not be reported as income, it is doubly attractive. Salaries of instructors and administrators range from $5,000 to $13,000; the headmaster receives $16,000. The budget totalled $750,000 in 1970-71, including meals and all other peripheral expenses. The salaries of 35 persons totalled $289,000—an average of $8,260; in 1971-72, this item rose to $341,000.

Life at Verde Valley, to say the least, seemed highly informal; many of the boys had long hair; and the dress of both sexes was sufficiently unconventional. Upon seeing one youth in derby hat and patched white overalls, like a plasterer, we missed our camera sorely. We saw groups of three or four, sometimes five or six, students sitting cross-legged on the floor, evidently deep in esoteric discussion.

Tuition is $4,000, which includes meals, room, various field trips, major medical insurance, the use of all school facilities, and one annual journey which lasts a full month and in which the entire student body and faculty journey in five school busses as far as Mexico City or Mississippi to study contemporary life and culture. Students must, however, provide for their own personal transportation to and from the school and pay for their books and ordinary dental, optical, and medical services. They also need at least $5 a week for incidental expenses. When all these items are computed, we estimated that the cost of keeping a son or daughter at Verde Valley must average at least $4,500 a year. If the school had a debt to be amortized out of income, the tuition would have to be increased or other sources of income found.

For the day students, tuition is $2,000.

Verde Valley is primarily a college preparatory. It offers a wide variety of courses in English, history, science, and mathematics, in the arts, various languages, and extra-curricular activities. Its graduates have been accepted at most of the leading colleges and universities in the United States and the school is proud of their achievements.

There is little doubt that most of the students come from fairly affluent middle-class families who seek for their offspring a more thorough grounding in the humanities than can be obtained at most public schools and who wish, also, to foster a wider outlook than is elsewhere to be attained.

Mr. Guarnaccia stated that in spite of the close proximity and constant companionship of the sexes, no pregnancy problems have arisen for years. He hinted, however, that some of the girls may be taking the pill.

The high cost of operation at Verde Valley is due, of course, in part to the generous salaries paid the staff, but much more to the extremely low pupil-teacher ratio. We believe that if a school is to have specialists in each subject where the enrollment is small, this situation is inescapable. In larger institutions, there are more students to fill classes for teachers specializing in every aspect of the educationnal process; and therefore, the per-pupil cost can be kept at a far lower level.

We must also note that the clientele at Verde Valley is definitely restricted; the instution does not, like a public school, enroll a cross section of the community; instead, it represents a select, expensive, and elite facet of American education.

2. Some Protestant Schools in San Bernardino, California

a. A Lutheran School

At 1820 Highland Avenue, San Bernardino, we found a beautiful, modern sanctuary belonging to the Lutheran Church of America; a part of its plant consisted of large and airy classrooms, all in excellent condition. There was also a large play area in the rear.

Mrs. Helen Weber, principal of the day school which used the facilities, stated that

(1) Enrollment had grown from 150 in 1963 to 184 in 1970; and that continued growth was expected.

(2) There were seven teachers in addition to herself; the average class-size was 26.3.

(3) Salaries ranged from $3,800 to $4,150; the principal received $5,600. Salaries totalled $32,350.

(4) The registration fee was $15 for the kindergarten and $20 for grades 1-6.

(5) Tuition, which included all costs, was: $230 in kindergarten; for grades 1-6, $300 for the first child; $410 for two children; and $510 for three or more.

(6) Only about 30% of the pupils were from church families.

(7) The school was completely self-supporting.

(8) All teachers were certificated either in California or in some other state.

(9) Music was taught a half day each week; the kindergarten had daily sessions from 9 to 12.

(10) The school operated two busses as part of its service.

(11) The per-pupil cost was between $250 and $255.

156

b. A Nazarene School

The Valley Christian School, operated by the Church of the Nazarene, had a kindergarten and 9 grades, an enrollment of 150, and a staff of 8, including the principal. The plant was large and well kept, with auditorium, cafeteria, playground, and parking area. Mrs. Dale van Nortwick stated that the salary schedule ranged from $3,400 to $4,000, and that all teachers were certificated by the state or by the California Association of Christian Schools. The institution was financed entirely by pupil-fees. Tuition in the kindergarten was $400; in grades 1 to 6, $330; in 7 and 8, $400; and $450 in the 9th grade. Members of the Church and children of ministers and missionaries received discounts of 20%; children from other Nazarene churches, 15%. The annual per-pupil cost approximated $350.

c. A Brethren School

The Grace Christian School was operated by the independent Grace Brethren (Bible) Church. The principal, Mr. Steve Mesarch, stated that enrollment began with 6 pupils in 1955, had grown to 145, and was expected to increase to 200 in 1971-72. The 8 full-time teachers, who were certified by the California Association of Christian Schools, would receive salaries ranging from $3,300 to $4,400 in 1971-72.

The school shared the cost of maintenance with the Church; but its operational costs were met entirely through tuition and registration fees. The latter were $17 for each child for the first semester and $10 for the second. Tuition was $320 in the kindergarten; for grades 1 to 6, it was $320 for the first child, $270 for the second, $210 for the third, and $50 for each additional from the same family.

The net cost of operation for 10 months in 1970-71 was $35,489—a per-pupil average of $244. Tuition was being increased slightly for 1971-72 to meet higher salaries and other increased charges.

The school received no subsidy from any source. Mr. Mesarch stated that every course was totally permeated with Bible religion and that any interference with such teaching would destroy the purpose of the school. "God," he said, "is present in every aspect of our study and instruction."

d. A Bible School

The Reverend Lester Wendt, Pastor of the Faith Bible Church and principal of the San Bernardino Christian School with 110 pupils, stated that, although it had a long waiting list, there was no plan to increase the size of the operation. The plant belonged to the Church, but the school was completely self-supporting. The registration fee was $18 and the tuition $280 for the first child; $12 and $200 for the second; $7 and $150 for the third. Only one-fourth of the pupils came from Church families; but "Bible religion" was taught to all alike. There were several Catholic children and some from "secular" homes. There were four teachers, a secretary, and the principal, all certificated by the CACS. Reverend Wendt declined to reveal the salary schedule or per-pupil cost; but the income apparently would not permit this to rise above $250.00.

3.   An American Lutheran Boarding School

Mr. Walter R. Reitan, Administrator of the Oak Grove Lutheran High School, Fargo, North Dakota, stated that the official enrollment was 202, had been increasing yearly, and would soon reach a maximum of 225. It was operated by a non-profit corporation of 56 members—elected by congregations in the State—who, in turn, elected a board of 15 regents. Sixty per cent of the students lived on campus at a cost of $1,400; tuition for day students was $700. The 1971-72 budget was $340,000, about $1,700 per pupil, of which nearly $1,300 was consumed in the educative process. The students paid $224,000; the National American Lutheran Conference gave the school $36,000; a publicity director raised an additional $85,000. Salaries for eleven full-time teachers ranged from $6,615 to $9,922—but in 1971-72, the maximum was to reach $10,363, in addition to fringe benefits worth at least $500. The school plant was without debt, and received no help of any kind from government sources.

Mr. Reitan was proud of his school; it has fielded an excellent football team every year, and in 1969 won the State Class B Basketball Championship by defeating every private and public school in its division. The school offered facilities and opportunities, he declared, beyond anything to be found in a public school. Costs may be somewhat higher, he admitted, but "Where," he asked, "will you find a school with 200 students which has a faculty and staff of 32? Where can you get the individual attention here provided and teachers with such dedication to work and principle? Where else will you find an institution where every one can strengthen and confirm his faith in the Lord?"

4.   The Golden West Christian School

In February, 1971, the Golden West Christian School—non- or inter-denominational— opened its doors in Phoenix, Arizona. The handsome buildings have 20 classrooms with a potential enrollment of 240, for pupils ranging from kindergarten through the 8th grade. During the first semester, there were 60; in the fall of 1971, 122. A capacity enrollment is expected in 1972-73.

This is the seventh of a privately owned, non-profit chain, known as the Hawthorne Christian Schools. Founded by the Reverend Carl Pike of Hawthorne, California, they are entirely independent. They stress the three Rs, strict discipline, and basic Christianity. The corporation also operates a Teacher's College, which prepares the religiously oriented instructors who man the system.

The oldest school is the Hawthorne, which began with 19 pupils in 1942, but now has more than 1,300. Combined enrollment of the seven schools now approximates 3,000.

Reverend Pike had been successful in various business enterprises, from which he accumulated a fortune; he then conceived the idea of using his wealth and energy to promote an elementary system of Christ-centered education. The income from several enterprises now subsidizes the schools; among these are radio stations, bookstores, an airplane service, and a fleet of charter busses known as the Fiesta Lines.

Mrs. Carl Pike, principal of Golden West, did not know the amount of capital invested or how much of the operational cost derived from subsidies. However, we estimated the value of the land and the two buildings at about $350,000.

At the opening of school in September 1971, the newspapers carried large advertisements soliciting pupils. Mrs. Pike stated that the school was planning on taking over a bankrupt radio station to bring its message to the people of metropolitan Phoenix.

Subjects taught are Bible, Reading, English, Spelling, Arithmetic, History, Phonics, General Science, Penmanship, and a language (Spanish or French). Music, Art, and Physical Education are also included in the curriculum. All pupils wear prescribed uniforms.

There are five full-time teachers, whose salaries averaged $2,700 for a 9-month year. Each one handles classes in all subjects at two grade levels.

The tuition is $55 a month for one child from a single family, $95 for two, $135 for three, and $166 for four, which includes all textbooks and transportation. The school owns three busses, which carry pupils to and from their classes.

Asked whether tuition was sufficient to meet all expenses, Mrs. Pike stated that it fell considerably short; but she assured us that there was no cause for worry, since the Lord cares for this enterprise and enables it to meet any exigency.

Since no financial statement was available at the local office, we did a little computation of our own. With a full enrollment of 240 and an average tuition of $450, there would be a gross income of $108,000. Ten full-time teachers would receive about $27,000; since maintenance, operation, textbooks, bus service, etc., probably would not exceed $40,000, there would be about $40,000 additional to amortize the debt and meet other obligations.

Should teachers and other personnel receive salaries comparable to those paid in the public schools, it is obvious that per-pupil costs at Golden West would at least be double what they now are. Since each teacher at present must cover many subjects and do so in two grades, there cannot be any specialization or much individual attention. Should the pupil-teacher ratios be comparable to those at Verde Valley or other elite schools, the cost would certainly quadruple.

There is little doubt that the *raison d'etre* of schools such as the Golden West is the desire of some parents for religiously oriented schooling and the expectation that their children will be taught good morals and drilled thoroughly in academic basics.

However, we must recognize that the economic structure of the school rests upon the dedication of devout teachers who are willing to work for approximately one-third of the salaries received by certificated personnel in the public schools.

160

5.   Two Seventh-Day Adventist Schools

a. The Fairview Junior Academy

The Fairview Junior Academy, 26,200 Date Street, San Bernardino, California, is a 10-grade school with excellent facilities, large classrooms, a parking area, and an extensive playground. Since there was no church in sight, it could have been mistaken for a public school. Mr. Allan Bohman, Superintendent, stated that it was supported by student fees and a subsidy of about $20,000 from four "constituent" churches; tuition was $360 in grades 1 through 8 and $560 in 9 and 10. There were 10 teachers, in addition to other personnel. He did not mention a per-pupil cost, but, since the enrollment, which had grown steadily, was 240, student fees and church subsidies totalled about $120,000; and probably reflected an operational per-pupil cost of about $500, in addition to amortization of investment and cost of bus service, which may have added $150 or $200.

Mr. Bohman stated that there were seven SDA schools in the general area, all maintained in the same manner; that all teachers are certificated either by the State or by the denomination. The salary schedule ranged from $6,400 to $9,100—comparable to that in the public schools.

b. An Elite Religious School

The Bakersfield Academy at 3333 Bernard, Bakersfield, California, is a 12-grade institution with a splendid plant which cost $350,000 and carried a debt of $200,000. Mr. Dave R. Cannard, Accountant, stated that the 1970-71 enrollment was 345, of whom 220 were in the elementary division. There were 24 teachers, including two principals; their salaries ranged from $7,500 to $8,800 and totalled $192,000. For 1971-72, the tuition was to be increased to $380 on the elementary level and to $770 on the secondary; this was in addition to the cost of music, cafeteria, and bussing.

Seven constituent churches paid subsidies totalling nearly $35,000 in 1970-71; the Central California Seventh-Day Adventist Conference paid another $24,000, plus $22,000 to cover one-third of the salaries of elementary teachers.

The school, therefore, received more than $241,000 in tuition and subsidies, which reflected a per-pupil operational cost of $710, in addition to bussing, music, and amortization, which would probably add another $200. However, since the Academy could absorb 150 additional pupils without expanding the plant or hiring many more teachers, per-pupil costs could be lowered materially.

Mr. Cannard stated that only 5% of the youth in his denomination who attend public schools remain in its fold; but that the retention rate among those who attend Church schools ranges from 80 to 90%. He added that about 25 of the Academy's high school students had left for the denominational boarding school at Monterey, which enrols about 450, and where costs are presumably substantially higher.

6.   **An Old Secular Institution**

The long-established St. Paul's Academy (secondary) at 1712 Randolph, St. Paul, Minnesota, operates as a unit with the Summit School (elementary), at 1150 Goodrich. These institutions are completely secular, wholly supported by student fees, individual contributions, and revenues from endowments. In May, 1971, a drive to raise $8 million was under way, of which $6.2 million had already been pledged or obtained. Tuition for 1971-72 ranged from $1,000 in the first grade to $1,550 in grades 7 and 8, and $1,600 on the high school level. Lunches and books were additional. However, the school catalog states that the "money the school receives through tuition only partially covers the full cost of educating a student. . . . With an enrollment of 638 and a student/teacher ratio of 8/1, the school provides small classes for a maximum of student involvement. . . ."

St. Paul's-Summit certainly offers an exclusive type of education. That the enrollment comes from wealthy families is obvious not only from the cost of enrollment but also from the fact that enormous sums were being successfully solicited from friends and former graduates for expansion, improvement, and increased endowment.

7.   **Two Missouri Synod Lutheran Schools**

a. **The St. John's Lutheran School of Bakersfield**

The St. John's Lutheran School at 1030–4th Street, Bakersfield, California, had 8 grades, 4 teachers, and 82 pupils, including several Negroes. Mr. Walter E. Peters, principal, stated that this was the only Lutheran school in Kern County; that only half of the pupils were from Church families; and that the year covered ten months. The enrollment had grown from 54 in 1965 to 100 in 1971-72. The teachers, who were certified and had bachelor's degrees, received salaries totalling $23,000, of which the principal, who also carried a full teaching load, received $8,395. For non-church members, tuition was $30 a month for the first child, $10 for the second and third, with additional ones free; for members, the charge was $15 and $5. The school was solely an operation of the parent church, which allocated $20,000 for the school. There was no other subsidy of any kind, except $86 from ESEA under Title II. Per-pupil cost was $356.

b. **The Grace Lutheran School of Fargo**

The Grace Lutheran School in Fargo, North Dakota, had a fine plant, entirely separate from any church sanctuary. Mr. John C. Leibert, principal, stated that it was established in 1948, had 75 pupils in 1968, and had since grown to 135. It was operated by the Grace Lutheran Church, the children of which received free tuition. There were five full-time and three part-time teachers; salaries totalled $33,000, and ranged from $4,200 to $6,700. There should be Title II ESEA money, but none had as yet been received. The school leased two busses at a cost of $7,200 a year; school maintenance cost $6,800; and taxes and assessment on property, including the principal's home, totalled $1,000; while instructional materials cost $3,000.

The budget of $53,000 was sustained by tuition and registration fees; by a subsidy of $10,000 from the Emanuel Lutheran Church; by another $20,000 from the operating Grace Lutheran Church; and by gifts from concerned individuals of $15,000. Per-pupil cost was $392.

8.   The Phoenix Country Day School

Quite different from any other institution described in the preceding pages is the Phoenix Country Day School, located at 3901 E. Stanford Drive, which was dedicated in October, 1961, as a non-profit non-sectarian independent institution enrolling pupils from kindergarten through the twelfth grade. It is one of the best in Arizona.

The school is organized in three divisions: (a) the Lower, which includes the kindergarten and grades 1 - 4; (b) the Middle, with grades 5, 6, and 7; and the Upper, for grades 8 -12 inclusive. All pupils are carefully screened, and only those believed to qualify as good college or university material are admitted or retained. The emphasis throughout is on academic achievement.

The first enrollment consisted of 93 elementary pupils; in 1965, this had grown to 320, with students in all grades. In 1969-70, the school had 380; however, when tuition was increased in 1971-72, enrollment fell to 340.

The school has eight buildings, two large athletic fields, and ample parking space in a site consisting of forty acres of valuable land in northeast Phoenix.

164

Mr. John L. Yellott, headmaster, stated that the net value of the plant in 1970-71 was somewhat in excess of $1 million—on which there was still a substantial debt. There was a small endowment; and gifts have averaged about $90,000 a year. The total budget in 1970-71 was $735,000, of which nearly half went for salaries. The per-pupil cost was $2,160.

There is an instructional staff of 37, consisting of four administrators and thirty-three full-time teachers. There are, in addition, at least a dozen other employees. Teachers' salaries range from $7,000 to $13,000 and average $9,000. The pupil-teacher ratio is approximately ten, which is higher than at Verde Valley but less than half of that in the public schools and about one-fourth of what we have observed in many parochials.

The school has five departments; and each section of each grade has a home-room teacher or supervisor; all academic subjects are taught by specialists. Counsellors are available for all students and individual tutoring is available when necessary.

Compared to Verde Valley, the Phoenix Country Day School seemed conventional and sophisticated; strict discipline is maintained; all pupils are smartly dressed; and a high value is obviously placed upon decorum. Furthermore, a rigid grading system is employed, with six well-defined classifications of scholastic performance. Pupils who fall below a required norm are simply dropped from membership.

The school publishes a long list of leading colleges and universities which have accepted its graduates and it is proud of the records they have established.

In 1961-62, the tuition ranged from $500 for the half-day kindergarten pupils to $1,200 for those in high school. For 1971-72, the tuition for kindergarten was increased to $700; $1,200 for grades 1-3; $1,400 for 4-6; $1,700 for 7-9; and $1,750 for 10-12.

However, this was by no means the total cost. The ninety students who availed themselves of bus service in 1970-71, paid $300 for this;[a] all students paid $145 a year for noon lunches; books and materials were supplied at the kindergarten level at $30 and at $60 a year for pupils in the grades. For all students in the Middle and Upper School, a general fee of $60 was imposed in lieu of individual fees for science, art, athletics, and student activities. On the high school level, therefore, those students who availed themselves of bussing paid $2,350.

The school undoubtedly offers a superior academic process: however, it does nothing that a public school, with similar pupils and objectives,

a. This extremely high cost results from the fact that students in a small private school are necessarily widely scattered. Public school pupils who need transportation at all can be carried at one-fifth the cost.

could not do at less than half the cost. As in the case of Verde Valley, the high price is due largely to the fact that, in order to have specialists with a small enrollment, there must be a very low pupil-teacher ratio.

The motivations which cause parents who can afford it to send their children to the Phoenix Country Day School are, we believe, the following: (1) the desire for superior academic training and discipline; (2) the wish to escape drugs and integration; (3) the ambition to have their offspring associate with teachers and with youth who respect and observe the amenities of "respectable" and conservative society; (4) the necessity of providing intellectual challenge for children with high IQs; and (5) the anticipation of social, intellectual, and economic achievement for them when they reach adulthood.

We know of at least one instance in which a bright boy, bored to frustration in the public school, became a serious problem in behavior. Sent to the Country Day School, however, he settled down to serious study, made phenomenal progress, and became a model of deportment and ambition.

SUMMARY

From our observation of a wide variety of private schools, secular and sectarian, we have concluded that the latter in all cases exist primarily to inculcate those religious tenets and disciplines which, it is hoped, will make the pupils into life-long supporting members of the communions or denominations which sponsor the schools. However, we found also that costs in such institutions vary greatly; they may be as low as $150 or $200 per pupil, or as high as $800 or $1,000, a difference depending on the kind of plant utilized, the type, salaries, and dedication of the teachers, and the kind of curriculum pursued.

The secular privates are intended specifically for an elite clientele, and are extremely expensive.

We found, also, that since all of these schools are necessarily quite small, they either have little specialization or the cost of instruction is very high. Furthermore, adequate equipment of any or all kinds is costly per pupil. For a school with a hundred or even three hundred pupils to offer the facilities possible and desirable in one with an enrollment of 2,000 is a very expensive undertaking. Finally, transportation for students scattered sparsely over wide areas costs several times as much as for those attending a neighborhood school, which the great majority can easily reach on foot.

We believe, therefore, that whatever advantages may be found in a private school with small enrollment, these cannot consist of adequate equipment, specialized instruction, or desirable location and service, except at enormous expense; and that it would, in consequence—with a given quality of instruction— be perhaps two or three times as costly to support many small schools as to maintain a single unified public system of education.

Part Two

Conclusions and Commentary

1

Enrollment: Past and Projected

Growth and Decline

Table I in the Appendix shows how the Great Depression caused such a reduction in the birth rate that it was more than 20 years before the baby-crop of WW II and the years following restored the public school enrollment to the level of 1930, when this was 25,678,153; in 1950, it was 25,111,427; in 1952, 26,562,663.

Then, however, as shown in Table III and XVI, a great expansion took place: public school enrollment rose to 30,528,323 in 1955, 36,086,771 in 1961, 42,173,764 in 1965, and 46,531,000 in 1969-70. Between 1952 and 1969-70, the combined enrollment in public and private schools increased from 28,660,250 to 51,432,313, or 80%. Private schools expanded more rapidly than the public; from 3,380,139 in 1950 to 6,304,722 in 1965, or 87%.

The Birth Rate

In 1935, there were 2,155,105 births, or 16.9 per thousand in population; in 1953, there were 3,902,120, with a rate of 24.6, which continued at approximately this level until 1961, when 4,268,000 children were born. Then, slowly at first, but with a gradually increasing tempo, the number of births declined, sometimes by more than a hundred thousand each year. In 1968, there were 3,502,000, a ratio of 17.3 per thousand, scarcely higher than in 1935, even though the Negro birth rate continued at about 26.

Since children are 5 or 6 years old when they are registered in a kindergarten or a first-grade class, the falling birth rate, which began after 1961-62, first became apparent in school enrollments about 1969-70. In 1971, Mr. Leroy Peterson, Director of the Iowa State Office of Planning, made a study of birth-trends in his state. He found that in all but two of the 99 counties there were fewer pre-school children than in 1961. In several, the drop was nearly 50 per cent. The result, he said, would be a great many half-empty schools.[a] We should note that the situation in Iowa is typical of that in many other states, especially the agricultural areas, as well as in large cities.

The same story comes from almost every corner of the country, except from areas like Scottsdale, Phoenix, or Albuquerque, where there has been a vast in-migration from the older sections of the nation.

From New York, Florence Flast, Vice-Chairman of the Committee for Public Education and Religious Liberty, wrote in May, 1971: "Here in New York City, there are close to 100,000 empty seats in the public school districts which have an aging population, a changing neighborhood, and a heavy percentage of non-public school enrollment."

In the industrial state of Michigan, for example, Dr. Stanley Hecher of Michigan State University, completed a study in 1971, which showed that between 1969-70 and 1970-71, total enrollment in all Michigan schools declined for the first time since the early Thirties: from 2,460,445 to 2,453,952. During the year, the public schools gained 14,874 and the non-public lost 21,367. On the basis of recorded live births, he found that during the following four years total enrollment would decline an additional 75,300.

Availability of Abortions

There is also another factor which is certain to reduce still further the school enrollment of the Seventies and the Eighties: the availability of legal abortions. There have, indeed, always been some terminations of pregnancy—legal or otherwise. But now that abortions are granted almost upon request, they are becoming more frequent; and it is possible, before the end of the current decade, that several hundred thousand otherwise certain births each year will not occur at all.

Projections

What this means for elementary and secondary education is not difficult to determine. Since children enter kindergarten or the first grade at 5 or 6, and continue in grade school until 14, those born during the years 1955-62 constituted the elementary enrollment of 1963-70. And since their high school years range from 14 to 18, those born between 1957 and

---

a.   Cf. the Des Moines *Register,* Sept. 2, 1971.

1962, which was the period of highest births, will supply the secondary enrollment between 1971 and 1975, after which this also will begin to decline quite rapidly.

Table XVII demonstrates what has already occurred and is certain to continue during the Seventies.[a] In 1970-71, total elementary and secondary enrollment was 51,432,000, a decline of 560,000 from the peak of 1969-70. In 1972, this total will not exceed 50,320,000. In 1974, it will drop to less than 49,000,000; in 1976, to 47,900,000; in 1979, to 46,855,000—five million less than in 1969-70.

Should every private school in the United States close before 1979, the total public school enrollment will be approximately the same as in 1970. In short, the flood of children who came into the schools, both Catholic and public, between 1950 and 1965, has abated; what we are facing now, by and large, is literally millions of vacant seats in the nation's classrooms.

---

a.   The New York *Times* News Service reported, 10-4-71, that the fertility rate during 5 months of the year was the lowest in the United States since 1935 and fell from 88.5 in 1970 per 1,000 women of child-bearing age to 77.5. During the first seven months of 1971, there were only 2,050,000 births, which was a rate of 16 per thousand, compared to 16.9 in 1935 and 24.6 in 1953. Although it is not known what impact therapeutic abortions have had upon the birth rate, there can be no doubt that this factor is becoming increasingly significant.

2

Can Public Schools Absorb Parochial Pupils?

The Actual Experience

In Part One, we saw what happened in 16 typical and representative cities. The public schools in Helena absorbed the entire Catholic enrollment of nearly 1,000, increased their own by 17%, and then for the first time had surplus room. Those in Butte absorbed 2,500, established a fine Vo-Tech with 1,232 students, yet increased their own enrollment by only 2,112. In Pueblo, they absorbed more than 4,000 in 6 years, yet increased their own enrollment by only 129. In San Bernardino, they accepted 1,300 students but lost enrollment. In Bakersfield, elementary registrations in the public schools remained static in a growing city while the Catholic dropped from 10% to 5.3% of the total. In Albuquerque, Catholic enrollment fell from about 9,000 to 4,400, but these transfers constituted so small a portion of the total increase in the public schools that it was not even noticed: meanwhile, the ratio of Catholic enrollment fell from 14.9% to 4.9%. The experience of Boise and Fargo shows that taxes in static communities which have few or no transfers will rise as rapidly as, for example, in Butte and Helena. In Duluth, the public schools absorbed nearly half of the 4,000 Catholic pupils; yet their enrollment increased only by the number in the new Vo-Tech. In Green Bay, where the Catholic schools enrolled 53.4% of all pupils in 1961, they had only 23.1% in 1971; and while the population of the school district increased by perhaps 20,000 between 1965 and 1971, the Catholic schools lost 3,778 and the public gained 5,234 pupils to maintain an almost static total enrollment. In Dubuque, where the ratio in Catholic schools declined from 60% to 35% and their enrollment from 11,000 to 7,500 in 5 years, the public increased by about 5,600, which reflected a greater interest in education on the part of Catholic parents. In St. Paul, in 6 years, the Catholic schools lost more than 14,000 pupils; but the public gained only 4,450—of whom 2,600 were in the new Vo-Tech. In Milwaukee, the Catholic schools lost nearly 23,000 in 5 years—but the public gained only 6,000. In Detroit, all schools declined: the Catholic by almost 50,000; the public by 13,000.

The Practical Result

We have found that when parochials close, the community unites to support the public schools. It was only when Catholic laymen decided that public schools were preferable, that large bond issues were voted for their support. This is what happened in Butte, Helena, Pueblo, Dubuque, St. Paul, and elsewhere: for many years, the public schools had been fed starvation rations; but when more and more empty seats appeared in the parochials, general bond issues were voted for the public so that they could finally be improved and expanded.

One of the classic illustrations of this is St. Paul. There, in 1967-68, the public school enrollment was more than double the Catholic; yet the Church schools had an investment of more than $3,000 for each pupil, while in the public sector it was only $870, a disparity which is now gradually and at long last being corrected during the Seventies.

An Extraordinary Accomplishment

We contemplate with mingled awe and admiration the stupendous achievement of our public **and** private schools during the period following 1950. Since the school plants, especially in the public sector, had long been neglected and had undergone very little improvement or expansion between 1930 and 1950, most of the buildings were antiquated, obsolete, and totally inadequate. And then, suddenly, about 1952, came a flood of children, which made a tremendous program of expansion mandatory. The achievements of the succeeding years were nothing less than phenomenal. In 18 years, enrollment increased by nearly 20 million.

What happened is shown in Table XVI. Between 1955 and 1970, while public school enrollment grew by 15,448,842, 1,126,385 new class-rooms—or stations—were constructed, for a net gain—after abandoning 333,385—of 793,000. Since, even at 25 pupils per room, this provided accommodations for 19,825,000 during this 15-year period, the public school plant in 1970-71 had an excess capacity of 4,370,000 on the same basis of utilization as in 1955-56. However, at that time and for a decade thereafter, double sessions were necessary in thousands of school districts. The 1970 *Digest of Educational Statistics* (p. 45) states that in 1964-65, an additional 98,300 classrooms would be necessary to provide one station for each 27.4 pupils on the elementary level and one for each 27.5 on the

173

secondary. In less than two years, however, enough rooms were built to supply this minimum requirement. During 1964-68 inclusive, more than 350,000 classrooms were built; and in 1970-71, there were 532,000 more teaching stations than in 1961-62.

With the new building under construction in 1972 and scheduled for completion by 1976, the public schools could then absorb virtually every pupil in the United States.

The Cost

To finance the expansion which occurred between 1950 and 1970, of course, enormous sums were necessary for capital outlay and interest on bonded debt. In 1949-50, these items totalled $1,114,754,000; in 1959-60, $3,151,300,000; in 1965-66, $4,546,442,000; in 1967-68, $5,233,601,000;[a] and in 1970-71, $6,350,000,000.[b] Since the average expenditure during the last 20 years has been at least $3.5 billion, we know that the taxpayers have granted the public schools more than $70 billion for expansion; and all these funds have been voted by the people, and very often by property owners alone.

Construction and Expansion

When we realize that all this has been done without any serious negative reaction from the taxpayers, it seems that any fear concerning future school financing is without foundation.

If what we have witnessed all over the country is a reliable criterion, it seems certain that the public school construction will continue during the Seventies at a rate comparable to that of the Sixties. However, the purpose of this will not be to meet the needs of a greater enrollment so much as to replace older buildings with the most modern facilities and to provide teaching stations for smaller classes.

Since it is incredible that anywhere near all Catholic schools will close, and since it is virtually assured that other private institutions will increase in number and enrollment, we deem it inevitable that there will be a considerable surplus of public school rooms and space during the Seventies, even if the general pupil-teacher ratio falls below 20, which would be an unlikely development indeed, if for no other reason than that school consolidation will continue and that taxpayers are not likely to finance partially used facilities or vote salary increases for teachers who have fewer than 20 pupils per class.

a.   Cf. 1970 *Digest, op.cit.,* p. 29.
b.   Cf. 1971 *SA* p. 102. The capital outlay alone was $5.2 billion.

The Conquest of Crises

Between 1965 and 1971, Catholic enrollment nationally declined from 5,662,000, or 11.6% of the total, to about 3,800,000, or 7.4%—a loss of 30%. In cities where the parochial enrollment does not exceed the 1971-72 national average, it is so insignificant that its transfer to the public sector could not cause disruption, and would, in fact, scarcely be noticed at all.

That we may realize more precisely what has already happened, we have combined the totals involved in Helena, Butte, Albuquerque, Duluth, Green Bay, Dubuque, St. Paul, Milwaukee, Pueblo, and Detroit, where, in some instances, from 40 to 60% of total enrollment was recently in Catholic schools. During 1964-65, the combined public enrollment in these cities was 634,082 and the Catholic 200,067; in 1971, these totals were 666,637 and 107,103 respectively. At the former date, the ratio of Catholic to public enrollment was 31.6%; at the latter, 16%. Total enrollment, in spite of many thousands in technical institutes which did not even exist at the beginning of the period, fell from 834,149 to 773,740; and while Catholic schools lost 92,864, the public gained only 32,555, or 5.1%. Total enrollment declined by 60,388, or 7.2%; the Catholic by 46.4%, compared to the national average of 30%.   Few statistics could be more significant. In these cities, the ratio of pupils in Catholic schools in 1964-65 was almost three times the national norm; and the subsequent decline greater than it would now be nationally in the private sector if all such schools should close. In spite of this, the developments in these ten cities during the last 6 or 7 years have not caused the slightest dislocation; on the contrary, they have been conducive to community harmony.

Conclusions

Precisely what developments will occur in the private sector during the Seventies, we cannot foretell; but we do know with certainty that by 1975 total school enrollment will drop by more than three million below that of 1969; and that by 1979, it will shrink by at least another million and a half.

The argument of parochiaidists, therefore, that public schools cannot provide room for parochial pupils without creating chaotic conditions or severe overcrowding is without validity.

Since the second great argument in support of parochiaid and subsidies for all private schools is that their termination will enormously increase the cost of public education and raise property taxes to unbearable levels, we turn now to a consideration of this question.

3

Actual Cost of Absorbing Parochial Pupils

Parochiaidists have a very simple method of computing the savings which their schools confer upon the taxpayers: they multiply their enrollments by average or reputed per-pupil costs in the public sector and the result is the amount saved. For example, in 1970, the National Catholic Educational Association issued a brochure entitled *If Catholic Schools Close. . . .*, on the reverse side of which there is a map showing the number of Catholic pupils in each state, the per-pupil cost of public school education there, and the consequent savings to the taxpayers, which averaged $801 per pupil and totalled $3,999,709,846.[a]

In Montana, according to the brochure, the cost of education during a five-year period increased by $12,046,290; since 8,008 parochial pupils were transferred, the implication is that the average cost of each was $1,504. However, we show in our study that the average total cost in Helena was only $660; that the average cost of absorbing 1,000 pupils and providing schoolhousing for them was only $400; that the property tax on an average house rose only $41.62; and that the cost of absorbing the whole Catholic enrollment was only $30 for the average family. Such was the total impact under the most extreme conditions imaginable.

The experience of Butte was similar. Through a careful analysis of all pertinent data, we found that the total average cost of absorbing 1,500 parochial pupils in 1968 and 1969 was less than $250 and that the State supplied half of this. Over a period of five years, 2,500 parochial pupils were absorbed at a cost of $63 a year to the owner of a $20,000 home.

In Pueblo, we found that the total per-pupil cost of absorbing 2,200 parochials was $200 each; and that State allocations will be sufficient to

---

a. In an article entitled "Should Catholic Schools Survive?" by John Deedy, Managing Editor of *Commonweal,* and published in the March 13, 1971, issue of *The New Republic,* the author states that the parochial schools, according to the reckoning of the Church, takes a load of $9 billion off the backs of the government, and the taxpayers.

enable the city to reduce the school millage. Had the parochiaid bill been passed, the beginning cost in Pueblo would have been $540,000.

Elsewhere, as in Bakersfield, San Bernardino, Albuquerque, Kansas City, and Duluth, in all of which there has been a substantial improvement and expansion in the public system and a gradual decline in the Catholic, the transfers from the latter have made no impact whatever; in all cases, the per-pupil cost has remained low or moderate; and the funds received from the states have been more than sufficient to offset any increase in local cost. Actually, such absorption has often meant a definite financial boon to the local taxpayers.

We note again that school taxes in Boise and Fargo, where there were virtually no transfers before 1970 and where the population remained static, rose at least as rapidly as in cities where massive transfers took place or parochial education was terminated entirely.

Milwaukee, St. Paul, and Detroit present special situations: in each of them, there was a heavy influx from parochial to public schools, but total enrollments fell so sharply that the transfers made little or no impact. In spite of vocational institutes, the total enrollment fell by 63,000 in Detroit; 11,000 in Milwaukee; and 9,000 in St. Paul.

Since this is the general national situation, any present or potential influx of parochial students into the public schools will not—except in very unusual cases—require expanded facilities, but only a somewhat higher utilization of those already existing.

Green Bay and Dubuque, again, presented special and different situations. Here we found Catholic school systems built during the last generation or two which recently enrolled 54 and 60% respectively of the city youth. Constructed at enormous sacrifice to Catholic laymen, these schools were standing almost half idle in 1971. And the same people who had paid so dearly for them were sending their children to the public schools and voting generous bond issues to improve and expand them.

In such circumstances, all discussion concerning cost is quite irrelevant. For reasons best known to themselves, the same Catholics who had previously supported parochial institutions had turned to public education. Since doing so must have involved increased expenditures, it should be obvious that the issue was not financial, at least not basically; it was a declaration in the most emphatic terms possible that Catholic parents preferred the common schools.

Such a decision was specifically apparent in the Western Dubuque Community School District. Here is a large and fertile agricultural region, which includes five or six towns, of which Dyersville, with 3,000 inhabitants, is the largest. During the century preceding 1960, this area had never known a public school; Dyersville still has none. In several of the villages, there was no school millage whatever. When the public school district was organized, it began with 600 or 700 pupils; it had more than 3,000 in 1971-72.

So here was a virtually total Catholic community, which paid almost no school tax at all, but which decided to establish public schools and thus to divert its educational funds to them through taxation, instead of making contributions for the same purpose to the parish churches and the diocese for disposition by clerical authorities.

Since cities like Bakersfield, San Bernardino, Kansas City, and Duluth are typical of the nation as a whole, their experience supplies an accurate barometer concerning the costs of absorbing parochial pupils. In all of these, the dwindling birth rate is leaving more and more vacant seats in the public schools; as the parochials shrink or close, some of these otherwise unused desks are occupied by the transfers. Instead of having 20, 21, or 22 pupils in a teaching station, the number may rise to 22, 23, or 24. In this manner, literally millions of private pupils can be absorbed without spending a dime for new equipment or engaging the services of a single additional teachers.

Actually, thousands of individual school districts will benefit financially by transfers because for each additional child enrolled they receive an allocation from state foundation funds. We have already seen the effect of this in Pueblo, Bakersfield, and elsewhere.

Those who discern the hand of Providence in the affairs of men may well detect its influence in what has occurred. Had the crisis in parochial education developed between 1955 and 1965, when the public schools were adding hundreds of thousands or even millions to their own enrollment annually, parochial transfers would indeed have constituted a very serious problem; and, under such circumstances, a legitimate computation of cost would have been one based upon per-pupil expenditure.

During the Seventies, however, this method is no longer valid. It is absurd to average current per-pupil costs and consider these the basis for each transfer. The only correct method is that we have used in this study: namely, to determine the actual cost of any additional facilities and personnel necessitated by the influx. In many cities, none whatever have been required for years; and will be called for even less throughout the Seventies.[a]

a.   The more discerning Catholic scholars are now admitting the fallacy of their usual method of computing the savings of parochial schools to taxpayers. According to an article of May 28, 1971, in *The Messenger*, published by the Belleville diocese in Illinois, Father C. S. Bartell, the noted Notre Dame scholar, is preparing a study similar to ours in which he concludes that transfer of parochial pupils to public schools may well be

178

There is also another significant element, which we will discuss in some detail in the next chapter: the federal and state subsidies already going to parochial schools. Since this already has mounted into hundreds of millions annually, all such funds will be diverted to public schools and constitute a significant element in their support.

We believe, therefore, that the data offered in this and the preceding chapter demonstrate (1) that the public schools can easily absorb any number of parochial pupils who may wish to transfer; and (2) that the cost to the taxpayers of so doing will be far less than any program by which private systems might be funded at public expense.

Since these are demonstrable facts, parochiaidists may no longer offer the financial argument to taxpayers in support of their demands for partial subsidies. Even if we did not know that these would soon blossom into demands for total support, this parochiaidist thesis would be without validity.

The proponents of private education must therefore retreat to other positions which in fact they have occupied for a century and a half and have been presented by such men as Archbishop Hughes, Archbishop Ireland, and Father Blum: namely, that unless Catholic schools are provided with public funds and allowed to operate as they wish, the religious conscience and the civil rights of Catholics, parents and children alike, are violated and desecrated.

But why, we wonder, are not the rights of Baptists, Methodists, Unitarians, Quakers, Muslims, and a thousand others equally disregarded when their specific doctrines are ignored in the public school? Why is it that Catholics are almost alone in believing that they cannot inculcate their peculiar beliefs in the minds of their children in the home, the church, and in religion classes operated by themselves outside the public schoolroom?

---

accomplished at minimal cost to **taxpayers**. He said, "Where public schools are already filled to capacity, absorption costs could exceed average costs. . . ." (We have shown that this did **not** happen in Helena or Pueblo.) "If, however," he continued, "excess physical capacity exists in a public school system and teachers are readily available, the costs of additional enrollment in public schools would approximate existing average instruction costs.

"On the other hand," Father Bartell said, "it is also possible that marginal instructional costs of transfer students might well be well below average cost-per-pupil already enrolled in the public system. This would be a likely possibility where excess physical capacity exists in the public schools and when pupil-teacher ratios are below the acceptable maximum levels. . . ."

Wonderful Devices

There is no method by which the value of direct and indirect public subsidies to parochial and other private schools can be accurately computed. Since the National Science Foundation publishes a *Report* covering *Federal Support to Universities, Colleges, and Selected Nonprofit Institutions,* we know precisely how much money is distributed to them under various federal programs.[a] However, when we investigate the public largesse to elementary and secondary schools, we find ourselves in a morass of confusion, uncertainty, and imponderables. This is true at least in part because direct aid to such institutions is prohibited by the First Amendment, by many Supreme Court decisions, and by the constitutions of almost all the individual states.

In order to evade or avoid such sanctions, a multiplicity of devices, marvellous for their ingenuity, have been adopted to spend tax-funds for the benefit of parochial schools or pupils; for this purpose, the Child-Benefit Theory has been pressed into yeoman's service. The Supreme Court has declared that bussing, textbooks, and lunches constitute aid to the child instead of to the school; on the same theory shared time and other programs have been utilized in a number of states.

ESEA

The greatest federal contributions to elementary and secondary education have been delivered since 1965 under Title I of ESEA, under which

---

a.   These totalled $3,453,000,000 in 1969.

public school teachers are sent into private schools in poorer areas to aid identifiably disadvantaged children, who are given instruction in special classes. However, even the Department of Health, Education, and Welfare knows only what funds are relayed through the **superintendents** of public instruction in the 50 state capitals. These, in turn, allocate funds to the school districts under their direction; and it is only on the local level that one can discover how much money is used for the benefit of parochial and how much for public school pupils. By and large, we found in the cities analyzed that allocations in both systems were approximately proportionate to enrollment.[a] Only a few schools in most communities were eligible to participate; in cities like Scottsdale, none at all. Sometimes, however, programs for individual schools are very costly: for example, we found at least two Lady of Guadalupe schools in which ESEA expenditures were greater than the entire private budget for their operation.

Title II of ESEA provides library books and audio-visual materials; and allocations ranging from about $1.25 to $2.50 per pupil are available to virtually every school, public or private, in the United States.

The purpose of Title III is to strengthen instruction in science, mathematics, languages, etc. Title IV, V, and VI furnish plans for decentralization; guidance, counselling, and testing; help in bilingual education; teacher-training; and various other forms of aid.

However, Title I is by far the largest and most important; and Title II spreads its largesse, albeit somewhat thinly, over the widest area. The *Progress Report* of the President's Commission on School Finance, dated March 22, 1971, states (p. 33) that approximately $1.2 billion had been expended annually for several years under Title I alone; and that 7,500,000 pupils had qualified for aid under its various programs in 1969-70: which would mean an average expenditure of $160.

Since, during the years 1965-70, Catholic schools enrolled about 10% of the total, we find that during this 5-year period, $600,000,000 of federal money was expended for their benefit: an average of $120,000,000 each year under Title I alone of ESEA.

Other Federal Subsidies

The publication cited above states also (p. 39) that federal aid to

---

a.   So far as we know, no Seventh-Day Adventist school has ever accepted such subsidies; and we have never found a Lutheran school receiving allocations under Title I of ESEA.

public and non-public elementary and secondary schools during the fiscal year ending June 30, 1970, totalled $3.3 billion, a sum distributed through 40 programs and administered by the Department of Health, Education, and Welfare; the National Science Foundation; the Office of Economic Opportunity; and the Bureau of Indian Affairs.

Since Catholic schools participated on an equal basis in virtually all of these, we compute their annual share during recent years at $300 million.

In addition to this, of course, we have the lunch program operated by the USDA and administered through state agencies. A document entitled *Child Nutrition Programs; Summary of Funds, Including Special Milk, Matching Requirements, and Participation in This Program* contains detailed information, some of which is reproduced in TABLE XVIII.

We find here that its total cost in 1947 was $218,588,894, of which the federal share was $67,902,894, the states', $20,616,000, local school boards', $17,532,000, and the children's, $112,540,000. Government subsidies therefore totalled $88,516,894, or about 40%. The amounts contributed by various sources grew annually and rapidly: in 1950, to $367,598,505; in 1960, to more than a billion dollars; and in 1971, to no less than $2,849,598,000.

Since we estimate the Catholic share of subsidized food for pupils proportionately to enrollment, this public expenditure for them would have been $15 million in 1950, $50 million in 1960, $70 million in 1965, and $90 million in 1971.

And since the various federal programs for Catholic elementary and secondary education in 1970-71 together with state and federal subsidies for lunches cost the taxpayers approximately $390 million; and since there were about 4,430,000 pupils in Catholic schools, we compute the per-pupil subsidy in them at about $90.

State Subsidies

In addition, there were, of course, a great variety of state programs even after the Supreme Court declared the principal form of parochiaid in Rhode Island and Pennsylvania unconstitutional and in spite of the fact that various forms of already enacted or potential subsidies for church schools were prohibited by referenda in New York, Michigan, and Nebraska. New York paid the Catholic schools $28 million for "Mandated Services"; and passed a Secular Education Services Act to provide an additional $33 million.[a] Ohio paid Catholic schools $50 per pupil in 1969-70;[b]

a. Both of these have been declared unconstitutional.
b. This sum was increased substantially in 1972, but has been declared unconstitutional.

Minnesota enacted a law[a] intended to give parents substantial tax-refunds, tax-credits or outright payments to reimburse them for the tuition required. Shortly after the Pennsylvania purchase-of-services law was declared unconstitutional, the state legislature enacted a tuition-reimbursement system to provide $47 million for Catholic schools.[b] At least a dozen other state legislatures will be considering some form of tuition-refund or voucher-payment system during 1972-73.

However, the most common forms of parochiaid consist of a great variety of auxiliary services. According to a release published by the National Catholic Educational Association, May 15, 1971, 24 states were then offering transportation to private pupils; 31 supplied health and welfare services; 7 "loaned" textbooks; 4 gave courses in driver education.

The November, 1971, issue of *Church and State* summarizes details concerning current parochiaid programs in the United States. Since the Idaho Supreme Court declared bussing unconstitutional on September 2, 1971, the number of states without parochiaid increased to 15 in the fall of that year, all located in the South or West.

Estimated Total Subsidies

We repeat that an accurate estimate concerning the total value of parochiaid is impossible. However, it is certain that if laws on the books in 1971 had been able to survive in Ohio, Pennsylvania, New York, and elsewhere, the total for all forms of parochiaid—state and federal combined—might well have exceeded $600 million in 1971-72.

Even so, by the most conservative estimate, the national average public subsidy for all Catholic pupils can scarcely be less than $125; the magnitude of this sum should be measured against the fact that total parochial per-pupil cost in most Catholic elementary parish schools was less than $100 in 1959-60; and in most of the cities we surveyed, did not exceed $200 or $250 in 1970-71.

When we realize that as private pupils transfer to the common schools, these vast sums, continually increasing, become available in support of public education, it is apparent that this factor should be recognized as a significant element in its total cost.

---

a.   This is now being challenged in the courts.
b.   This has now been struck down by the courts.

5.   Why Catholic Schools Are Declining

The Laity on Strike

Several facts, etched sharply against the historical background, cannot be challenged: (1) that despite constant urging by seven provincial councils, Catholics between 1829 and 1849 failed or refused to establish parochial schools; (2) when ordered to do so under severe sanctions by the Third Plenary Council of Baltimore in 1884, the decree was ignored by nearly 65% of all parish churches during the following generation; (3) that during the great period of Catholic immigration (1840-1920) nearly three-fourths of the newcomers belonging to that faith abandoned it; (4) that its greatest period of proliferation and educational expansion occurred after WW II between 1946 and 1965; and (5) that since then there has been a steady decline in its schools and finally—for the first time in American history—an actual loss of membership. In the fall of 1971, school enroll-ment fell to a point below that of 1955.

In the course of this study, we show (1) that at certain periods in the past, Catholic laymen must have contributed a very large portion of their incomes to the Church; but (2) that during recent years, especially since 1964, they have simply refused to support the programs sponsored by the hierarchy.

As to the reasons for this, speculation may vary widely: as to the fact itself, there can be no dispute. From one unimpeachable source after another, we have learned that a large proportion of Catholic laymen con-tribute no more than one per cent of their gross income to the Church; and many give even less, or nothing at all.

Why is it that a new generation of Catholics have closed their purses whereas their fathers paid for an enormously costly educational plant and their grandfathers gave a large portion of their earnings to construct huge cathedrals and an amazing complex of schools, rectories, convents, monasteries, seminaries, colleges, retreats, and mother houses? and, in addition, send large but undivulged sums to Rome for the support of the Papacy and its world-wide apostolate?

Has the younger generation of Catholics fallen in love with material things and rejected spiritual values? Or has it begun to doubt the theology, mission, or authority of the Church? Are they refusing indoctrination in their preference for a secular education? Are they in revolt against a system of education over which they have no control? Have they decided that some aspects of their foreign-based Church are irrelevant in America? Are they listening to such voices as those of Emmett McLoughlin, James Kavanaugh, or Mary Perkins Ryan?

One thing is certain: the causes of the educational crisis in the Catholic Church are internal. In the words of two prominent Catholics, sociologist Father Andrew Greeley and attorney William Brown: "the basic problem facing Catholic schools in the United States is not loss of external support, but the internal collapse of morale. There is a loss of nerve, a loss of conviction, a loss of faith, a loss of enthusiasm. This is the root of the problem of Catholic education."[a]

Where a man's heart is, there will he place his treasures. Catholic laymen once gave the Church their most cherished sons and daughters, who, despite vows of poverty, chastity, and obedience, have recently been leaving it in droves. Not so long ago, laymen placed their worldly goods also at the disposal of the Church; but now they are deposited on other altars and for different purposes.

A Pointed Commentary

On October 4, 1971, *Newsweek* published an article entitled "Has the Church Lost its Soul?" A Gallup poll is cited, according to which 52% of Catholics now go to Mass only on Sundays and Holy Days; 63% rarely go to confession; 58% believe that one can ignore the Pope's condemnation of artificial birth control and still be a good Catholic; 60% state that it is no sin for a divorced Catholic to remarry; 78% believe that salvation may be found outside the Church; 92% knew of no important decision of the National Conference of Bishops; 94% read no Catholic literature, or virtually none; 53% declared that priests should be permitted to marry; 73% stated that sex education should be taught in parochial junior high schools; and only 38% even knew who the Berrigan brothers were.

---

a.   *Can Catholic Schools Survive?*, Sheed and Ward, p. 22.

We believe that these responses are an accurate index to the malais of the Catholic Church. It no longer controls the minds of its communicants, as once it did so utterly. "There was a time," the article declares, "not so long ago, when Roman Catholics were very different from other Americans. They belonged not to public school districts, but to parishes named after foreign saints; and each morning parochial school children would preface their Pledge of Allegiance to the Flag with a prayer for Holy Mother the Church. . . .

"The Catholic Church was a family then, and if there were few brothers in it, there were lots of sisters—women with milk-white faces of ambiguous age, peering out of long veils. . . . Alternately sweet and stern, they glided across polished classroom floors. . . , virginal 'brides of Christ' who often found a schoolroom of 60 students entrusted to their care. At home, 'Sister says' was a sure way to win points in a household argument.

"Even so, in both church and home, it was the 'fathers' who wielded ultimate authority. . . .

"There were sins that only Catholics could commit, like eating meat on Friday, or missing Sunday Mass. But mostly, the priests were there to pardon common failings of the flesh, which the timid liked to list under the general heading of 'impure' thoughts, desires, and actions. . . .

"In less than a decade, however, the 'unchangeable' U. S. Catholic Church has changed very much indeed. The Latin Mass, fish on Friday, and regular monthly confession are now merely memories to most Catholic adults—and only folklore to their children. What Sister says in class, using strange new catechisms, is more likely to create arguments at home than settle them. . . . and on other public issues such as abortion and aid to parochial schools, conflict has replaced concensus. . . ."

The author continues that for every five priests who die, retire, or leave the priesthood, only two seminarians are ordained; that many Catholics are now saying that laymen ought to elect their bishops and limit their tenure; that more Catholics are listening to Billy Graham than to their own pastors; and that a considerable number are turning to Pentecostalism or the underground church.

The Finances of the Catholic Schools

When the Catholic Church declares that its schools are saving the American taxpayers $4 billion or $9 billion, are not lay Catholics likely to conclude that their educational system is costing them too much? Would not the hierarchy be wiser if they told their own people how little it costs them to obtain quality education in the Church? Although these proclamations are beamed at non-Catholics, they fall equally upon the ears of everyone. Although Catholics are not told what savings and other benefits would accrue to them by sending their children to the common schools, we believe that they have pondered this question for themselves and have arrived at definitive decisions.

Catholic schools do not, of course, cost $9 billion or $4 billion; nevertheless, they do involve a considerable expenditure. The National Catholic Educational Association states that for operation alone the per-pupil cost in 1969-70 was $241.71 on the elementary level and ranged from $481.00 to $612.57 on the secondary. The cash outlay to educate 1,000,000 high school and 3,500,000 grade school pupils was therefore $1,400,000,000.[a] However, should we add the normal value of facilities used, the cost would probably rise to $1.75 billion; and should we add further the value of contributed services, the total would perhaps rise to $2.25 billion.

In 1971, the Catholic Church claimed 48,214,729 members, which would mean about twelve million families. Since the mean per-capita income in the United States was $3,700, Catholics should have been earning $168 billion. The total operating cost of all Catholic schools, therefore, would require considerably less than 1% of their income—which could have been contributed as a tax-deductible item to the parish church or a diocesan or private high school.

And since the different schools have various sources of revenue in addition to tuition fees and parish subsidies, the conclusion seems inescapable that millions of Catholics are now refusing to contribute more than an infinitesimal portion of their earnings for religious education.

In our conversation with Mr. Lewandowski in Milwaukee we obtained, for the first time, a crystal-clear insight concerning what has been taking place in Catholic education. High tuition charges were not the cause, but the direct result, of pupil-withdrawals. In the early Sixties, tuition in parish schools, at least in any substantial amount, was virtually unknown. Then, about 1965, parents began transferring their children to the public schools for reasons entirely unrelated to cost. As a consequence, those parents whose children were in public schools refused to make heavy contributions to the parish church for the operation of the school. The

---

a.   In his book, *Wordly Goods,* James Gollin estimates the income of the American Catholic Church at $3 billion, of which 40%, or $1.2 billion, is used for education. He estimates parish income at $2.1 billion, or $166 from the average family, which would be slightly more than 1.5% of income.

pastor was therefore forced to charge tuition for the children who remained. Since it was impossible to collect a sum sufficient to meet rising costs through fees and tuition, the church continued to subsidize the school in part: this caused conflict and polarization; and still more parents transferred their children to the public schools.[a]

When this process reached a certain point, it became mandatory to close the school in order to save the church itself from disruption, heavy losses, or even dissolution.

This is the untold story of Catholic school decline; and it has been and is being repeated in thousands of parishes across the nation.

There can be no doubt that while the Church was building new schools by the thousands following WW II and enrolling millions of additional pupils, its laymen must have been contributing at least 10% of their income to support its activities. Now the majority refuse to contribute anything at all for parochial education; and this has become the symbol and the measure of their independence and emancipation.

The issue, therefore, which the Catholic hierarchy has placed before the American people is simply this: will non-Catholics subsidize the schools which the Catholic laymen reject?

At this point, we wish to add a few words concerning two widely discussed programs in which the public schools collaborate with the parochial: shared- and released-time.

The latter, under which pupils may leave the campus during school hours to receive religious instruction, has been declared constitutional by the Supreme Court. And since the 1971 *Official Catholic Directory* states that 1,303,032 high school students and 4,181,416 elementary pupils were attending classes under released time, we took this to mean that all of these were actually leaving the school premises during school hours for this purpose. We discovered, however, that nothing could be further from the truth; the practice was not prevalent or even in existence in any of the 16 cities covered in this study. We heard of only one area where it was in general use (Pocatello and Idaho Falls); and there, as in Utah, it had been

---

a.   In the article by John Deedy, already cited, he says: "Once a unifying bond, the school is now a source of conflict, a polarizer of Catholics. And it will continue to be a polarizer, one fears, since the issue transcends the level of finances. . . . For liberals. . . , the parochial school is an octopus, sucking up more and more revenue to educate fewer and fewer of the Catholic school-age population. . . strangling energies . . . which might more profitably be directed to the renewal of parish life."

188

established, not for the benefit of Catholics, but for pupils in the Church of Jesus Christ of Latter Day Saints. We were told, however, that Catholics also took advantage of the provision there. We believe that the millions said to be under released time are simply—at least for the most part—receiving some kind of instruction after school hours or on the week end.

As for shared-time, on which the Supreme Court has not yet ruled, it is regarded with ambivalent attitudes. Such Catholic educators as Virgil Blum condemn it severely; and public school administrators are apt to regard it simply as a stopgap measure which serves a more-or-less desirable purpose during the transition period while more parochial pupils transfer to the public schools in preparation for the ultimate abolition of the church-related.

Only in the Detroit Archdiocese and outside the city itself; and in Dubuque, Iowa, did we find any substantial shared-time programs in operation. By and large, these also, like released time, have not proved entirely satisfactory to the parties concerned.

Part Three

Two Centuries of Controversy

1.   Introductory

During the last hundred years, elementary and secondary education in the United States has grown much faster than the population and its cost has been rising even more rapidly. In 1870, in a population of 37,818,449, the enrollment was 6,871,522, the expenditures $63,397,000, and the operational per-pupil cost $9.37. As shown in Table I in the Appendix, enrollment expanded to 21,578,000 in 1920, the total cost to $1,036,151,000, and the per-pupil expense to $64.16. However, it was only after WW II exerted its irrepressible inflationary force that costs really began to skyrocket: in 1950, the total per-pupil outlay advanced to $258.85; and in 1960 to $472.17. But even this was only the beginning: in 1969-70, when enrollment reached 45,904,000 and the costs $42,057,457,000, the per-pupil operating cost rose to $858; including expenditures for interest and capital outlay, it was $954.

Thus, while the price-index of all consumer items advanced 400% between 1870 and 1970,[a] the per-pupil educational costs increased nearly 7,000%. Between 1945 and 1969-70, total expenditures for education at all levels rose from $4,167,597,000, or 2% of the Gross National Product, to $69,500,000,000, and it consumed 7.5% of the GNP.[b]

Table II traces the growth and evolution of the instructional staff in public elementary and secondary schools, together with their salaries and pupil-ratios. In 1869-70, there were 201,000 teachers, with an enrollment ratio of 34.2, but an Average Daily Attendance ratio of only 20.3. Over

---

a.   Data from *Historical Statistics of the U. S.*, 1789-1945, published in 1952 by the Department of Commerce; and from the 1970 *Statistical Abstract*, p. 339.

b.   Including private and higher education, cf. 1970 *Digest of Educational Statistics*, p. 21.

the years, however, the gap between enrollment and ADA lessened sharply, indicating that attendance gradually became more regular; in 1919-20, the ratio of staff to enrollment fell to 31.8; but the teacher-ADA ratio increased to 24.6. Thereafter, all ratios continued to decline; in 1969-70, the staff-enrollment and teacher-ADA ratio fell to 20.9; and the staff-ADA to 19.7.

The annual salary of teachers averaged $189 in 1869-70; however, compensation in few occupations has risen more dramatically. The average rose to $252 in 1889-90, $871 in 1919-20, $1,441 in 1939-40; and the post-war era has given schoolmen an unprecedented expansion of income: $5,174 in 1959-60, $8,560 in 1969-70, and $9,265 in 1971.

In 1967-68, when all current (i.e. operating) expenses for elementary and secondary public education totalled $26,877,162,000, the cost of instruction alone was $18,375,762,000, or 69%.

Table III traces the development of public and private enrollment during the last 90 years. In 1880, the total was about 10,600,000, of whom some 92% were in government schools and 405,234 in Roman Catholic. During the first year for which we have complete records—1900—the total enrollment was 16,961,249, of whom 93% were in public schools and 854,523, or 5%, in Catholic. During the following decades, the public schools continued to expand, but the Catholic did so more rapidly: from 1,237,251 in 1910 to 2,464,467 in 1930—an increase of almost 100%.

It should be noted that the public schools increased rapidly and continuously until 1929-30, when they enrolled 25,678,015. Then, however, the Great Depression caused the birth rate to drop so sharply that it was more than twenty years before this total, in spite of a much larger high school attendance, was again attained. By 1959-60, however, the baby-crop following WW II had increased public school enrollment to 36,087,000, and this rose to 42,173,764 in 1965 and to 45,904,000 in 1970.

In the meantime, an extraordinary development was occurring within Roman Catholic education. It had long been its proclaimed ideal to enroll every Catholic child in a Catholic school. However, in spite of every effort, this objective had never even been approached. Catholic enrollment actually declined, along with the public, between 1930 and 1940.

Following WW II, however, the Catholic schools enjoyed a period of tremendous growth. Enrollment, which had been 5% of the national total in 1900, rose to 6.3% in 1910, 7.3% in 1920, and leaped to 3,066,387 in 1950, which was 10.7%. In 1961, it rose to 5,369,540 and attained its highest ratio of 12.8%; in 1965, it reached its numerical apogee of

5,662,328, which was 11.6% of the total. During the early Sixties, hundreds of thousands were turned away;[a] according to the *National Catholic Almanac* of 1966 (p. 85): in "1964-65, 78 dioceses, which kept track of rejections, reported that 133,000 grade school and high school applicants were turned away for lack of space." Cardinal McIntyre of the Los Angeles Archdiocese could observe with infinite satisfaction the completion of another school every week within his jurisdiction alone; and it seemed as if the ideals of the Third Plenary Council of Baltimore were at last to be achieved. Instead, by the fall of 1971, enrollment dropped to about 3.8 million, which was less than 7.5% of the national total and less than the total of 1955.

Table V, VI, and VII trace the development of the Catholic Church from 1809 to the present time (1971). While its school enrollment increased from 405,234 in 1880 to 5,662,328 in 1965, its membership proliferated from 6,143,222, or 12.5% of the population, to 48,214,729 in 1971, or 23.5%. However, the greatest expansion began only after virtually all immigration from Catholic countries was terminated in 1924. Between 1936 and 1965, while the population grew by 45%, Catholics increased by 117%—to about 45 million; and their school enrollment by 135%, from 2,408,081 to 5,662,000. During the same period, the public schools increased from 25.3 to 42.2 million—about 65%.

About 1944 or 1945, the leaders of the Catholic Church mounted a determined crusade for public funds to support their various institutions. Under the Hill-Burton Act, its hospitals have received federal grants totalling hundreds of millions of dollars. In 1948, Cardinal Spellman declared that pupils in parochial schools were entitled to a lunch and a ride and that the Church would never ask for anything more.

Certainly, the agitation of the prelates has borne rich fruitage. In 1963, the Higher Facilities Education Act was passed, under which religious colleges and universities, notably the Catholic-Jesuit, have received billions of dollars.[b]

---

a.   Neil G. McCluskey, in *Catholic Education in America,* 1964, Columbia University Press, states that among the 144 dioceses and archdioceses in the United States, 7 alone turned away 35,469 would-be pupils during the preceding year.

b.   St. Louis U. (Jesuit), which reported a plant-value of $72,133,000 and revenues of $26,013,191 in 1966, received $7,324,000 in federal subsidies in 1969 (*A Report to the President and Congress,* published by the National Science Foundation). Other Catholic institutions received sums as follows: Catholic U. of America, $5,686,000; Marquette U., $3,955,000; Notre Dame, $8,126,000; Fordham, $2,252,000; Boston College,

Mr. Kenneth H. Simon, Chief of the Reference, Estimate, and Projection Section of the Department of Health, Education, and Welfare, issued Circular No. 692 in 1962, in which he assumed that the progression of 1960-61 would continue indefinitely; he therefore declared that in 1964-65, enrollment in the public elementary and secondary schools would be 42,207,000 and in the non-public, 7,942,000; while this projection was fairly accurate for the public it was 1,640,000 too high for the private. A combination of forces had begun to exert an influence as early as 1962 which confounded the prognosticators, who were therefore bogged down in a morass of error: whereas Mr. Simon predicted a 1969-70 public enrollment of 47,032,000 and a private of 9,682,000, the former rose only to 45,900,000 and the latter to about 5.5 million. For 1974-75, he foresaw a private enrollment of 11,639,000 and a public of 52,823,000; and for 1979-80, totals of 13,802,000 and 59,733,000. Assuming that the birth rate would continue to rise, and believing that Catholic schools would go on expanding as before, he overestimated enrollment for 1979-80 by about 17 million. His estimate for the private sector in 1970 was nearly 4,200,000 too high.

Interestingly enough, the same Mr. Simon in his 1970 *Projection of Educational Statistics to 1979-80,* estimates the public enrollment at the latter date at 51 million and the non-public at 5.4 million.

While Catholic enrollment declined from 5,662,328 in 1965 to 4,429,323 in 1970-71 and to 3.8 million in 1971-72, we find that other private schools enjoyed a remarkable expansion, as shown in Table IV. Non-Catholic private schools enrolled 626,753 in 1961-62; 826,764 in 1965-66; 903,789 in 1968-69; and an estimated 1,099,000 in 1970, an increase of 76%. Non-Catholic, church-related schools increased their enrollments from 386,802 to 537,632, or 39%. Perhaps the greatest expansion of all occurred in the highly evangelical churches, organized, for example, in California as the Association of Christian Schools. In 1967, they comprised 102 institutions with 14,659 pupils: an average of 143. In

---

$5,501,000; Loyola of Illinois, $5,029,000; and dozens of others, smaller amounts. SMU received $3,290,000 and Emory (also Methodist), $11,865,000; Baylor U., $16,973,000, and Wayland U. (both Southern Baptist), $7,134,000; Brigham Young, $1,218,000; Loma Linda University (SDA), $3,924,000. Among Jewish institutions, Brandeis received $6,737,000 and Mt. Sinai Medical, $10,750,000. The leading state and secular universities received the largest allocations: for example, MIT was given $97,604,000 and Harvard $69,558,000. More than 2,000 colleges and universities shared in the largesse: some received as little as $2,000 or $3,000.

1970, there were 162, with 29,486—an average of 183—and an overall increase of more than 100%, and an average growth of 30%. Between 1961 and 1969, Lutheran school enrollment increased from 161,045 to 195,690; Jewish, from 39,830 to 66,724; Christian Reformed, from 39,964 to 63,000; and that of the Evangelicals, lumped together as "Other," from 30,189 to 59,899.

To explore and determine the ultimate and proximate causes of this development, we made the on-site analyses reported in Part One. In the following pages, we trace the historic evolution of the vast drama which has unfolded in American education during its two-hundred-year history.

2. The Early American School in Conflict

The Colonial Period

The average American may find it difficult to realize the pervasive and tenacious hold which sectarian religion exercised upon the state as well as upon education during this nation's formative period. In Virginia, the Anglican-Episcopal was actually an established church before the Revolution; under its influence, laws had been passed which made it a penal offense for parents to refuse baptism for their children or for Quakers to assemble. The latter were ordered into exile upon pain of imprisonment; and were legally subject to the death-penalty upon a third return. Men like Madison[a] and Jefferson led the battle for religious liberty and separation of church and state; the latter introduced a Bill for Establishing Religious

---

a.   In 1784, a bill was introduced into the Virginia Assembly to assess a tax against all property for the support of the clergy. In 1785, Madison wrote his *Memorial and Remonstrance against Religious Assessments,* addressed to the Honorable, The General Assembly of the Commonwealth of Virginia, in which he declared in part: "We maintain therefore that in matters of religion, no man's right is abridged by the institution of Civil Society, and that Religion is wholly exempt from its cognizance. . . .

". . . if religion be exempt from the authority of Society at large, still less can it be subject to that of the Legislative Body.

". . . it is proper to take alarm at the first experiment with our liberties. . . . Who does not see that the same authority which can establish Christianity, in exclusion of all other religions, may establish with the same ease any particular sect of Christians to the exclusion of all other sects? That the same authority which can force a citizen to contribute three pence only of his property for the support of any one establishment, may force him to conform to any other establishment in all cases whatsoever?"

196

Freedom in 1779, which was enacted into law by the Assembly in 1786.[a]

In Massachusetts, the Puritan-Presbyterians, ruling with an iron hand, drove Roger Williams into the wilderness; and passed severe laws against Anabaptists and other dissidents. Although public schools were established almost as soon as the colony was organized, they remained, in substance parochial institutions. This should not be surprising, since the state was controlled by a Calvinist civic-ecclesiastical polity, a two-pronged power similar to the church-state unions which had ruled European nations for many centuries. The Charter of 1628 specified that the state must promote religion, especially in the schools; and in May, 1631, the General Court enacted a law under which only members of the dominant church were permitted to vote, thus creating a coterminous civil-ecclesiastical polity.[b]

Other colonies followed suit: laws were passed in Connecticut to enforce orthodox doctrine to a degree even surpassing those in Massachusetts or Virginia. The New Netherlands (New York) Charter of 1640 provided that no religion should be permitted except the Reformed, as then preached and practised under public authority.

The experience of Maryland is intriguing: colonized by Catholics under the leadership of Lord Baltimore in 1634, it was soon invaded by others of differing persuasions and the original settlers found themselves becoming a minority; for this reason, in 1649, while still in control of the legislature, they passed an Act of Toleration, which gave all sects the right to exist, but also provided the death penalty for anyone who denied the Trinity or spoke disrespectfully of the Blessed Virgin, the Mother of God. By 1673, political power had passed from Catholic control; and in 1704, a Protestant-dominated legislature enacted laws under which deportation was threatened against any "Papist" who should operate a school, board pupils, or give religious instruction to children.

---

a.   This declared that "to compel a man to make contributions of money for the propagation of opinions he disbelieves and abhors, is sinful and tyrannical"; and "that all men shall be free to profess, and by argument to maintain, their opinions in matters of religion, and that the same shall in no wise diminish, enlarge, or affect their civil capacities."

b.   Cf. *Public Funds for Private and Church Schools,* by R. J. Gabel, S.T.D. (a doctoral dissertation at the Catholic U. of America), 1937, which contains a resumé of early American education and the religious controversies which raged over it.

In New Jersey, there were no schools before 1820 except those owned and operated by churches.

In fact, only three of the original thirteen colonies were based on principles involving any substantial church-state separation: Rhode Island, founded by Roger Williams, who became a Baptist; Pennsylvania, settled by Quakers under the leadership of William Penn; and Delaware, organized and ruled by Swedish libertarians.[a]

During the waning decades of the 18th century, most of the current education was carried on by church or *ad hoc* religious societies.[b] As a result, those of other beliefs were often forced to consign their children to illiteracy or have them indoctrinated with tenets which they rejected or abhorred.

The one and outstanding exception to this situation was Virginia, where, under the leadership of Thomas Jefferson and James Madison, a statewide system of common and wholly non-sectarian schools was established following the passage in 1779 of the Bill for the More General Diffusion of Knowledge. The same men, therefore, who were chiefly responsible for writing our Declaration of Independence and winning the War of the Revolution, were also the creators of the earliest system of truly public schools that appeared upon this continent.

The Battle for Religious Neutralism

After the Founding Fathers submitted the Constitution to the states for ratification in 1787, it soon became apparent that certain additions, consisting of the First Ten Amendments and known as the American Bill of Rights, would be mandatory. The opening words of this addendum declare that "Congress shall make no law respecting an establishment of religion or prohibiting the free exercise thereof. . . ."

This double-edged sword of liberty not only separates church from state by making the latter neutral in the sectarian field: it also confers a power accorded no other category of activity: the supreme right to worship in whatever manner the individual conscience may dictate; or, what may be equally crucial, not to do so at all.

---

a.   A Swedish contingent, sent by Gustavus the Second Adolphus, arrived in 1624, and established the first permanent settlement in Delaware.

b.   Cf. *Public Funds for Parochial Schools?* by George R. LaNoue, published by the National Council of Churches, 1963, P. 12.

This principle was adopted because of the multiplication of religious sects and denominations—as well as the progress of rationalism, or enlightenment, especially among the educated classes. Most of the men who devised the Constitution—such as Franklin, Madison, Jefferson—were deists, and might now be classified as Unitarians or Ethical Culturists. However, their influence alone would not have been sufficient to create a constitution which ignores religion except to say that Congress may not legislate in any manner concerning it. By 1790, there were at least seven important Protestant denominations, but none comprised more than a significant minority. Therefore, since none could dominate, all agreed that religion, left to the home and the church, should be maintained by voluntary contributions.

Thus it was that religious neutralism was established as a great American principle. It was not adopted as protection against potential aggression by Catholics, who then comprised only one-half of one per cent of the population. It was established to protect all Protestants as well as the religiously uncommitted from such aggression as had already been inflicted by Calvinists and Episcopalians upon non-members; the purpose was to make sure that no religious group should ever be able to use the state to enforce its will upon others or to compel them, directly or indirectly, to contribute so much as a penny for the support of their activities.

In 1696, there were only seven Catholic families in New York City; as late as 1775, their descendants were forced to journey to Philadelphia or even to Baltimore to receive the sacraments. In 1785, in an American population of 3,600,000, only 18,200 were Catholics, of whom 15,000 were in Maryland, 1,500 in New York State, 700 in Pennsylvania, and 200 in Virginia.[a]

By 1810, when the population had grown to 7,239,881, there were still only 150,000 Catholics.[b] Table V traces the early growth of the Church;[c] in 1808, there was only a single diocese (Baltimore) with 68 priests, 80 churches, two seminaries, two literary institutes for boys, and two female academies. In 1820, almost two centuries after Lord Baltimore came to Maryland, the Church still had only 124 congregations, compared to 10,680 belonging to other denominations.[d] Even in 1830, the Catholics

---

a.   *Catholic Yearbook of 1828*, p. 111.

b.   *Ib.*

c.   Beginning in 1817, an annual or at least a semi-annual almanac or directory of the Catholic Church has been published; year by year, this has grown more detailed and comprehensive. We have used this source of information throughout this study.

d.   Cf. Gaustad's *Historical Atlas of Religion in America*, pp. 160-161.

outside of Maryland were too few to influence public policy: they had only 9 seminaries, 8 "colleges" for boys,[a] and 20 female academies. Since by this time, they had 230 churches, it is clear that the parochial school, as later developed, was unknown. It is unlikely that as many as 10% of Catholic youth were enjoying Church education and indoctrination.

Historians know that social processes are not governed by law alone, but by the inner propulsions of those who manage social and political institutions: and it was simply inconceivable to the great majority, who were practising Protestants, that morality or good citizenship could be inculcated in the public schools without religious indoctrination. The conflicts which ensued did not come from rationalists, Unitarians, or others without religious commitments so much as from those who, cherishing fervently their own specific doctrines, believed that others must share them or suffer eternal damnation.

Following 1785 in New York, therefore, various Protestant denominations, especially Quakers, Lutherans, Congregationalists, Episcopalians, Presbyterians, and Dutch Reformed, operated their own schools, received public funds for their support, and conducted virtually all elementary education. In 1805, however, the Free School Society, founded by DeWitt Clinton, mayor of New York, established a number of non-sectarian schools, for the purpose of providing free education for poor children not enrolled in any church institution; and public funds were allocated to these on the same basis as to those owned and operated by churches.[b]

After this dual system had been in operation for about 20 years, the Free School Society was replaced by the Public School Society, a corporation with a much broader base, which included many public-spirited citizens, and which soon commanded very wide support; and in 1825, when the Board of Aldermen in New York City received authority from the state legislature to allocate educational funds, the Society was entrusted with this responsibility. In a radical departure from previous practice, it approved funding only for those schools which were operated by the government and which were entirely independent of any religious entity. In short, the Free Schools of Clinton developed into a system which commanded all available public funds.

---

a.   These were actually on the high school or secondary level.
b.   It should be noted that the existence of the First Amendment did not, at this time, prevent public funding for sectarian schools.

As Protestant parochials became public institutions in New York and elsewhere, they continued, quite naturally, to bear the imprint of their former ownership and were, therefore, highly offensive to the slowly increasing Catholic community. In spite of their origin, however, the secularization of the common schools made rapid strides after 1825; first, because no group of Protestants would tolerate any specific teaching which conflicted with their own distinctive tenets; second, because a growing secular community was determined to exclude all religious indoctrination of whatever kind from the curriculum; and, third, because Catholics would not tolerate even the slightest vestige of non-denominational Protestantism.

Although the Public School Society encouraged Scripture readings and the recitation of prayers, it was adamant against the payment of public funds to any church-related institution. Intentionally or not, therefore, its influence hastened the complete secularization of the public school. In 1842, a Special Committee of the New York Legislature ruled that no money could be given to any religious school on the ground that "if religion be taught" there, it would lose "one of the characteristics of a common school, as all religious and sectarian studies have a direct reference to a future state, and are not necessary to prepare a child for the mechanical or any other business. No school," continued the Committee, "can be common unless parents of all religious sects, Mohammedans and Jews, as well as Christians, can send their children to it to receive the benefit of an education, without doing violence to their religious belief."[a]

But before this consummation was attained, a tremendous drama was enacted to its spectacular denouément in New York, to which we now turn our attention.

Archbishop John Hughes, Crusader for Parochiaid

Perhaps the bitterest and most decisive battle over parochiaid ever fought on American soil occurred in New York during 1840-42. Under the leadership of John Hughes, then Coadjutor of the New York diocese, the Catholics came within an eyelash of victory; and almost everything that has since been said on the subject, pro or con, was aired in acrimonious debate. Before the conflict was finally resolved, the City wavered on the brink of civil war.

---

a. *Public Funds for Private and Church Schools, op.cit.* p. 356.

These were the early years of the great Irish immigration; and the clash of ideologies had grown ominous. As early as 1835, Samuel F. B. Morse, an artist and the inventor of the telegraph, wrote that "there is good reason for believing that the despots of Europe are attempting, by the spread of Popery in this country, to subvert our free institutions. . . ."[a] In 1844, a conflict broke out in Philadelphia, in which "Native Americans" confronted Catholics: churches, rectories, and convents were burned. James Gordon Bennett, famous as journalist, publisher, and sponsor of international yacht racing, declared that there were dungeons under the old St. Patrick's Cathedral in which Protestants were to be tortured when the Catholic Church gained political ascendancy.[b]

Such was the atmosphere in New York City when the storm over parochiaid broke into the open in 1840.

We have already noted the establishment of the private, Protestant-oriented Free School Society which, beginning in 1805, had a virtual monopoly over the distribution of State funds for education in New York City. As we have also noted, this was replaced by a corporation called the Public School Society in 1825, after which public funds were denied to any school controlled by a church or religious organization; and the teaching of any denominational tenet was forbidden in the common schools. The corporation consisted of a 56-member board of trustees; a five-man executive committee, who were also its officers, exercised general supervision over its affairs.

Since New York was heavily Protestant during the early years following the formation of the Public School Society, the Catholic issue had then not arisen. But with the arrival of Irish immigrants, the stage was set for the fierce confrontation which ensued.

The raging controversy was ignited over the use of the King James version for Scripture readings and the content of textbooks used in the public schools. The Catholic clergy had complained that these were punctuated with terms like "Papists" and "Popery" used as terms of contempt. In order to remove all such objections, the trustees of the Public School Society invited the Catholic clergy to expurgate all offensive passages.

On May 14, 1840, a Committee of the Public School Society held a meeting attended by the Catholic Vicar-General, Father Power, who agreed to examine all school texts and make recommendations for their expurgation. However, the Committee waited in vain for two months for a

a.   *Foreign Conspiracy against the Liberties of the United States*, p. 51.
b.   *Complete Works of the Most Reverend John Hughes, D.D.*, edited by Laurence Kehoe, New York, 1866, Vol I. pp. 125-126.

reply of any kind. Instead, the Vicar-General published a vitriolic article in *The Freeman's Journal,* in which he excoriated the Committee, the Public School Society, and the common schools.[a]

When asked why the Catholics took this course, Hughes declared that he would not assume the odium of censorship; and that, furthermore, no one had the right to make such a request of him (Kehoe I 58). Finding their most strenuous and long-continued efforts to obtain advice from the Catholics unavailing, the trustees of the Society appointed a committee to perform the task; and everything which seemed to have the slightest anti-Catholic bias was deleted. This, however, only seemed to enrage the proponents of parochiaid the more (*ib.* I 68).

Hughes was certainly at least forthright: "No Catholic who believes in the truth of his religion," he declared, "can allow a child of his to frequent the public schools . . . without wounding his own conscience and sinning against God. . . ." Catholic children who have been indoctrinated in them "have no feelings in common with their Church"; they are ashamed of it because in the school books and from the teaching there they hear nothing but insults to their faith (*ib.* I 57).

He made it clear that the infidelity fostered in the common schools was far worse than vagrancy or crime. In a letter to the *Evening Post*, September 3, 1840, Hughes declared that "thousands of children of poor Catholic parents are growing up without education simply because the law, as interpreted and administered under the Public School Society requires a violation of their rights of conscience. The number of such children may be from nine to twelve thousand. Of these, the Catholics, by bearing a double taxation, educate four or five thousand; a few hundred have attended the Public Schools, and the rest may be considered as receiving only such education as is afforded in the streets of New York" (*ib.* III 34). Since Catholic parents were forced to choose between ignorance and infidelity for their children, it was better that they grow up as petty criminals than attend a public school (*ib.* 19).

To make a child an infidel, he declared, it was only necessary to cage him up in a public schoolroom and give him a secular education (*ib.* III 67). He accused the schools of favoring only the Secularism of Infidelity; and of leaving the pupil free to riot in fierce and unrestrained lusts, which could only produce dangerous citizens (*ib.* 77). He condemned the schools because the Holy Scriptures were read in them without commentary or

---

a.   *Public Money and Parochial Education,* by V. P. Lannie, Western Reserve University Press, 1968, p. 23. *The Freeman's Journal* was published by McMaster, the virulent crusader for Catholic parochial schools.

specific tenet. "The Catholic Church," he declared emphatically, "tells her children that they must be taught by authority"; but "the Sectaries say, Read the Bible, judge for yourselves." Thus, he inferred, Protestant principles were slyly inculcated and the schools were used for their propagation. Public education was nothing but "Socialism, Red Republicanism, Universalism, Deism, Atheism, and Pantheism, anything, everything, except religionism and patriotism."[a] Elsewhere he stated that by teaching children to judge the Bible for themselves, they were being taught the principles of infidelity (*ib.* II 63).

In 1839, Hughes had been made Administrator Apostolic of New York; and shortly thereafter, he left for a tour of Europe. While he was absent, a group of Catholic laymen presented a petition to the council of aldermen demanding that their eight schools share equally in the funds administered by the Public School Society.

Governor William Henry Seward had not only encouraged this petition: he was also planning a system of state schools that would allocate funds to the parochials. His ostensible purpose was to make it possible for the thousands of children now roaming the streets as vagrants and delinquents to obtain a basic education.[b]

When the governor published this proposal, much of the press condemned him; and Protestant pulpits reverberated with thunderous anathemas. He was branded as the ravager of the common schools, the enemy of Protestantism, and the subverter of free American institutions. Nativist ministers declared that his proposal was intended to finance the Catholic Church; and that Jesuit priests would be installed as instructors of innocent children, who would fall prey to the wiles of the Scarlet Lady (Lannie 23).

Militant Protestant groups proclaimed that if money were given to Catholic schools, they would re-establish their own and demand an equal share of the public funds (*ib.* 34-36). However, during the early stages of the controversy, the Catholics themselves were divided on the issue, and it was only on the return from abroad of the dynamic Hughes and his assumption of leadership that the Catholic community became united in the struggle for public funds.

On July 28, 1840, Hughes called a mass meeting, which was held in the basement of St. James Church and at which the following resolutions were vociferously and unanimously adopted:

---

a.   Quoted by Neil McCluskey, *Catholic Education in America*, p. 14.
b.   In 1840, the population of New York City was 312,719. The importance of New York State may be realized from the fact that it had a population of 2,428,921 in a national total of 17,069,453.

(1) That the operation of the Common School System in New York is a violation of the civil and religious rights of Catholics.

(2) That Catholics are not worthy of their proud distinction as Americans unless they resist such invasion of their rights by every lawful means.

(3) That in seeking a redress of grievances, they are only carrying out the principles of the Constitution, which secures equal civil and religious rights to all.

(4) That a Committee of eight be appointed to propose a report on the injustice which had been done to the Catholics in their civil and religious rights in the operation of the Common Schools.

(5) That a Committee of three be appointed to propose a report on public moneys expended by the State on schools to which Catholics have contributed, but from which they have derived no benefit.

Under the tutelage of Hughes, the Committee of Eight prepared an elaborate petition (Kehoe I 48-53), which was presented to the council of aldermen and which declared in part:

"Your Petitioners . . . regard the public education which the State has provided as a common benefit, in which they . . . feel that they are entitled to participate . . . . The Public School Society has the monopoly of public education . . . in the city of New York; and the funds provided for that purpose at the expense of the State, have passed into the hands of this private corporation. . . . they profess to exclude all sectarianism from the schools. If they do not. . ., they are avowedly no more entitled to the school funds than your petitioners, or any other denomination of professing Christians. If they do . . . , they exclude Christianity—and leave to the advantage of infidelity the tendencies which are given to the minds of youth. . . .

". . . they tell us . . . 'that they are aware of the importance of early religious instruction,' and that none but what is 'exclusively general and scriptural in character should be introduced into the schools under their charge.' Here, then, is their own testimony that they did introduce and authorize 'religious instruction' in their schools. . . .

"In their Annual Report, they tell us that . . . their schools are uniformly opened with the reading of the Scriptures, and the classbooks are such as recognize and enforce the great and generally acknowledged principles of Christianity. . . .

"Even the reading of the Scriptures in those schools your petitioners cannot regard otherwise than as sectarian; because Protestants would certainly consider as such the introduction of the Catholic Scriptures, which are different from theirs, and the Catholics have the same ground of objection when the Protestant version is made use of.

"Your Petitioners have to state further . . . that many of the selections in their elementary reading lessons contain matter prejudicial to the Catholic name and character. The term 'Popery' is repeatedly found in them . . . as one of insult and contempt. . . .

"The Public School Society . . . allege that they have proffered repeatedly to make such corrections as the Catholic Clergy require. . . . They allege, indeed, that with the best intentions they have been unable to ascertain the passages which might be offensive to . . . your petitioners" who therefore "submit . . . that this Society is eminently incompetent to the superintendence of public education. . . .

"For these reasons . . . your petitioners cannot, in good conscience . . . intrust the Public School Society with the office of giving 'a right direction to the minds of their children.' And yet this Society claims that office, and claims for the discharge of it the Common School Funds, to which your petitioners, in common with other citizens, are contributors" but "are not only deprived of any benefit in return, but their money is employed to the damage and detriment of their religion. . . . Hence the establishment by your petitioners of schools for the education of the poor. The expense necessary for this, was a second taxation, required not by the laws of the land, but by the . . . demands of their conscience . . . since they were reduced to the alternative of seeing their children growing up in entire ignorance, or else taxing themselves anew for private schools. . . .

"Your petitioners have to deplore, as a consequence of this state of things, the ignorance and vice to which hundreds, nay thousands of their children are exposed. . . .

"It is objected that though we are taxed as citizens, we apply for the benefit of education as 'Catholics'. . . . It has been contended by the Public School Society that the law disqualifies schools which admit any profession of religion, from receiving any encouragement from the School Fund. . . .

"The members of that Society, who have shown themselves so impressed with the importance of conveying their notions of 'early religious instruction' to the 'susceptible minds' of Catholic children, can have no objection that the parents of the children, and teachers in whom the parents have confidence, should do the same. . . .

"Your petitioners therefore, pray that your Honorable Body will be pleased to designate, as among the schools entitled to participate in the Common School Fund . . ." St. Patrick's, St. Peter's, St. Mary's, St. Joseph's, St. James', St. Nicholas', Transfiguration, and St. John's schools.

On this petition, an emotion-packed hearing took place on October 29, 1840, from 4 to 10 P.M.; and continued the next evening from 5 P.M. almost until midnight. Hughes was the principal spokesman for the Catholics; a number of prominent individuals appeared in opposition.

Hughes declared over and over that he wanted no money for a religious or sectarian purpose, but only for the secular studies required by the state (*ib.* I 58). Furthermore, he proclaimed a fervid support for the principle of church-state separation, and maintained most stoutly that public money for Catholic schools was precisely the best method of guaranteeing its perpetuation (*ib.* III 126).

It was his opinion that if other sects wished to establish their own schools, they should be permitted to do so with public funding (*ib.* I 70). He emphasized that he was not opposed to Scripture reading as such, but to the Protestant version "without note or comment" (*ib.* 62).

In this connection, he expatiated at some length on one of the basic differences between Catholics, on the one hand, and all sectaries on the other. The latter may have differences among themselves, but they all agree that "the Bible alone, as understood by each individual, is the rule of faith" (*ib.* 96). Protestant ministers are not teachers, but only preachers. "They take the Bible—give out their opinions. . . " and this leads to more "opinion, opinion. Here is the difference between us. With us the doctrines of Revelation are facts . . . confirmed by the unanimous faith of the Church from the days of Christ. . . ." (*ib.* II 45). God has not vouchsafed his promises and his spirit to everyone, but only to the Church collectively; and "therefore we do not receive the Bible except what the Church guarantees. . . ." (*ib.* 72). And he twitted his opponents by saying that Trinitarians and Unitarians use the same Scriptures to prove their opposite theologies (*ib.* 71).

When told that history could not be taught at all or even studied without referring to facts highly embarrassing to the Catholic Church, Hughes retorted that instead of describing the burning of Huss, he would give children a chapter on the character of Charles Carroll of Carrollton as a reading lesson; and, he asked, "would that be teaching them of purgatory?" (*ib.* II 62).

Hughes lamented that Catholic children went to school "with perhaps only the fragment of a worn-out book, thinly clad, and bare feet on the frozen pavement"; but with money, all this could be remedied (*ib.* III 18).[a]

Again and again, he reverted to the question of indoctrination: "If the public schools could have secured a perfect neutrality on the subject of religion, then we should have had no reason to complain. But this has not

---

a.   In spite of this poverty, however, the Catholic laymen of New York shortly thereafter paid for the construction of the enormously costly St. Patrick's Cathedral, for which Archbishop Hughes laid the cornerstone.

been done, and we respectfully submit that it is impossible" (*ib.* III 18). Elsewhere he declared: "If the children are to be educated promiscuously, as at present, let religion in every shape and form be excluded. Let not the Protestant version of the Scriptures, Protestant forms of prayer, Protestant hymns, be forced on the children of Catholics, Jews, and others as at present, in schools for the support of which their parents pay taxes as well as Presbyterians" (*ib.* 125).

During his presentation before the Council, Hughes used language almost identical to that found more than a century later in the works of Virgil Blum: "We contend for liberty of conscience and freedom of education. We hold that the laws of nature, of religion, and the very constitution of the country, secure to parents the right of superintending the education of their own children.

"This right we contend for, but we have hitherto been obliged to exercise it under the unjust disadvantage of double taxation. If the State, considering our children its own, grants money for their education, are we not entitled to our own portion of it when we perform the services which are required?"

When we read the statements made by opponents of parochiaid at the hearings, we realize how little the basic issues have changed. "If the school money should be divided among the religious denominations generally," asked one speaker, "what will be left for the support of schools of a purely civil character? . . . there would be no public school in which to educate our citizens" (*ib.* I 67).

"By granting a portion of the School Fund to one sect to the exclusion of others," declared another, "a 'preference' IS at once created, a 'discrimination' made, and the great object of constitutional guarantees is defeated; taxes are imposed for the support of religion, and conscience, directly trammelled and confined, is no longer in the perfect and unshackled state which our systems of government were intended to establish and perpetuate" (*ib.* I 78).

A spokesman for the Public School Society declared that "An extension of the bounty asked for by the petitioners would be . . . repugnant to the principles of our government. If the doctrines of all religious denominations in the state were taught, in the slightest degree, at the expense of the people, under the authority of law, there would still be a legal establishment, not confined to one or a few sects, it is true, but concerning many. Taxes, under such a system, would still be raised for religious purposes; and those who professed no religion, or belonged to no sect, would be taxed for the benefit of those who did" (Lannie 49-50). The Public School Society maintained that the Catholic clergy rejected the public schools, not because religious doctrines were taught in them, but precisely

208

because their own peculiar tenets did not dominate the curriculum (Kehoe I 38).

"But when," another speaker asserted, "all the Christian sects shall be satisfied with their individual share of the public fund, what is to become of the children whose parents belong to none of these sects, and who cannot conscientiously allow them to be educated in the peculiar dogmas of any one of them? It must be plain to any impartial observer that the applicants are opposed to the whole system of public education." Furthermore, "it will be found that the uncharitable exclusiveness of their creed must ever be opposed to all public instruction which is not under the direction of their own priesthood" (*ib.* I 60).

There were also speakers who charged the Catholic Church with having laws permitting the murder of heretics; and who maintained that no history of Europe could be taught covering the last ten centuries without mentioning facts unfavorable to it; what its clergy were demanding, therefore, was a total falsification of history (*ib.* I 61).

A Committee from the Public School Society reported that it had visited three of the Catholic schools and found them lamentably deficient in accommodations, textbooks, and teachers; the rooms were excessively crowded, badly ventilated, the books much worn, and general conditions deplorable (*ib.* I 97).

The Council deferred its decision on the petition until January 11, 1841, when its members voted 15 to 1 to reject. They passed a resolution stating that the Catholic schools had a right to operate, but no right to public funds.

Instead of subduing Hughes, this rebuff spurred him into frenetic political activity. On October 29, 1841, at Carroll Hall, he organized the Church and State Party, which, amidst frenzied applause, nominated a slate of 2 senators and 13 assemblymen to represent New York City in the state legislature. A campaign marked with hatred and bigotry ensued. The Catholic clergy denounced the incumbent politicians as "partisans of an intolerant monopoly, notorious as the irreconcilable foe of their and their children's rights" (*ib.* III 116). However, the opposition raised such a clamor as had never before been heard in New York; the Bishop, it was said, was plotting the subversion of the Constitution by effecting a union between the State government and the Catholic Church (*ib.* 117). The public was warned that dreadful feuds and murderous outbreaks would certainly ensue unless the Catholics would permit their children to enter the public schools, which the Roman clergy continued to denounce as centers of Protestant indoctrination or hotbeds of infidelity. The Public School Society was branded a monopolist power, the purpose of which was to destroy all civil and religious liberty (*ib.* III 117).

When the votes were counted, it was found, to the consternation of the Protestants and the jubilation of the Catholics, that the entire slate of Church and State Party candidates had been elected. And when they assembled in Albany for the session of 1842, they were in virtual control of the legislature. It seemed as if total victory perched upon the banners of John Hughes.

The occasion seemed particularly auspicious because he had a powerful ally in Governor Seward, who sponsored a bill which would extend State control over education to New York City by abolishing the Public School Society and which would set up boards of education in every community empowered to establish public schools dedicated to the tenets of whatever denomination could muster enough votes to elect the members of such boards. In other words, there would be in each geographical entity a publicly supported school which would, in effect, be a parochial institution representing the majority sect or denomination of the area.

This proposal, known as the Maclay Bill, passed the Assembly 65 to 16 on March 31, 1842. It seemed indeed as if the non-denominational common school was doomed. However, after the bill reached the Senate Committee on Education on April 1st, that body added an amendment which altered drastically one of its provisions: the teaching of any specifically denominational tenet in a State-funded school was proscribed.

The crucial battle, however, was yet to be fought on the floor of the Senate. At midnight, April 8, a vote was taken on the amended bill. One senator, pledged to support the Assembly version, absented himself; the amended form was approved, 13 to 12, after acrimonious debate. Faced with this ultimatum, the Assembly concurred with the Senate version, and it became law in the State of New York.

By an incredibly narrow margin and almost in a manner miraculous, the greatest drive for parochiaid in American history was thus defeated.

The Public School Society of New York was abolished; a board of education was set up in every community; sectarian instruction was outlawed in the common schools; and a truly universal system of education was established.

However, this was not the final repercussion. As soon as word reached New York concerning the events of April 8 in Albany, ugly mobs began gathering in the streets. Organized on one side as the Spartans and, on the other, as Catholic militants, they rioted, looted, and fought each other for several days.

At last, however, calm settled on the strife-torn city. Hughes retired from the political arena. Made bishop of New York on December 20,1842, and archbishop on July 19, 1850, he devoted his energies to building a large system of Catholic education and creating the greatest and richest diocese in the entire world. He laid the cornerstone of the great St. Patrick's Cathedral on August 15, 1858; he died January 3, 1864; and his bones were transferred to a crypt in that monumental structure on January 30, 1883.

Horace Mann and the Secular School

Battles, similar to the conflict in New York, were raging in other states, notably in Massachusetts, where the Unitarian, Horace Mann, a leading proponent of public education, was State Secretary of the Board of Education from 1837 to 1848. In general agreement with the Public School Society of New York, he argued that there was a basic system of Christian tenets and ethics which could be taught without offense to anyone and the elaboration of which could be left to the home and the church. The public schools would therefore inculcate a non-sectarian Christianity, which could never be identified as Methodist, Lutheran, Presbyterian, Congregational, Quakerite, Calvinist, Baptist, Episcopal, Unitarian, Universalist, Deist, or Catholic.

The result, however, was not entirely what he had hoped for. Instead of uniting the various groups, the differences among some of them were simply accentuated. He was assailed by some for secularizing the schools; by others, for encouraging the teaching of religion. What finally survived was a thin belief in a deity, the recitation of the Lord's Prayer, something akin to the Golden Rule, and lip-service to the Ten Commandments. Mann's influence simply accelerated the total religious neutrality and the complete secularization of the common schools.

It must have been galling indeed for the leaders of the Roman Church to see their children educated in the gradually burgeoning public schools; and this was especially true whenever they retained any vestige of Protestant influence either in their textbooks or their devotionals.

We turn, therefore, to the gigantic effort exerted by the Catholic Church to establish its own educational system.

The Catholic Councils

To the Catholic clergy, the Protestant influence in, and the secularization of, the public schools were equally anathema and to be avoided as the plague. Seven times between 1829 and 1849, the bishops convened in provincial councils in Baltimore. In the first, they emphasized the fearful dangers to which Catholic children are exposed through attendance at the public schools. They urged all parishes to establish their own to protect their offspring from heretical contamination. In their agony, the reverend Fathers exclaimed: "How would your hearts be torn with grief did your minds foresee, that throughout eternity" your children may "be cast into outer darkness, where there is weeping and gnashing of teeth! . . . Believe us, it is only by the religious education of your children that you can train them up, as to ensure that, by their filial piety and steady virtue, they may be to you the staff of your old age, the source of your consolation, and reward in a better world."

They admitted, however, that the public school would prepare the children who attended them for greater affluence and success in this temporal vale; and could fit them for a career replete with honor and importance. But how can all this, they pleaded, "console you in the progress of eternity to recollect that you had for a time beheld them elevated to power, applauded by fame, entrusted to command, swaying nations, dispensing wealth and honours; but misled by vice and now tortured . . . for eternity? If you would avert this dreadful calamity, attend to the teaching of your child. . . ."

The Second Provincial Council held in 1833 and the Third in 1837 issued pastoral letters emphasizing the same theme. The Fourth, held in 1840, assured the faithful that "we have always deemed it to be one of our most pressing obligations to . . . provide establishments where" our children "may be carefully educated by competent persons . . . in that path which leads to heaven. . . . The great evil" in attending non-Catholic schools, declared the Council, "is the danger to which they are exposed by having their faith undermined . . . and their exposure during their tender youth to the fatal influence of . . . those who undervalue our creed." And, it continued, "we can scarcely point out a book in general use in the ordinary schools . . . wherein covert and insidious efforts are not made to misrepresent our principles, to distort our tenets, to vilify our practices, and to bring contempt upon our Church and its members."

In 1843, the Fifth Provincial Council issued more concrete commands: "You must, therefore, use all diligence that your children be instructed at an early age in the many truths of religion, and be preserved from the contagion of error. We have seen with serious alarm, efforts made to poison the fountains of public education by . . . accustoming children to the use of a version of the Bible made under sectarian bias. . . . We admonish parents of the awful account they must give at the divine tribunal, should their children, by their neglect or connivance, be imbued with false principles, and led away from the path of salvation. . . ."

In making the King James version of the Bible a crucial issue, we would suggest that the Council was something less than ingenuous: for the disparity between this and the Douay is neither extensive nor decisive. The point was, as Hughes had pointed out, the Protestant indoctrination was based primarily upon the Scriptures without commentary or interpreta-

212

tion, thus permitting the Word to speak for itself. Catholic indoctrination, on the other hand, consisted almost entirely of dogmas developed by its ecumenical councils and papal promulgations. "The great Protestant majority," writes Jesuit Neil G. McCluskey, "was easily persuaded that Catholic efforts to eliminate the Protestant Bible from the schools and to get public money for their own, represented a concerted attack on the foundations of the republic."[a] He might have added that it was also regarded as an attack upon Christianity itself: for many Protestants were fully persuaded that the Catholic Church represented a total subversion of their religion. Catholic clergymen denounced their Protestant opponents because the *New England Primer* used long before in states where there were virtually no Catholics, had carried the stern admonition, "Child, behold that Man of Sin, the Pope, worthy of the utmost hatred." The English Puritan pamphleteer, Reginald Prynne, had stated about 1650 that the English bishops were the toenails of Antichrist, who, of course, was the pope. Material of this kind was used very effectively by the Catholic clergy to convince their laymen that they should not send their children to the public schools.

In his argument before the aldermen of New York, Hughes explained only in small part why Catholic children must not be exposed to simple readings from the Scriptures—any version of them: for it is a fact that Catholic schools made no such use even of their own. The answer is not far to seek: this ancient collection of documents knows nothing of Papal Infallibility, of ruling cardinals, holy fathers, or popes; of the Mass, relics, the Real Presence, the confessional, purgatory, or indulgences; of the Immaculate Conception, the Physical Assumption of the Virgin, or her Perpetual Virginity as the Mother of God, who hears our prayers and pleads with her Son for mercy to repentant sinners; of venial or mortal sins; of beads, rosaries, genuflections, or "holy crossings"; of saintly celibate orders, convents, or monasteries; of prayers and Masses for the dead; of the seven sacraments, which require the ministrations of the Church and its clergy throughout the life of the individual; of schools operated by nuns and priests and owned by the bishop; or of a hundred other dogmas, disciplines, and rituals unknown in Protestant Christianity. What if Catholic children, left in a total vacuum concerning all these distinctive and sacred teachings, should conclude that they are unnecessary—in fact, detrimental—to salvation?

When the Seventh Provincial Council convened in 1849, Europe was in a state of turmoil or revolution; the Catholic Church itself was in dire peril, and the Pope, disguised as a footman, had fled through a postern of the Vatican in order to preserve his life from the wrath of his angry

a. *Catholic Education in America*, p. 14.

people. During this hour of crisis, the American prelates issued a Pastoral in which the faithful were exhorted and admonished, in return for the pure and living doctrine which they had received from the Holy Father, "to furnish the exiled Pontiff with temporal things in the time of distressed affliction." And they continued: "We exhort you, brethren, to continue to cherish the Mother of God, since the honor given to her is founded on the relation which she bears to him. . . . The more highly you venerate her, as the purest and holiest of creatures, the deeper sense you manifest of his divinity.

"When we survey the Christian world, and see thrones overturned . . . . we are afflicted with the utmost despondency; but when we raise our thoughts on high to the kingdom of light and love, where Mary stands enthroned near the throne of her Divine Son, we are inspired with confidence that she . . . will effectually plead our cause . . . . .

"Let us therefore ask that the hydra head of heresy may be crushed forever. . . . Let us pray that all divisions and strife may be brought to an end, and that all professors of the Christian name may be reunited in one religious communion. . . ."[a]

The Protestants, however, ignoring all such suggestions and invitations, continued to go their own way in stubborn intransigence.[b]

Meanwhile, the secularization of the public schools continued apace. As the 1929 edition of the *Encyclopaedia Britannica* observes, this "was not purposed, but incidental. . . . Whenever a minority . . . has chosen to object, on what are averred to be conscientious grounds, to some religious element in the . . . curriculum in the public schools, that element has forthwith been eliminated. . . . Each religious group has been . . . con-

a.   The pastoral letters of the various councils are printed in the almanacs and directories of the Church for the years in which they appeared, as well as in other compendia.

b.   During this period especially it was a general belief among the American Catholic clergy that Protestantism would soon be eradicated and that all the heretics would soon be reunited in the sweet communion of Mother Church. In 1850, Archbishop Hughes delivered a lecture entitled "The Decline of Protestantism and Its Cause," in which he declared: "Everybody should know that we have for our mission to convert the world— including . . . the commanders of the army, the Legislatures, the Senate, the Cabinet, the President, and all! We have received from God a mission that the Protestants have never received. . . . God will reconduct to the fold of Christ those . . . unhappily wandering brethren, who are wasting their strength, their lives, in the folds of Protestantism. . . . If it had not been for these awful errors of Protestantism. . . Christianity would by this time have absorbed all the nations of the earth." (Published by Dungan and Brother, New York, 1850.)

cerned to see to it that the public schools should not contain anything out of line with its peculiar beliefs. . . . The result has been to strip the public schools almost completely of religious teaching and worship."[a] In short, the dozens of sects and denominations which multiplied under the benign banner of the first Amendment agreed finally on only one principle: No religion at all is infinitely preferable to any form thereof in the public schools which deviates in the slightest from that of the protesting dissident.

As their numbers and influence grew, the Roman Catholics probably became the most insistent among these protestors; and there can be no doubt that they contributed decisively to administering the ultimate *coup de grace* to religious instruction of any kind in the public schools.[b]

In 1850, the Catholic Church had 30 dioceses, 1,073 churches, 29 seminaries, and 108 schools for girls and boys. Sensing its rapidly growing power, it convened the First Plenary Council in 1852 in Baltimore, attended by 6 archbishops and 35 suffragan bishops, who declared: "If your children, while they advance in human science, are not taught the science of the saints, their minds will be filled with every error, their hearts will be receptacles of every vice, and that very learning which they have acquired . . . will be an additional means of destroying their happiness . . . and weakening the foundations of the social order."

Parents were warned: "Guard carefully these little ones of Christ. . . . You are to watch over the purity of their faith . . . guided . . . by the authority of God's Church . . . . give your children a Christian education . . . . accompanied by religious practices. . . ."

In 1850, with the recent accretions from Ireland, the Church numbered 1,233,350 communicants, who constituted a powerful pressure group in a nation of about 23,000,000. However, this was only a herald of things to come: for the invention of the steamship made it possible for the multi-million Catholic masses, oppressed and starving in Europe, to traverse the ocean. In the Eighteen-Fifties, therefore, the Church arrived at the threshold of power; and, as its voice grew stentorian, it exercised ever-increasing influence in the social, economic, and political arena of the expanding nation.

---

a.   Fourteenth Edition, Vol. 20, pp. 12-13.

b.   McCluskey, *Catholic Education in America*, p. 16, states: "In opposing Catholic influence in the public schools, they [the Protestants] were forced to stand by . . . as all religious influence disappeared and a totally secular philosophy moved in."

The Consolidation of the Catholic School

As mid-century approached, two traumatic events occurred in Europe which altered profoundly the course of American history: (1) the devastating Irish potato famine of 1841-45 and (2) the fierce political upheavals of 1848-49 in Central Europe. Between 1841 and 1860, 1,894,830 Irish immigrants came to these shores;[a] and between 1850 and 1870, 2,467,317 Germans, who were predominantly Catholic, arrived. Between 1830 and 1920, 29,675,238 persons came to America of whom 22,962,194 were born in wholly or overwhelmingly Catholic countries. After Ireland and Germany had disgorged their millions, other countries followed suit during the remainder of the 19th century, and well into the 20th: between 1901 and 1920, Austria, Hungary, Russia, Poland, and Italy alone supplied this country with 8,716,272 new citizens,[b] of whom the great majority had been baptized into the Catholic faith.

The Irish, however, remained the decisive influence in the Catholic Church; of its outstanding clergy, at least 75% are still of Hibernian descent.

In spite of the impassioned pleas and directives issued by eight American councils, the educational enterprise of the Church developed very slowly. Even in 1860, the 2,385 parishes still had few parochial schools. We find, instead, 148 seminaries and 166 convents preparing young men and women for vocations or the priesthood; beyond this, there were only 89 literary "colleges" for boys and 202 "female academies."

We may say, however, that by 1880 the Catholic Church had come of age. Following 1850, its membership increased by 400% in 30 years to 6,143,222—or 12.3% of the population; and it had 55 bishops, 5,989 priests, 6,407 churches, and 24 seminaries with 1,186 students. It also had 663 academies or institutes, and 2,246 parochial schools with 405,234

a.   Cf. the 1925 *Statistical Abstract*, p. 85.
b.   *Ib.*

pupils. However, in spite of conciliar pressure, more than 4,000 parishes were still without schools; and only a fraction of Catholic youth were enrolled in Church institutions.

It must, furthermore, have been a tragedy of major proportions to the prelates that so many Catholics abandoned their faith after breathing the new air of these United States. Despite the enormous immigration, the Church still claimed only 8,579,966 members in 1891. In an article published in *The Catholic Mirror*, September 17, 1904, this organ of Cardinal Gibbons of Baltimore lamented: "If all the descendants of our Catholic forefathers had remained in the faith, there would be more than 40,000,000 Catholics in the United States today." In that year, the Church claimed only 11,887,317 communicants, including children, of whom probably less than one-half were active in the Church.

When the Second Plenary Council met in 1866, it reiterated in more strident language the necessity of establishing parochial schools. And, with the arrival of millions of additional Catholics, another problem—but one of long standing—reared its ugly head higher than ever before. Since Catholic youth were still being reared in ignorance in preference to attending public schools "It is a melancholy fact," declared the assembled bishops, "and a very humiliating avowal for us to make, that a very large proportion of the idle and vicious youth in our principal cities are the children of Catholic parents. . . . certain it is, that a large number . . . appear to have no idea of the Christian family, and the responsibility imposed on them of providing for the moral training of their offspring. . . .

"Day after day, these unhappy children are caught in the commission of petty crimes, which render them amenable to the public authorities; and . . . they are transferred by the hundreds . . . to distant localities, where they are brought up in ignorance of, and most commonly in hostility to, the Religion in which they have been baptized."

During the decades following the first Plenary Council, James A. McMaster, a layman who edited and published the *Freeman's Journal* of New York, prosecuted a tireless and fervent crusade, the object of which was to place every Catholic child in a Catholic school. His publication was widely read, extremely influential, and in complete harmony with the thinking of Pius IX, who promulgated the *Syllabus of Errors* in 1864.[a]

---

a.   Although this is used as a text to be memorized in Spanish and other Catholic state schools, it has never been translated into English or made available in any form by the Church to the American laity.

Since the repeated admonitions of nine councils had not produced the desired results in spite of the direst eschatological threats; and since only a small minority of Catholic children were as yet in Church schools, it became necessary to take more drastic action.

The American bishops therefore requested authoritative guidance from Rome which was supplied in a document dated November 24, 1875,[a] and entitled "Instruction of the Congregation of Propaganda." This declared that "The Sacred Congregation of Propaganda has been many times assured that for Catholic Children of the United States of America evils of the greatest kind are likely to result from the so-called public schools" which are "most dangerous and very much opposed to Catholicity. For the children in those schools . . . can neither learn the rudiments of the faith nor be taught the precepts of the Church. . . .

"Again, these schools being not under the control of the Church, the teachers are selected from every sect indiscriminately . . . so that there is nothing to stop them from infusing into the young minds the seeds of error and vice. Then evil results are certainly to be dreaded from the fact that . . . children of both sexes must be in the same classrooms and sit side by side. . . . the children are fearfully exposed to the danger of losing their faith and . . . their morals. . . .

"Unless this danger can be rendered remote, instead of proximate, said schools cannot in conscience be used. . . .

"It only remains, then, for the prelates to use every means in their power . . . that the faithful may more freely contribute the necessary expenses . . . to provide Catholic schools. . . .

"However, the S. Congregation is not unaware that circumstances may be sometimes such as to permit parents to send their children to public schools. Of course, they cannot do so without having sufficient cause. Whether there be sufficient cause in any particular case is to be left to the conscience of the bishop.

"Further, before a child can be conscientiously placed at a public school, provision must be made for giving it the necessary Christian training and instruction . . . dwelling particularly on those truths of faith which are called most in question by Protestants and unbelievers; children beset with so many dangers they should guard with tireless devotion to the Blessed Virgin, and on all occasions animate them to hold firmly by their religion. The parents . . . must keep them from . . . familiarity with . . . other school children whose company might be dangerous to their faith or morals. . . .

---

a.   Published in translation in *The Pastor* (June, 1886).

218

"Parents who neglect to give this necessary Christian training and instruction to their children . . . if obstinate, cannot be absolved. . . ."[a]

After this *ex cathedra* promulgation had been thoroughly digested, the Third Plenary Council was convened in Baltimore in 1884. It declared that "In days like ours, when error is so pretentious and aggressive, every one needs to be as completely armed as possible . . . that they may withstand the noxious influences of popularized irreligion. . . ."; and it adopted a fourfold Resolution, which provided:

(1) That every church should within two years establish and thereafter maintain a parish school, unless the bishop should decide that a delay was permissible.

(2) That a priest who fails to accomplish this objective deserves to be removed.

(3) That any church, which fails to carry out this directive is to be reprimanded.

(4) That all Catholic parents are bound to send their children to the parish school, unless the bishop approves another institution.

It is evident that the American prelates either would not or dared not enact a decretal in the full spirit of the "Instruction." A new pope, Leo XIII, with more moderate views, had replaced Pius IX, and it is possible that the less stringent language now used stemmed from his prudence in dealing with the American laity. Had the Third Plenary Council followed the rigid line proposed by McMaster in the *Freeman's Journal* and by the Vatican in 1875, millions of otherwise loyal Catholics might have been driven from the Church. On the other hand, although the Resolution of 1884 unquestionably furnished a tremendous impetus in the construction of parish schools, we need only look at the record to discover that it was dishonored in the breach more often than honored in obedience. In 1891, as shown in Table V, there were still only 3,277 elementary schools in 7,631 parishes: which is to say that 4,354, or 57%, had refused or failed to

---

a.   It is difficult to see how this could be interpreted to mean anything other than that the sacraments would be denied to parents sending their children to the public schools. It is certain that the "Instruction of the Sacred Congregation" caused heated controversy in the American church and probably significant loss of membership; and this is definitely implied from the much softer tone of the Fourteen Propositions sent to America in 1892 by Archbishop Francis Satolli.

obey the Council.[a] Nor did matters improve with the passage of time: in 1905, there were 11,387 churches and missions but only 4,235 schools—a ratio of 37%. It was not until 1920, when 10,680 churches had 5,852 schools, that more than half had achieved the ideal of 1884.

As controversy continued to rage, Rome offered a compromise in May, 1892, in the form of Fourteen Propositions presented by Archbishop Francis Satolli. In general, these reinforced the Resolutions of the Third Plenary Council. There were, however, several substantive changes: Section V strictly forbade all priests and bishops to take any step which would exclude from the sacraments any parent whose children were not in Church schools. Sections VI and X actually expressed approval or at least toleration for the public school so long (Section XII) as the "hundreds of thousands of Catholic children in the United States" who "attend schools which are under the control of State boards," are given a "religious and moral education according to Catholic principles. . . ." This was to be accomplished by teaching the catechism to them during free time in the public schools; by conducting classes in other buildings; or by having the parents themselves inculcate the faith at home. Finally, Satolli urged that Catholic schools and teachers be developed to a point where they would be equal to or even superior to their public counterparts.

During the years following the Third Plenary Council, various prominent Catholics expressed their views concerning their schools. Filled with enthusiasm and optimism, Archbishop James Edward Quigley of Chicago gave vent to the following dithyramb, which was printed in the Chicago *Tribune*, May 5, 1903: "Within twenty years, this country is going to rule the world. . . . The West will dominate this country, and what I have seen of the western parochial schools has proved that the generation which follows us will be exclusively Catholic. When the United States rules the world, the Catholic Church will rule the world."

Even at that time, Catholic theories concerning public funds for parochial schools had been definitely formulated, and were thus stated by the Jesuit father, James S. Hayes: "Every school that does the work of education in a way to satisfy the requirements of the state in all the secular branches of instruction is entitled to state support, no matter to what religious denomination the school managers may belong. . . ."[b]

---

a.   The 1967-70 *Data Bank*, published by the National Catholic Educational Association, p. 4, states that 37% of the parishes had schools in 1884, 44% in 1891, but only 36% in 1900.

b.   *The New World*, Feb. 6, 1904.

Intermixed with paeans for Catholic education and demands for public funds, fierce denunciations were sometimes levelled at the public schools: "The state schools are the curse of filial piety and obedience and the breeding places of anarchism and rebellion. They unfit the mind of the child with contempt for their helpless parents, who have nothing to say . . . . what a conglomeration of boys and girls are gathering in the public schools! The children of thieves, murderers, and criminals sit side by side with the children of the honest and upright; the Jew and the Christian, the infidel and the devout. . . .

"Oh, what cursed negligence of otherwise sensible parents to allow such a commingling! . . . they risk their innocent offspring with the . . . corrupt scum of humanity merely because the state offers to relieve them of the education of their children. Before another generation grows up, our public schools will be sinks of corruption from which lecherous, impious, and scoffing humanity will issue forth and poison our country." [a]

How could Catholics who absorbed such propaganda live at peace with Protestants who were persuaded that the Great Church was none other than the Whore That Sitteth upon the Seven Hills of Rome?

The Secular Counteraction

1. The Know-Nothings and the American Protective Association

The rapid growth of Catholic churches, membership, and political influence, together with the widespread fear of its potential power, created movements and fostered the spread of opinions intended to curb its expansion on American soil. Thus it was that a very significant anti-Catholic development took form as The American Party, organized in 1852 or 1853 under the slogan America for Americans. In due course, it became known as the Know-Nothing Party, because its members refused to discuss their beliefs with strangers or outsiders.

In 1854 and 1855, the Party won elections in 9 states; under its prodding, the Massachusetts General Court made Bible reading mandatory in all public schools. For several years during the Sixties, hatred engendered by the Party was so intense in Baltimore that the city had to be placed under martial law and occupied by federal troops.

The Party advocated the ownership of all church property by boards

---

a.   *Ib.*, April 9, 1904.

of trustees; [a] the denial of the franchise to the foreign born; the reading of the Bible and some interdenominational religious instruction in all public schools; the outlawry of any organization that gives fealty to a foreign government or ecclesiastical polity; the taxation of all church property, including the sanctuary; and the abolition of sectarian schools, or, at the very least, the absolute denial of any tax funds to them.

Because of various divisions concerning subsidiary issues, the American Party disintegrated within twenty-five years of its inception; however, it had a successor, called the American Protective Association, which, at a convention held in Bloomington, Illinois, January 23, 1894, adopted the following platform: (1) that no one should be elected to public office who owes allegiance to any foreign king, potentate, or ecclesiastical authority; (2) that we should maintain a single, non-sectarian school system and oppose all attempts to supplant it by sectarian education; (3) that no public funds should under any circumstances be used for a sectarian purpose; (4) that all church real estate, with the exception of the sanctuary itself, should be subject to taxation; and (5) that all parochial and other

---

a.   The ownership of Catholic church property was a burning issue for decades following 1785, when a group of laymen in New York City purchased a site, built a church, and hired their own pastor. In 1800, most Catholic church real estate in America was vested in boards of lay trustees. The Jesuit Bishop John Carroll, who had returned to the United States in 1773 when the pope dissolved and suppressed the Order, who was the first primate of Baltimore, and who founded Georgetown College in Washington, led the battle against lay ownership of Catholic property. On August 22,1822, Pius VII issued a decretal in which he stated: "that trustees and laymen should arrogate to themselves the right . . . of establishing pastors and also of removing them . . and of bestowing revenue upon whom they please, is a practice new and unheard of in the Church . . . in that case . . . laymen would usurp the power which was given by Almighty God" to the Church alone. The Fourth Provincial Council of Baltimore decreed in 1840 that thenceforward no church should be consecrated unless the deed thereto had previously been made in trust to the bishop. In 1842, Bishop John Hughes of New York took up the crusade to implement this decree; he bewailed the fact that in this country alone a system of trustee ownership prevailed, without parallel in the Catholic Church; and he declared that this was terribly injurious to religion. He was successful in eradicating lay control or ownership. By 1855, almost all Catholic properties were held in the names of the bishops. Actually, one of the objectives of the Know-Nothings was to help groups of Catholic laymen to obtain title to their Church real estate and to establish control over their pastors and revenues.

private schools as well as convents and monasteries should be opened for inspection by public officials.[a]

2. Ulysses S. Grant, the "Blaine Amendment," and Theodore Roosevelt

The movement to enforce a complete separation of church and state spread across the country from 1853 to 1900 and enrolled among its exponents many in the highest echelons of government. One of these was Ulysses S. Grant, who declared in a message to Congress, December 7, 1875:

"I recommend that a Constitutional amendment be submitted to the legislatures of the several states for ratification, making it the duty of each . . . to establish and forever maintain free public schools adequate to the education of all the children in the rudimentary branches . . .; forbidding the teaching in said schools of religious, atheistic, or pagan tenets, and prohibiting the granting of any school funds or school taxes, or any part thereof, either by legislative, municipal, or other authority, for the benefit or in aid, directly or indirectly, of any religious sect or denomination, or in aid, or for the benefit of, any religious object of any nature or kind whatever. . . . We declare church and state forever separate and distinct, but each free within their proper spheres. . . ."

In 1876, Congress enacted a law requiring all new states to write into their constitutions provisions for public schools which must forever remain free from sectarian influence or control. Although the proposal of the President, embodied in the so-called Blaine Amendment, never obtained the two-thirds vote necessary for submission to the states for ratification,[b] at least forty of them in due course wrote its basic provisions into their

---

a.   This demand became widespread at the time because of the Maria Monk scandals and other similar emotional disclosures.

b.   Different versions of the Blaine Amendment came up for a vote in Congress twenty times and once failed by only a single vote to obtain the two-thirds necessary for submission to the states.

charters.[a] One of the versions of the so-called Blaine Amendment contains the following language:

"No public property and no public revenue of, nor any loan of credit by or under the authority of, the United States, or any State, Territory, District, or municipal corporation, shall be appropriated to, or made or used for, the support of any school, educational, or other institution, under the control of any religious or anti-religious sect, organization, or denomination, or wherein the particular creed of any religious or anti-religious sect or denomination shall be taught; and no such appropriation or loan or credit shall be made to any religious or anti-religious sect, organization, or denomination, or to promote its interests or tenets." [b]

Theodore Roosevelt, another strong proponent of church-state separation, declared: "We stand unalterably in favor of the public school system in its entirety. . . . We are against any division of the school tax fund and against any appropriation of public money for sectarian purposes. We are against any recognition whatever by the State in any shape or form of State-aided parochial schools. But we are equally opposed to any discrimination against or for a man because of his creed. . . . The very reasons that make us unqualified in our opposition to State-aided sectarian schools make us equally bent that in the management of our public schools, the

---

a. The Montana Constitution adopted in 1889, contains the following language:

ART. V, Section 35: "No appropriation shall be made for charitable, industrial, educational, or benevolent purposes to any person, corporation, or community not under the absolute control of the state, nor to any denomination or sectarian institution or association."

ART. XI, Section 8: "Neither the legislature, assembly, nor any county, city, town, or school district, or other public corporation, shall ever make, directly or indirectly, any appropriation, or pay from any public fund or moneys whatever, or make any grant of lands or other property in aid of any church, or for any sectarian purpose, or to aid in the support of any school, academy, seminary, college, university, or other literary, scientific institution, controlled in whole or in part by any church, sect, or denomination whatever."

b. Since there had already been a great deal of debate as to what the First Amendment actually meant or how far it was intended to go in erecting Jefferson's Wall of Separation, the so-called Blaine Amendment was an attempt to write into the federal Constitution provisions which would spell this out in terms acceptable to the strongest proponents of church-state separation. It is indeed interesting to note that most modern Supreme Court decisions have been written basically in the spirit of the "Blaine Amendment."

adherents of each shall be given exact and equal justice, wholly without regard to their religious affiliations." [a]

Catholic Critics of Parochial Education

1. Orestes Brownson, Caustic Journalist

It would indeed be an error to assume that all Catholics have been or are now unanimously in support of the school system envisioned by the American councils or the "Instruction of the Congregation of Propaganda de Fide." Some of the most articulate and best-informed must be numbered among the severest critics of the parochial schools.

One of these was Orestes A. Brownson, a fanatically loyal convert who entered the Church in 1844 when he was 41 and who published his *Quarterly Review* in New York for many years. His ferocious pen made enemies and created controversy, but he left an indelible mark upon the Church he adored, but whose schools he excoriated.

The bishops, he declared, [b] had established their system of education simply as a means of "promoting Catholic interests, and of converting the whole country to the Catholic faith. Yet, strangely enough, they are very far from receiving the hearty and undivided support of our whole Catholic community. Great dissatisfaction has been expressed by not a few whose love of Catholicity and devotion to the Church cannot be questioned" and they "refuse to join in the movement for parochial schools . . . under the care of the clergy. . . . Whence comes it that so many amongst us prefer the public schools. . . ?

"We hazard little in saying that our so-called Catholic schools . . . do not educate their pupils to be at home and at ease in their own age and country, or train them to be living, thinking, energetic men, prepared for the work that actually awaits them in either church or state. As far as we are able to trace the effect of the most approved Catholic education of our days . . . it tends to repress rather than to quicken the life of the pupil, to unfit rather than prepare him for the active and zealous discharge either of his religious or his social duties. They who are educated in our schools seem misplaced and mistimed in the world, as if born and educated for a world that has ceased to exist. They come out ignorant of contemporary ideas . . . and large numbers of them sink into obscurity, and do nothing

a.   From *American Ideals*, G. P. Putnam Sons, New York, 1924, pp. 63-64.

b.   In an article which appeared in Brownson's *Quarterly Review,* January, 1862.

for their religion or their country; or, what is worse, abandon their religion, turn their backs on the church, and waste all their energies in seeking pleasure. . . .

"Catholic education . . . aims to restore . . . an order of things which the world has left behind, and which it is neither possible nor desirable to restore. . . .

"In scarcely any part of the Christian world can we find men who are earnest Catholics . . . among the active and influential men of the age . . . . Catholic education . . . fails to produce living men, active, thinking men, great men, men of commanding genius, of generous aims, and high and noble aspirations; and hence it also fails to enable the Church to take possession of humanity, and to inspire and direct its movements. . . .

"Our Catholic population is practically a foreign body and brings with it a civilization foreign from the American and in some respects inferior to it. . . .

"Now the objection to Catholic schools . . . is that they tend . . . to perpetuate the association of orthodoxy with this inferior civilization . . . because what is wanted by their founders and supporters is not simply the preservation of orthodoxy, but the perpetuation of the foreignism hitherto associated with it. . . .

"These are some of the reasons which have led many of our most intelligent, most earnest, and devout Catholics to form their unfavorable judgment of Catholic schools and Catholic education . . . and prove that, from the seminary down to the primary school, it stands in need . . . of a wide, deep, and thorough reform. . . ."[a]

2. John Ireland, Archbishop of St. Paul

Orestes Brownson was only a layman, albeit an influential one; but when the Archbishop of St. Paul, John Ireland, one of the giants of the Church, advocated the abolition of the parochial school, he created a controversy almost unparalleled in scope and bitterness. He stated his views in an address entitled "State Schools and Parish Schools,"[b] which was delivered in St. Paul at the 1890 Convention of the National Education Association; his words still reverberate within and outside Catholic circles. Since proposals similar to his have since been advanced by various parochiaidists, they merit our careful consideration. What he was advoca-

a.   It should be noted that he stopped just short of demanding the complete abolition of the parochial school.
b.   Reprinted in *The Church and Modern Society*, Vol. I, pp. 215-232, D. H. McBride, New York, 1903.

ting was essentially a system based on that proposed by Governor Seward in New York in 1842.

"I am," he declared, "a friend and an advocate of the state school. In the circumstances of the present time, I uphold the parish school. I sincerely wish that the need for it did not exist. I would have all schools . . . to be state schools. . . .

"I concede the necessity of the state school. The child must have instruction. . . . Universal instruction implies free schools in which knowledge is to be had for the asking; in no other manner can instruction be brought within the reach of all children. Free schools! Blest indeed is the nation whose vales and hillsides they adorn, and blest the generation upon whose souls are poured their treasures. No tax is more legitimate than that which is levied in order to dispel mental darkness. . . .

"I am unreservedly in favor of state laws making instruction compulsory. . . . It were idle for me to praise the work of the . . . free school of America! Withered be the hand raised in sign of its destruction. . . .

"I turn to the denominational or parish school. It exists. I again express my regret that there is a necessity for its existence. In behalf of the state school I call upon my fellow-Americans to aid in the removal of this necessity.

"Catholics are foremost in establishing parish schools. . . . Lutherans, also, exhibit great zeal for parish schools. Many Episcopalians, and not a few of other Protestant denominations, command and organize parish schools. . . . God forbid that I should desire to see in America the ground which Protestantism now occupies swept by the devastating blast of unbelief. Let me be your ally in warding off . . . irreligion, the destroyer of Christian life and of Christian civilization. . . . Irreligion is abroad, scorning the salvation which is offered in the teachings and graces of Christ Jesus. . . In our fear lest Protestants gain some advantage over Catholics, or Catholics over Protestants, we play into the hands of unbelievers and secularists. We have given over to them the school, the nursery of thought. Are we not securing to them the mastery of the future?

"The state school is non-religious. . . . The school deals with immature, childish minds, upon which silent facts and examples make deepest impressions. The pupil sees and listens, and insensibly forms the conclusions that religion is of minor importance. Religious indifference becomes his creed; his manhood will be, as was his childhood in the school, estranged from God and the positive influence of religion. . . .

"Accidentally, it may be, and unintentionally, but, in fact, most certainly, the state school crowds out the Church. The teaching of religion is not a function of the state; but the State should, for the sake of its people,

227

and for its own sake, permit and facilitate the teaching of religion by the Church. . . .

"Secularists and unbelievers will demand their rights. I concede their rights. I will not impose upon them my religion, which is Christianity. But let them not impose upon me and my fellow-Christians their religion, which is secularism. . . .

"I come to the chief difficulty. The American people at large are Christians; but they are divided among themselves. Not to speak of other differences, there is the vital and radical one between Catholics and Protestantism of all forms. . . . Well-meaning men propose as a remedy to teach a common Christianity in the schools. This will not do. In loyalty to their principles, Catholics cannot and will not accept a common Christianity. To Catholics, what does not bear on its face the stamp of Catholicity is Protestant. . . . Is it not a thousand times better to make a compromise than to allow secularism to triumph and own the country? . .

"It is no honor to America that ten million of its people are forced by law to pay taxes for the support of schools to which their conscience does not give approval, and are, furthermore, compelled, by their zeal for the religious instruction of their children, to build school houses of their own, and pay their own teachers. It is no honor for the fifty millions to profit by the taxes paid by the ten millions. The cry that the State schools are open to Catholics, if they silence their conscience, is not a defense that will hold before the bar of justice. . . .

"I solve the difficulty by submitting it to the calm judgment of the country . . . and in the spirit of peaceful compromise. . . . I would permeate the regular state school with the religion of the majority[a] of the children of the land, be this religion as Protestant as Protestantism can be, and I would, as is done in England, pay for the secular instruction given in denominational schools. . . .[b] This is not paying for religious instruction, but for the secular instruction demanded by the state. . . .

"Another plan: . . . In Poughkeepsie the city school board rents the

---

a.   Here the Archbishop was certainly involved in a fatal contradiction; for, since, in the United States, the Protestants were and are the majority, not only as a whole, but also in most school districts, this proposal would make the public or state schools anathema to Catholics. And how, under this arrangement, could the rights of secularists and unbelievers be protected?

b.   This is very similar to the arrangement which existed in Rhode Island and Pennsylvania and which the Supreme Court declared unconstitutional in the *Lemon* and *Dicenso* cases.

228

buildings formerly used as parish schools, and from the hour of 9 A.M. to that of 3 P.M. the school is in every respect a state school—teachers being engaged and paid by the board, teachers and pupils being examined, state books being used, the door being always open to the superintendent and members of the board. There is simply the tacit understanding that so long as the teachers, Catholic in faith, pass their examinations and do their work as efficiently and as loyally as other teachers under the control of the board, they shall not be replaced by teachers of another faith.[a] During school hours no religious instruction is given. Christian doctrine is taught outside the hours for which the buildings are leased to the board. The State pays not one cent for the religious instruction of the pupils. In the other schools, Protestant devotional exercises take place in fullest freedom before the usual school hours. . . .

"Allow me one word as a Catholic. . . . Not one stone of the wondrous edifice which Americans have reared in their devotion to education would Catholics remove or permit to be removed. They would fain add to its splendor and majesty by putting side by side religious and secular instruction, neither of them interfering with the other, each of them borrowing from the other aid and dignity. Do the schools of America fear contact with religion? Catholics demand the Christian State school:in so doing, they prove themselves the truest friends of the school and of the state."

We need not be surprised that the Archbishop was assailed from almost every side by his fellow-bishops for advocating the abolition of a system for which so much sacrifice had been endured and from which so rich a fruitage was expected. And, since his proposals were no less abhorrent to the proponents of church-state separation, they only injected more hot fuel into the already raging fires of controversy. Perhaps it was as a result of this crossfire, that the Archbishop during his later years became a leading proponent of total Catholic education, which he continued to be until his death in 1918.

3. Father Jeremiah Crowley, Excommunicate

If the declarations of Orestes Brownson and John Ireland caused pain among devout Catholics, what would be their reaction to the phillipics of the Reverend Jeremiah J. Crowley, who, in 1904, published a book called *The Parochial School, A Curse to the Church—A Menace to the Nation.*

---

a.   Here again the Archbishop would establish a completely sectarian principle at public expense: he would bar any teacher in the quasi-public schools of this kind who are not of the Catholic faith. In short, he would establish a religious and sectarian prerequisite for employment in a public operation.

Here was a man of Celtic-Norman stock, who had been ordained to the priesthood in Ireland, where he had been sentenced to prison for defending the civil rights of a Protestant. In Chicago, he was excommunicated by Archbishop Patrick A. Feehan because he made charges, supported in writing by 25 other priests, against the greed, corruption, venality, and scandals prevalent among the clergy. Every diocese, he declared, had its priestly devotees of Bacchus and Venus; and many of the means they employed to obtain money, which they used in the service of Satan, were not only scandalous, but often criminal.[a] Instead of being investigated, his charges only led to his removal from office and even his physical expulsion from attendance at Church services.

Father Crowley professed undying love for his Church; and declared that he wished only to save it from self-destruction at the hands of corrupt ecclesiastics, who were also determined to destroy the American public school (p. 21).

The Catholic laity, he said, never wanted parochial schools; it was the prelates who insisted on them because they realized (1) that there could never be a union of church and state in America as long as its citizens are products of the public schools; (2) that Catholic indoctrination can be carried on only under Church control; (3) that the parochial school enables the hierarchy to keep from the children the truth concerning clerical greed and corruption; and (4) that they can use the school as a means of immense graft (p. 73).

Catholic parents send their children to these schools chiefly for fear of hell-fire, threatened by the councils and from the pulpit; and some priests even deny the sacraments to parents whose children are in the public schools.

The Catholic clergy, declared Crowley, do everything in their power to bring the public schools into disrepute (1) by calling them godless, vicious, corrupt, heretical; (2) by trying to secure funds for their own schools; (3) by encouraging other sects to demand money for theirs; (4) by placing Catholics on public school boards and in their teaching staffs; and (5) by securing jobs for nuns and monks in the public schools.

Crowley observed that when the Bible was read in the public schools, Catholic ecclesiastics denounced the practice and this was the chief reason it was abandoned. And so, having eliminated God from the public schools,

---

a. Crowley stated that it was a common practice, when a priest became involved in scandal or crime, simply to shift him to another parish, sometimes under an assumed name, so long as he remained loyal to the hierarchy and never criticized any of its scandals or those who were guilty of them.

230

they charged them with being Godless and unfit for the education of Catholic youth. The next step was to erect parochial schools, which depleted the pocket-books of the poor (p. 89).

Father Crowley left few stones unturned in his crusade. "Some pastors make an annual pretence," he charged, "of giving their congregations" a financial report; "but those who have inside knowledge . . . know that they are monumental pieces of deception. . . . the laity have no voice in the temporal affairs of the parish. They dare not ask for a complete financial report. All they can do is pay up and shut up" (p. 200).

Crowley charged that not as many as two per cent of the parochial school principals could pass an examination to teach in a public school. "The parochial school," he averred, "is totally defective in the teaching staff. . . . The sisters . . . coax and urge their pupils to become nuns . . . (p. 215). Recruits, as a rule, are immediately put to teaching. Without training, without pedagogic ability, and without experience, they are placed over Catholic children to impart to them secular knowledge and religious instruction" (p. 247). Furthermore, the secular instruction is deplorably weak; the teachers are completely under the thumb of the pastors, who can discharge them at will" (p. 248). "I assert that the parochial school has been the most potent factor in the loss of millions of communicants which the Catholic Church has sustained in America" (p. 322).

Since the laity supplied the money, argued Father Crowley, they should know what becomes of it and they should control the schools. There is only one way to regenerate them and that is by placing ownership and management wholly in the hands of the laity. Until that "is done," they "will continue to be a curse to the Church and a menace to the nation. . . ." (p. 372). "The Catholic parochial school should never have been started. It will go out of existence when the Catholic laity are emancipated. . . ."(p. 373).

In conclusion, Father Crowley offered a philosophy and an analysis that remain forever cogent: "Statistics show that there are almost 150 different denominations in the United States. Imagine the public school abolished and each sect educating its own youth! . . . What kind of citizens would be produced: Two generations wholly educated in sectarian schools would mean the disruption of the United States. The youth would enter the arena of citizenship filled with bigotry. . . . each sect and religious body would become a caste. There would be falsehood in instruction originating in ambitions for advantage over other bodies or for greater control of individual adherents. . . . the public school safeguards the best interests of the Catholic Church in America, as, indeed, it safeguards the best interests of all the other sectarian and non-sectarian bodies. . . ."

231

4.   The Nature and Rationale of the Parochial School

Its Aura and Composition

It is certainly a phenomenon worthy of note that as late as 1905 the Catholic Church claimed only 12,461,793 communicants in the United States; and that even in 1920, when it had 10,608 churches and 5,852 elementary schools, it still had only a claimed membership of 17,701,213. Had all the Catholic immigrants and their offspring continued in the faith, they would certainly have numbered not less than 60 million, a decisive majority of the population. In 1936, there were 20,735,188 communicants and 12,720 parishes, of which 7,490, or 58.9%, had schools. In 1946, there were 24,403,136 members in 13,132 parishes, of which 7,597, or 55.3%, had schools; in 1964, the Church came nearest to realizing its century-old ideal concerning education, when 17,445 parishes had 10,902 schools—a ratio of 62.5%. In 1971, the number of parishes had risen to 18,244, but those with schools had declined to 9,271, or less than 50.9%. In 1971-72, the ratio fell well below a moiety.

Concerning one fact there can be neither question nor dispute: there is little point in operating a sectarian school unless it inculcates a sectarian faith in order to retain the youth so educated for future membership in the communion. This is candidly admitted by the Seventh-Day Adventists, Lutherans, and Apostolic evangelicals who operate their own schools. As an illustration, we cite Mr. William A. Kramer in an article published by the Education Committee of the North Dakota Catholic Conference in its 1970 *Nonpublic Education Report.* "The state must continue to achieve its purpose and allow church-related schools to achieve theirs . . . but not to sacrifice their religious purposes. 'Secular purpose' does not mean secularization. . . . Legislation can and should be so worded as to permit also a church-related school to preserve its own purposes while still serving the public purpose of state and community."

232

The California Association of Christian Schools offers a case in point; its 1971 *Directory* proclaims as its statement of faith that (1) the Bible is inspired, the only infallible, authoritative Word of God; (2) there is one God, eternally existent in three Persons, the Father, Son, and Holy Spirit; (3) we believe in the deity of Christ, in His Virgin Birth, in his sinless life, in His Miracles, in His vicarious atoning death, in His resurrection from the dead, in His ascension to the right hand of the Father, and in His personal return in power and glory; (4) because of the exceeding sinfulness of human nature, there is an absolute necessity of regeneration by the Holy Spirit for salvation; (5) the saved shall be resurrected into life, but the lost unto damnation; and (6) there is a spiritual unity of believers in Christ.

The Catholic parochial school is indeed a highly distinctive institution; even if it were not its purpose to permeate every subject with the sacred odor of sectarian doctrine, it would still be as different from the public school as day is from night. Almost always it is attached to its operating parish church; the children are usually clad in uniforms; they are marched in formation from the school to the sanctuary to partake in religious rituals; the classrooms are decorated with the pictures and images of the Virgin, usually with the Christ child, or of St. Joseph or the Holy Family, and with the statues of saints; until recently, almost every teacher, especially on the elementary level, was a sister; the school is owned by the bishop and authority is vested in the parish pastor; the school itself is a retreat where juveniles, totally segregated from the world outside, grow up under the impression that the Catholic Church is the only institution on earth that is either salutary or invested with importance and authority.

The very names of the schools constitute an important factor in the emotional and intellectual formation of the child. Whereas the public school—which may be only a block away—may be called the East, the West, the South, or the Central, or the Washington, Lincoln, Jefferson, Madison, Eisenhower, Roosevelt, Longfellow, Emerson, Whitman, or some other name redolent of American tradition, its Catholic counterpart will bear a title such as St. Mary's, Our Lady of Perpetual Help, Our Lady of Sorrows, Our Lady of Redemption, Our Lady of the Rosary, Our Lady of Heaven, Our Lady Queen of Angels, Our Lady Queen of Heaven, or St. Margaret-Mary; or it bears the name of some obscure saint who lived centuries ago on another continent, such as Lawrence, Nepo, Cantius, Bosco, Joachim, Ignatius, Hilary, Hedwig, Gerard, Francisco, Dominic, Cecelia, or Christopher. The greater the number of parishes in a city, the more bewildering is the array of saints. For the Mexicans, there is Our Lady of Guadalupe; for the Irish, St. Patrick; for the French, St. Louis; for the Italians, St. Anthony; for the Poles, St. Casimir and St. Stanislaus; for the Bohemians, St. Vitus; for the Slovaks, St. Wendelin; for the Negroes,

St. Peter Claver and St. Benedict the Moor; for the Scandinavians, St. Brigid. Since there is such a plethora of male and female saints and since the Blessed Virgin has been adorned with such a multiplicity of honorific titles, it is seldom necessary to dedicate more than one school in any diocese to a single adoration—or at least in the same city. Catholic secondary schools are usually diocesan and therefore named after some bishop or other Church dignitary—as the Brady, Murray, or Hill in St. Paul; or the Ryan, Timon, Fallon, Colton, Carroll, McMahon, and Daugherty in Buffalo; or the St. Pius X in Albuquerque or the Roncalli in Pueblo. Sometimes high schools are owned by orders and therefore classified as "private" and may be named after a wealthy donor, like the Jesuit Brophy Prep in Phoenix, Arizona.

The purpose of the parochial school was vividly described by Archbishop John Ireland during the later period of his ministry: "Mere secular education is a peril and a menace . . . nothing but daily drill in the teachings of the faith, and the daily influence of an atmosphere permeated with the spirit of faith, will sink religion so deeply into the soul of the child that it will remain there through life, unaltered and unwavering. . . ." It cannot be achieved, he emphasized, by "the perfunctory and superficial instruction which is usually given by parent or priest outside the Catholic school. . . . We cannot but look with alarm to the future of religion in America, when we recall that a large proportion of Catholic children are educated outside Catholic schools, and how little is done for the religious training of such children. The losses to the faith will be immense unless much more be done for our little ones. . . . The hope of the Catholic Church in America is in Catholic schools. . . ."[a]

However, such institutions have been assailed by many critics, among whom we find a fervent spokesman for evangelical Christianity, Loraine Boettner, who declares: "In the 19th century, the Roman Church began a vigorous campain to drive Bible reading out of the public schools. The real objection, of course, was not to the teaching of religion, as such, but to the fact that the Roman Catholic religion was not taught. And now that the Bible and religion have been driven out of the public schools, the Roman Church denounces them as 'godless,' 'socialistic,' 'immoral,' and 'un-American.' " "The parochial schools, with their intense indoctrination of the young, are . . . the 'secret weapon' by which the Roman Church hopes to control the nation's future citizens and so win the victory over

---

a.   *The Church and Modern Society,* II, 243, 320-21.

Protestantism."[a] He adds that children are regimented in the Catholic schools; that they are administered by the clergy; that teachers have no tenure or rights whatever; and that the people who pay for them have no voice in their control or operation.

The Catholic parochial school still bears the unmistakable imprints of its origin when, more than a century ago, it began serving its various ethnic minorities. Often in close proximity, we may still find the tall spires of German, Irish, Czech, French, Polish, Italian, Bohemian, and other churches in which, for decades, these national minorities continued to worship and to conduct schools in their own language and according to the culture and heritage they imported from Europe. The Catholic community was thus often divided against itself in hostile and contending camps.

For many years, even in the United States, the Church was obsessed with the dangers of sex; and it therefore separated boys from girls either in different areas of the school or in entirely different buildings or institutions. To this day, many of the secondaries are for a single sex, as, for example, the St. Joseph's academies for girls.

As the Catholic community developed, some parishes or certain segments of the laity became more affluent; thereupon, they erected more commodious schools for their children. Thus, while the public schools offered substantially similar facilities to rich and poor alike, regardless of sex, creed, race, poverty, affluence, or national origin, the parochial schools became segregated not only on sectarian, but also on sexual, ethnic, and economic bases as well.

Nor was this all. Since Negroes were attracted much more by evangelical fervor[b] than by the austere rituals of the Great Church, few indeed were the black children enrolled in Catholic schools; nor were their parents likely to choose costly private education in preference to the free schooling supplied by the government. The result was two-fold: first, the Catholic schools were virtually all white; and, second, in the few instances of substantial minority enrollment, the schools which had them were of a single race and found in the city ghettos. Sometimes, as whites fled the Inner City, a few Negroes entered the abandoned parochial schools. The overall result, however, especially in some large cities, has been devastating

---

a.   *Roman Catholicism*, Presbyterian and Reformed Publishing Co., pp. 363 and 368.
b.   Cf. *Churches and Church Membership in the United States*, Series A, No. 2, published by the National Council of Churches. In 1950, 10,892,694 American Negroes—or 75% of the total—were communicants either in Baptist or Methodist churches.

for the public schools. As we noted in our analysis of Detroit, the Negro ratio there in 1970 was 64%. In 1969-70, nationally, the Negro ratio in public schools was 14.5%; but in the Catholic schools, it was 4.8%, or 197,780 out of 4,089,658. Meanwhile, since even these were concentrated in a few schools, the great majority of parochial schools remained virtually all-white.

In Pennsylvania there are 9 dioceses with a total 1970 Catholic school enrollment of 481,452.[a] However, there were only 14,928 black pupils in the system, a ratio of 3.3%.[b] In Philadelphia, where 34.6% of the population had become black in 1970, Mayor Dillworth noted in 1967 that the public schools, which were to become a principal vehicle to promote integration, had been thwarted in that objective because certain people enrolled their children in private schools, which resulted in placing an abnormally large proportion of Negroes in the public. In his city, the Negro ratio was 30% in 1967, but in the public schools, it was already 57%.[c] In Washington, D. C., the black ratio was 53.9%; but in the public schools it was 93.3% in 1970; meantime, in the Catholic, the proportion was only 19.2%.[d]

The Catholic secondary schools, in addition to their religious preference, enjoy the privilege of selectivity: problem pupils or those with poor elementary academic records may be consigned to the public schools. The Catholic schools have also been found to practice discrimination on the basis of race, affluence, family, and ethnic origin.[e]

The Authority of the Church

At the opening of this chapter, we offered statistics which show that the ideals of the Third Plenary Council, since they proved quite unenforceable in the United States, were never even approached. However, this does not mean that the laws of the Church have been altered or ameliorated: the point is that they can be implemented in any country only to the degree that it has influence over the people or can exercise political control through concordats or other means. All Catholic authorities, now and

---

a. Cf. the *Official Catholic Directory* of 1971.
b. Cf. *Data Bank, op. cit.,* of 1967-70, p. 55.
c. *Should Public Monies Be Used to Support Non-Public Education?* by A. D. Swan, 1967, p. 38.
d. Cf. *Church and State,* Feb., 1971, p. 7.
e. For a discussion of this, cf. *Public Funds for Parochial Schools?* by LaNoue, *op. cit.* p. 34.

in the past, agree officially that every Catholic child should (or must) be in a Catholic school; and that no religious instruction except the Catholic should or may be given in any educational institution whatsoever. They agree also that all subjects in Church schools must be permeated thoroughly by religious ideology in such a manner that the entire educational process becomes an integrated whole.

Especially in the field of education, the claims of the Church are virtually without limit. For example, *The Syllabus of Errors* (promulgated by Pius IX in 1864), which has never been rescinded and the Propositions of which have been reinforced by countless subsequent promulgations, anathematizes the following mortal errors: (1) that "Public schools in which the youth of the republic are trained . . . are and ought to be controlled by civil authority. . . ." (2) that "The best interests of Society demand that public schools, which are open to all children of every class . . . shall be free from clerical control. . . ."; (3) that "Catholic men may approve of a kind of education that is separate from the Catholic faith and the power of the Church. . . ."; and (4) that "The Church must be separated from the State and the State from the Church." (No. 45, 47, 48, 55.)

Canon Law No. 1374 states that no Catholic parent may send his child to a non-Catholic school without the consent of his bishop; 1381 declares that the religious training of youth in all schools is subject to the supervision and authority of the Catholic Church; that its bishops are empowered to prevent any teaching in any school which is contrary to the Catholic faith; and that they have the right and the duty to demand the removal of all teachers and textbooks failing to meet with their approval.

In his famous encyclical on *The Christian Education of Youth*, promulgated in 1929, Pius XI declared: "It is evident that both by right and in fact the mission to educate belongs to the Church . . . by reason of its double title, in the supernatural order, conferred exclusively upon her by God Himself; absolutely superior, therefore, to any other title in the natural order."

In its Declaration on Christian Education, Vatican Council II declared: ". . . this Sacred Synod proclaims anew what has already been taught . . . namely" that "the duty of educating belongs to the Church . . . because it has the responsibility of announcing the way of salvation to all men. . . ."

Non-Catholics have often observed the crucial importance of its schools to the Church. In commenting on the Everson Case, Mr. Justice Jackson of the United States Supreme Court remarked: ". . . the parochial school is a vital, if not the most vital, part of the Roman Catholic Church. If put to the choice, that venerable institution, I should expect, would forego its whole service for mature persons before it would give up the education of its young. . . ."

The Operation of Catholic Schools

Since, obviously, Canon law is inoperative in many countries, how does the Church reconcile its demands there with its own professed objectives? We can only observe that the Church is a vast and flexible organism which operates in accordance with current conditions. It asks for the maximum it believes attainable: when it receives less, it prepares maneuvers to obtain more. In the meantime, it makes every effort to conceal its ultimate objectives; when its own Canon Law is brought to its attention, it declares emphatically that it does not have the slightest desire to implement anything of the kind in the United States.

In Sweden and Mexico as in Communist lands the Church is forbidden to operate any parochial school: under such circumstances, it pleads humbly for the minimal privilege of paying in full for its own education—as it did also in Oregon in 1924, when parochial schools were banned by the voters.

However, as soon as it obtains the full right to operate educational institutions, it begins demanding fringe benefits, as in the United States: lunches, textbooks, transportation, remedial services, released time, shared time, purchase-of-services, pay for secular instruction by its own teachers, income-tax rebates for the parents of parochial children, and finally ever-larger tuition-vouchers, which will eventually cover the total operational cost of elementary and secondary education. On the college and university level, it has demanded and obtained vast subsidies.

In countries where the Church is stronger or has been more successful in pushing its demands, as in England, Western Germany, France, and the Netherlands, the Catholic schools receive approximately the same support as do the public—in some cases, as in Germany, even larger allocations.

In some of the Canadian providndces, as in Saskatchewan, the Catholic schools not only enjoy parity with the public for operational costs: they also receive public funds for the construction of their facilities. At first, such money was given only for elementary education, but then it was paid for secondary schools also. Furthermore, Catholics sit on boards which determine what textbooks may be used in the public schools.

In Italy, the public schools indoctrinate all pupils with Catholic ideology; there are some private schools, but they may not teach anything offensive to the Church.

In the heavily Catholic and French-speaking Quebec, the Catholic parochials, which have about 90% of the total enrollment, **are** the public schools. Theoretically, at least, Protestant schools may be established on the same basis. Quebec, therefore, represents the next to the final step in the direction of total Catholic education, which is found in countries like Spain and Portugal, where concordats have established the full Canon Law and where children are often required to commit the *Syllabus of Errors* to memory. Here every public school is a Catholic school, manned and operated by the clergy; and no other similar institution may exist.

Thus, as the Church progresses in power, it advances from a small privately operated academy to a monopolistic system, in which every deviationist form of religion or ideology is forbidden under the extreme penalty of law.

The Grand Concept of Permeation

While our public schools teem with the American heritage, the Catholic, in contrast, are submerged, enveloped, and permeated by the history, doctrines, and traditions of the Church; and by an overriding imperative dedicated to the formation of the People of God, the living body of Christ.

That these are the basic principles upon which Catholic education is founded is abundantly clear from official statements bearing the highest credentials. In 1897, Pope Leo XIII declared in the encyclical *Militantis Ecclesiae*: "It is necessary not only at certain times to teach Catholic religion to children, but all other subjects must also be made fragrant with the odor of piety. . . . If this holy habit should not pervade and permeate the souls of both teachers and pupils, little benefit will accrue. . . ." In his 1929 encyclical, *The Christian Education of Youth,* Pope Pius XI reinforced this statement: "It is necessary not only that religious instruction be given to the young at certain fixed times, but also that every other subject taught be permeated with Christian piety."

The scholarly Jesuit, Joseph H. Fichter, Professor of Sociology at Loyola University of the South, describes how the teacher can orient every subject toward the relationship between God and man. Textbooks are written, he says, specifically from the Catholic point of view and are oversaturated with the religion of the Church; the child has little opportunity indeed to become acquainted with the English classics read in the common schools. Every possible method and technique is employed to channel the flow of religion into the whole curriculum. Each day the children are taken to Mass and receive the sacraments; teachers, add Fichter, never cease from urging—"pestering"—the girls to become nuns.[a]

A book published by the National Council of Churches states that "Empirical research into parochial textbooks has demonstrated that

a. *The Parochial School—A Sociological Study,* Notre Dame Press, 1958, pp. 86, 88.

religious symbols, concepts, and doctrines, are frequent in such subjects as science, mathematics, and languages. . . . There is no legislative method of separating secular from religious subject matter across the board in religious schools."[a]

In a carefully documented study, the Catholic scholar, Ernest Bartell, declares: "Arguments for expansion of the present form of 'total' education in the Catholic schools state or imply that the secular and religious benefits are inseparable. . . . To the extent that the two classes of benefits are actually inseparable, then for purposes of our analysis they must be treated as joint products. . . ."[b]

In their widely heralded book, *S.O.S. for Catholic Schools,*[c] Father C. Albert Koob, President of the National Catholic Educational Association, and Mr. Russel Shaw, Director of the Division of Information of the United States Catholic Conference, make it clear that teaching in Catholic schools is an apostolate, rather than a profession (p. 5, 99, etc.); and that the basic purpose of Catholic education has always been "to form their students into good Catholics. . . ." (p. 128).

The authors state further that the ". . . ideal of 'integrating' religion into the Catholic program . . . should mean this vision of the Christian community underlying every aspect in Catholic education. The school is the place where the child . . . learns . . . the reality of the People of God. . ." (p. 21).

In their highly regarded work, *Can Catholic Schools Survive?*[d] Mr. William E. Brown and Father Andrew W. Greeley declare that Catholic education is the most important mission of the Church; that it must be conducted by the bishops (p. 59); and that religious instruction cannot be left to the parents, because they "simply will not do the job." (p. 67). The authors emphasize that there are no "secular subjects in Catholic schools— that all are religious or secular-religious" (p. 67); that the purpose of such education is to teach the truth of the Catholic faith, which is authentic Christianity (p. 82); that virtually every "secular" subject will be permeated with religious values (p. 89); and that this permeation is absolutely essential (p. 160). "A school established for the purpose of forming children to become mature Catholics . . . should confront every point of view expressed in literature, every tenet of philosophical systems, every description of human beings. . ., institutions, and . . . customs with positive

---

a.   *Public Funds for Parochial Schools? op. cit.,* p. 31.
b.   *Costs and Benefits of Catholic Elementary and Secondary Schools,* University of Notre Dame Press.
c.   Holt, Rinehart, and Winston, New York, 1970.
d.   Sheed and Ward, New York, 1970.

Catholic criticism. If the Church is what she claims to be, she has the right to pass judgment. . . ." (p. 89-90).

Neil G. McCluskey, S.J., perhaps the most articulate Catholic spokesman to emerge in recent years, declares that Catholics will continue to support their schools because "the objectives of religious education can best be realized in an atmosphere wherein spiritual and supernatural realities hold their proper place in the hierarchy of values. . . . Christianity offers a **life** which envelops the whole person. . . the Catholic school serves as a primary conduit of Christian culture—a way of looking at total reality."[a]

Elsewhere the same author states: "the public school has had to adopt a theoretical neutrality between those who believe in the God of the western tradition and those who do not. Yet the public school is not really neutral, for it gives an equivalent denial to the question by actually taking another starting point and aiming at another goal. What is worse, the public school, by default, facilitates the entry of a naturalistic religion of democracy, or secularist cult of society, into the vacuum, so that only the child from a secularist family can feel perfectly at home in the common public school. . . . The point to be made here, however, is that the philosophy of public school education is being dictated by those forces in society which, wanting no other goal for it, have nearly succeeded in quarantining the public school from the churches. . . ." (p. 20-21).

The Catholic Philosophy of Education

In 1919, a Washington convocation of American Catholic prelates set forth the purpose of an ideal education which, it declared, "is indeed a holy work, not merely a service to the individual and society, but a furtherance of God's design for man's salvation. . . our educators will recognize the advantage which concerted effort implies both for the Catholic system as a whole and for each of its allied institutions. . . .

"Our system is based on certain convictions that grow stronger as we observe the testing of all education. . . .

"**First**: The right of the child to receive education and the correlative duty of providing it, are established on the fact that man has a soul created by God. . . .

"**Second**: Since the child is endowed with physical, intellectual, and moral capacities, all these must be developed harmoniously. . . .

---

a.　　*Catholic Education in America*, p. 24.

"**Third**: Since the duties we owe our Creator take precedence of all other duties, moral training must accord the first place to religion, that is, to the knowledge of God and His law, and must cultivate a spirit of obedience to His commands. . . .

"**Fourth**: Moral and religious training is most efficacious when it is joined with instruction in other kinds of knowledge. It should so permeate these that its influence will be felt in every circumstance of life. . . .

"**Fifth**: An education that unites intellectual, moral and religious elements, is the best training for citizenship. . . .

"Our Catholic schools . . . aim, openly and avowedly, to preserve our Catholic faith; they offer to all our people an example of the use of freedom for the advancement of morality and religion."[a]

After its meeting of 1950, the American hierarchy issued the following carefully worded statement: "The child must be seen whole and entire . . . as a citizen of two worlds. He belongs to this world surely, but his first and highest allegiance is to the kingdom of God. From his earliest years he must be taught that his chief significance comes from the fact that he is created by God and is destined for life with God in eternity. . . .

"First of all, it will arouse in him a consciousness of God and of eternity. . . . Second, it will give him a continuing purpose in life. . . . Third, it will induce in him a deep sense of responsibility. . . . Finally, religion will challenge him to sanctify whatever walk of life he chooses and to seek and accept the will of God in whatever way it may be manifested. . . .

"Parents, therefore, should make early provision for the child's growth in God. . . . Morning and evening prayers, grace before and after meals, the family rosary . . . the reverential making of the sign of the Cross, the inculcation of respect for the crucifix and other religious objects—all these are practices which should be encouraged in the religious formation of the child. . . .

"In helping parents . . . the Church . . . initiates the child into the life of grace . . . by providing Catholic schools for each stage of his educational development. . . ."[b]

---

a.   From the "Pastoral Letter of the Archbishops and Bishops of the United States," published by the National Catholic Welfare Council in *The National Pastorals of the American Hierarchy,* 1923.

b.   From *Our Bishops Speak,* published 1952, by the Bruce Publishing Co., of Milwaukee, Wisconsin.

5.   The Catholic School: Costs and Staff

Wherever we have gone, in city after city, the local board of education has complete and detailed statistics concerning cash on hand, sources and amounts of revenue, every property asset and encumbrance, and each item of expenditure, no matter how minute, together with totals in all categories. Making a study of past and present public school costs and budgets is often a painstaking procedure: but the information is available.

Although Protestant and other private schools generally do not publish or furnish such elaborate data, we have found them very cooperative in supplying information concerning sources of income, salaries, mortgage encumbrances, tuition-charges, per-pupil costs, etc. However, this has usually been conveyed orally rather than in prepared documents.

Although Catholic administrators have been less communicative, there is now among them also a tendency toward greater disclosure. They have been happy to divulge their salary schedules, their tuition rates, estimated per-pupil costs, parish subsidies, and the amount of current debt. However, none of them ever supplied documents with financial information even remotely comparable to the reports available from public schools.

Indeed, for many years it has been one of the bitter complaints of Catholic critics and lay parishioners that they not only have no control or influence in the operation of the schools, but that they cannot obtain any adequate financial report or accounting.

Perhaps, in part to meet the demands for such information, a number of studies have been made during recent years by Catholic scholars. The University of Notre Dame Press in 1966 published Reginald A. Neuwien's *Catholic Schools in Action*, which has a chapter discussing "The Staff of Catholic Schools" and contains considerable information concerning teacher preparation and salaries. *Catholic Education in the Western World*, edited by James Michael Lee, 1967, provides a description of Catholic schools in various countries; and it includes a chapter on those in the

United States, with some financial data. In this category, however fragmentary it is, the study by Ernest Bartell, *Costs and Benefits of Catholic Elementary and Secondary Schools,* is the most detailed. But it covers only two dioceses (Youngstown and San Francisco) for the years 1958 to 1963, and is therefore out of date.

The most important source of financial and other statistical information concerning Catholic schools is the Research Department of the National Catholic Educational Association, located at One Dupont Circle, N. W., Washington, D. C., which, in 1970, published its first edition of *Data Bank, a Statistical Report,* and, in 1971, a sequel, with the sub-title *A Report on U. S. Catholic Schools.* Although these contain a mass of statistics, they are in no way comparable to the reports available from every public school district in the United States or from the United States Office of Education.

While making this study of Catholic parochial schools, past and present, we have arrived at two conclusions: (1) that it was once a far less expensive operation than its public counterpart; but (2) that the gap separating them in per-pupil costs has been narrowing substantially, even dramatically, during recent years. The reasons for the first deduction are principally the following: (a) the cheaply constructed facilities, once so common, were integral parts of the church-plants; (b) classes were extremely large—often with a PTR of 60 or 70; (c) the instructors were almost exclusively sisters who had little preparation and whose compensation was bare subsistence; and (d) the curriculum was limited to a few secular basics, catechetical instruction, and religious indoctrination and rituals.

During recent years, especially since 1955-56, and particularly on the secondary level, this situation has been changing—rapidly and decisively. According to Bartell (Table XIII) the average salary of a sister was $750 to $900 in 1958, which rose to $1,000 or $1,200 in 1963. The *Data Bank* states that this norm increased to $1,285 in 1967, $1,450 in 1968, and $1,995 in 1970-71; and we found that sisters in some dioceses were receiving up to $2,500 or even $2,750, in addition to housing and various other fringe benefits. Furthermore, the number of lay teachers now exceeds the religious; and, although their pay has advanced considerably over the level of 1962-63, when, in Ohio, it was $2,388 less than in the public schools (Bartell p. 100), it is still well below public school parity. This, and the fact that there is no tenure in Catholic schools, has resulted in an enormous turnover—about 250% greater than in the public (p.112).

According to Bartell's findings, elementary per-pupil costs increased in San Francisco between 1958 and 1963 from $97.37 to $126.30; on the secondary level, from $243.39 to $262.54. According to *Data Bank,* this

244

rose to $240.81 in 1970-71 in the elementary level; to $481 in the diocesan, and to $612.57 in the private secondaries. But when the "contributed services" are included, the *Data Bank* found that the true per-pupil cost in elementary schools was $309.35 in 1970-71; $650.85 in diocesan and $819.63 in the private secondaries. In the United States as a whole, in all public schools, the per-pupil ADA cost was $472 in 1960 and $954 in 1970—including the capital outlay and amortization of debt. In 1960, the operational cost was $375 and in 1970, $858.

As lay teachers have replaced religious and the salaries of both have risen in Catholic schools, the component of "contributed services" has become smaller. For example, in 1967-68, when elementary per-pupil cost was $246.00, the cash outlay was $145 and the contributed factor $101. In 1970-71, the cost rose to $309.35, of which the contributed portion fell to $68. In the diocesan high schools, the shift was even more decisive: of the $579.40 cost in 1967-68, $244.50 was contributed; in 1970-71, only $168.85 of $650.83 was so classified.

Since it seems that this process must continue, the difference each year between per-pupil cost in Catholic and public schools will undoubtedly decline. Among reasons why they have not yet reached parity, the following seem obvious:

(1) The pupil-teacher ratio in Catholic schools is still, in spite of considerable reduction, far higher than in the public. For example, in the latter it was 25.2 in 1939-40, 24.4 in 1949-50, 23.4 in 1959-60, and 20.9 in 1969-70. In the Catholic, it was 37.9 in 1962-63 and 26.4 in 1969-70.

(2) Although the salaries of sisters and men religious have been increased, their "contributed services" still constitute a significant element. If present trends continue, however, the religious will cost more and more or they will be replaced by lay teachers, whose compensation, unless their work is to be highly inferior, must become at least somewhat comparable to those in public education.[a]

(3) Since lay teachers in Catholic schools have no tenure, receive only minimum salaries, and rarely have any provision for retirement, they are extremely restive and there is a huge turnover. If the Catholic schools are to achieve parity with the public, they must in time pay comparable salaries—which will increase per-pupil cost materially.

---

a.   We found that most teaching brothers receive from $4,000 to $4,500, plus housing, transportation, health insurance, and other fringe benefits, which, in some cases, increased their total cost to more than $6,000—in addition to the expense of their education and preparation. And it should not be forgotten that they pay no Social Security or Income Tax and that they can purchase many items at discount prices.

(4) Catholic schools or pupils are already receiving substantial subsidies directly or indirectly from the public purse, as shown in Part Two. None or little of this is usually computed as a component in per-pupil cost.

(5) Whereas public schools usually supply free textbooks and other valuable desiderata for which Catholic students either pay or do without, this is another important differentiating element in total cost.

(6) Since the parochial school can be as selective as it wishes, it need have no worry concerning problem children, the mentally retarded, the juvenile delinquents, the pregnant girls, etc., who cause a great deal of additional expense in the public schools. If the parochials were required to accept a cross-section of the population, their operating costs would increase enormously.

(7) Since Catholic schools are almost entirely white, they do not have to grapple with the problem of racial friction or the lower Negro academic achievement.

(8) Many Catholic schools are lacking in programs comparable to those in the public schools such as in music, debating, athletic contests, and other cultural programs, which are expensive and require elaborate facilities. The place of these is taken largely by a dedication to religious formation and instruction.

(9) Catholic schools are generally deficient in the expensive equipment necessary for laboratory work in chemistry, physics, etc.; and this is one of the reasons why shared-time programs, as in Dubuque and the Detroit Archdiocese, have become popular.

(10) One of the most costly types of education now carried on in the public sector consists of the rapidly expanding technical institutes, which are springing up all over the country and which involve enormous investments in sophisticated equipment. These schools, established for high-school students or graduates and older adults, are never found in any parochial school system.

For reasons like these, per-pupil costs in Catholic schools have been less than in the public. However, as it has become increasingly necessary for the parochials to supply services at least somewhat comparable to those in public schools, the base for their lower costs has been eroding rapidly.

Probably the private Catholic high school comes nearest to its public counterpart. Here, without including various expenditures which public schools must sustain, the per-pupil cost of $819.63 in 1969-70 included $207.05 for contributed services. Since it is certain that this component will continue to decline, the day cannot be far distant when per-pupil cost there will rise to parity with that of the public high school.

Should such private institutions be publicly funded, it seems very likely that they would become similar to the elite secular schools which dot the land and where per-pupil costs are frequently double or triple those in the public domain.

It is particularly noteworthy that whereas tuition charges were almost unknown in the Catholic elementaries as late as twenty or even ten years ago, these have become more and more prevalent. We found only one city—Dubuque—where there was still none in the grade schools. Bartell states that there was no such charge in Youngstown as late as 1963. The *Data Bank* reports that in 1969-70, 21.8% of all Catholic elementary school income derived from tuition, 5% from fees, 64.4% from subsidies, and 8.8% from other sources. On the secondary level, 59.4% came from tuition, 21% from subsidies, and 19.6% from other sources. It states also that 42.8% of all parochial schools charged less than $50 in 1969-70 and only 4.2% as much as $200. Thus, Catholic high schools are financed chiefly through tuition, but elementary schools are still maintained principally by subsidies from the operating churches. We found this to be true in every city where we interviewed Catholic educators.

Table VIII shows the pupil-teacher ratios in the Catholic educational system together with the number and proportion of lay and religious instructors and personnel from 1920 to 1971. We see here that the proportion of pupils to staff dropped from 38.8 in 1920 to 31.3 in 1961, and 22.1 in 1971. However, "staff" here includes not only administrators, but all part-time teachers; when these factors are taken into account, the ratio becomes very different, as shown in Table IX, based on statistics supplied by Neuwien and the *Data Bank*, where we find that the true PTR was 36-40 on the elementary level and 26.0 on the secondary in 1962-63; 33.4 in 1967-68 and 29.2 in 1969-70 on the elementary; and 20 in 1967-68 and 18 in 1969-70 on the secondary. This gives a composite ratio of 37.9 in 1962-63 and 26.4 in 1969-70, which contrasts with 23.4 in 1959-60 and 20.9 in 1969-70 in the public schools.

Since both PTRs and PSRs are considerably higher in Catholic than in public schools, it would seem that the latter probably offer a wider selection of courses, more extra-curricular activities, or greater individual attention. And when we take into account the time devoted in parochial schools to specific religious studies and rituals, the disparity in academic education appears to be sharply intensified.

The second fact which emerges is the tremendous increase in the ratio of lay personnel in Catholic schools: this was 7.9% in 1920, 9.3% in 1945, 12.6% in 1950, 18.9% in 1955, 31.3% in 1961, 37.7% in 1965, and 53.4% in 1971.

To discover how pupil-staff ratios have evolved in Catholic schools during the last hundred years, we consulted Catholic directories for reports from each school in Dubuque, St. Paul, and Milwaukee. Although some variations emerged, the development in all three has followed a similar course: in Dubuque, the pupil- staff ratio gradually dropped from 40.4 in 1905 to 25.7 in 1971; meanwhile, the number of lay teachers increased from 2 in 64, or 3.1%, to 163 in 308, or 52.9%. In St. Paul, the lay teachers increased from 1 among 166 in 1905 to 494 in 866 in 1971, or 57%, ratios which vary only slightly from the national norm. In Milwaukee, lay instructors increased from 3 among 405 in 1910 to 688 among 1,274 in 1970, who then comprised 54.1% of the teaching staff. It is therefore probable that the experience of these cities very nearly parallels that in hundreds of others.

The data in Table VIII and IX combine Catholic elementary and secondary enrollments. However, we should point out that in the parish elementary schools, which enrolled about 80% or more of all Catholic pupils, lay teachers were virtually unknown until after 1950; and the pupil-teacher ratio was very high. In many of these, between 1880 and 1920, we commonly find 3 or 4 sisters for 120 or even 150 pupils; for example, in 1905, St. Raphael's in Dubuque had 16 sisters for 678 pupils; St. Mary's, 15 sisters, and 1 lay teacher, for 665 pupils; Sacred Heart, 12 sisters and 1 lay teacher for 640 children: a total of 45 teachers for 1,995, a ratio of 44.3. Even in 1920, there was only a slight improvement: St. Raphael's then had 17 sisters for 502 pupils; St. Mary's, 16 for 604; and Sacred Heart, 15 for 667: 48 for 1,973, a ratio of 41.1.

In St. Paul, the ratio in many schools was even higher: in 1905, the Cathedral school had 12 sisters for 612 pupils; St. Agnes, 19 for 1,100; St. Mary's, 11 for 550; and St. John's, 5 for 265—47 for 2,507, a ratio of 54.8. In 1920, these four schools had 53 sisters for 2,494 children, a ratio of 47.1.

In Milwaukee, the pupil-teacher ratio was 66.2 in 1892; 46.6 in 1920; 35.3 in 1964; and 24.8 in 1970, including a considerable but undisclosed proportion of part-time teachers.

In 1889-90, the PSR to enrollment in all American public schools was 34.9 and to ADA 22.4; in 1920, they were 31.8 and 24.6 respectively; in 1970, both were 20.9.

Even in the early part of this century most public school teachers were certificated; and by 1920, virtually all of them were so. Since 1930, the bachelor's degree has become virtually mandatory, even on the elementary level; and since 1950, it has become almost universal. For years, a large proportion of all teachers have had master's degrees as well.[a] In Arizona, for example, a teacher's certificate is voided after six years unless a master's degree has been obtained. Many other states have similar requirements.

Before 1920, a certificated nun was indeed a rarity; and even in 1969-70, 31.3% of religious full-time instructors and 43.5% of lay teachers were uncertified in the elementary Catholic schools; on the secondary level, these respective ratios were 28.6 and 29.6%.[b] Since there were 104,137 religious and 90,066 lay teachers in 1968, there must have been nearly 70,000 at that time who could not have been eligible to teach in a public school.

---

a.   The 1970 *Digest of Educational Statistics,* p. 40, reports that 69.6% of all public school teachers had a bachelor's degree in 1965-66 and that 21.9% had a master's; that 7% had certificates without a 4-year degree; and that .1% had doctorates.

b.   *Data Bank* for 1967-70, p. 16.

The Argument in Justification

1. A Liberal Educator

Robert M. Hutchins, formerly president of the University of Chicago, and later head of the Center for the Study of Democratic Institutions at Santa Barbara, California, declared: "The Wall Jefferson erected in the name of the First Amendment[a] rose no higher than was necessary to wall off the religious opinions and practices of citizens from interference by government. His letter does not suggest that he would have opposed public expenditures that might benefit schools under religious management."[b]

2. The Ecumenical Council

Since the highest authority in the Catholic Church is presumably an ecumenical council, we quote passages from three declarations issued by Vatican II (1962-1965):

---

a.   In his letter to the Danbury Baptist Church Association, Jefferson wrote: "Believing with you that religion is a matter that lies solely between man and his God, that he need account to none other for his faith or his worship, that the legislative powers of government reach actions only, and not opinions, I contemplate with sovereign reverence that act of the whole American people which declared that their legislature should 'make no law respecting an establishment of religion or prohibiting the free exercise thereof,' thus building a wall of separation between church and state."
b.   In an article in the *Saturday Evening Post,* June 8, 1962, entitled "A Liberal Calls for Aid for Church Schools."

From the Declaration on Religious Freedom

"Parents, moreover, have the right to determine, in accordance with their own religious beliefs, the kind of religious education that their children are to receive. Government, in consequence, must acknowledge the right of parents to make a genuinely free choice of schools and of other means of education, and the use of this freedom of choice is not to be made a reason for imposing unjust burdens on parents, whether directly or indirectly. Besides, the rights of parents are violated, if their children are forced to attend lessons or instructions which are not in agreement with their religious beliefs, or if a single system of education, from which all religious formation is excluded, is imposed upon all."

From the Declaration on Christian Education

". . . the public power, which has the obligation to protect and defend the rights of citizens, must see to it, in its concern for distributive justice, that public subsidies are paid out in such a way that parents are truly free to choose according to their conscience the schools they want for their children.

"The Church reminds parents of the duty that is theirs to arrange and even demand that their children be able to enjoy these aids and advance in their Christian formation to a degree that is abreast of their development in secular subjects. Therefore, the Church esteems highly those civil authorities and societies which, bearing in mind the pluralism of contemporary society and respecting religious freedom, assist families so that the education of their children can be imparted in all schools according to the individual and religious principles of the families. . . .

"Therefore the State . . . must always keep in mind the principle of subsidiarity so that there is no kind of school monopoly, for this is opposed to the native rights of the human person. . . .

"The Catholic school . . . retains . . . the utmost importance . . . . Consequently, this Sacred Synod proclaims anew what has already been taught . . . namely, the right of the Church freely to establish and to conduct schools of every type and level. . . .

"The Council also reminds Catholic parents of the duty of entrusting their children to Catholic schools wherever and whenever it is possible, of supporting these schools to the best of their ability, and of cooperating with them for the education of their children."

From the Declaration of Conscience

"The right of parents to choose the religious schools and education in which their children will be reared should not merely be supported, but guaranteed. The state MUST contract to protect this right and not merely consent to it."[a]

3. The Massachusetts Advisory Council on Education

In March, 1969, this entity representing the Catholic point of view, issued an elaborate study[b] dealing with parochial education, the impact on public schools when the private close, and the probable costs to taxpayers should they be compelled to assume all educational costs. This Report declared: "A mark of genius in American society is its pluralism—that quality which welcomes diversity. . . . The excellence of our educational system and its service to all levels and elements of our people is due to the combination of public education with our independent systems of religious and secular schools."

4. A Catholic Schoolman

The Reverend John F. Gilbert, Superintendent of the St. Paul Archdiocese, declared in the course of an intricate argument: "The test, then, is not whether the agency or organization receiving the [public] funds is private, or under private control, but whether the specific activity carried on by that body is essentially one in the public interest. . . . We find the decisions of the federal and state courts fully supportive of our conclusion that the state may spend funds on public-interest activities being carried forward by private organizations."[c]

---

a.   Since Canon Law categorically forbids any Catholic parent from sending his child to a non-Catholic school without the consent of his bishop and since, in countries such as Spain and Portugal, Catholic schools enjoy a complete monopoly, it would seem that these declarations are intended only for countries like the United States, Sweden, Mexico, or those with Communist regimes.

b.   *The Measurement of Alternative Costs of Educating Catholic School Children in Public Schools.*

c.   *In "A Philosophy of Education," published by the N. Dakota* Nonpublic Education Report of 1970.

5. An American President

In spite of the fact that on election eve, President Richard M. Nixon declared himself unalterably in favor of church-state separation, he soon invited Catholic educators for conferences at the White House and he has issued a number of statements dealing with parochiaid, of which the following is typical: "The non-public elementary and secondary schools in the United States have long been an integral part of the nation's educational establishment. They supplement . . . our public school system. They provide a diversity which our educational system would otherwise lack. . .

"There is an equally important consideration: these schools—non-sectarian, Catholic, Jewish, Protestant, and other—often add a dimension of spiritual value to education by affirming a moral code by which to live. No government can be indifferent to the potential collapse of such schools."[a]

On August 18, 1971, the President declared in an address to the Knights of Columbus in New York, who gave him a standing ovation, that he was on their side and that they could depend on him to help them get parochiaid.

6. The Founder of Citizens for Educational Freedom

Father Virgil C. Blum, S.J., the originating spirit of CEF, has probably stated the rationale of parochiaid more fully and in more specific detail than any other protagonist. His *Freedom in Education*[b] covers every facet of the subject and purports to establish an irrefutable logical, moral, and juridical basis for public subsidies for church-related elementary and secondary schools.

He summarizes the many grants by which the federal government is already subsidizing education, especially on the college and university level. Since almost every one now accepts the validity of such programs (p. 147), it should be obvious, he declares, that similar support for elementary and secondary church-related schools is even more compelling; and that there cannot be any constitutional objection to conferring similar benefits for the study of secular subjects (159), especially when given in the form of vouchers to parents. The objection that such aid might nable the sectarian school to release funds for religious instruction is entirely irrelevant (169).

---

a. Statement issued April 21, 1971.
b. Published 1965, by Doubleday.

Father Blum describes in detail the nature of the God-centered, church-related school, where religion is a permeating reality which gives meaning and significance to the entire course of study. For this reason, he rejects all shared-time programs, because, when the child is subjected to them, he partakes of two totally different and incompatible religious orientations (26-27). Shared-time, therefore, involves compromises which upset the Catholic conscience; it destroys the principle that education must be an integrated whole (35); and it may lead to a condition of moral and religious schizophrenia, in which all values will be rejected (38).

Perhaps the crux of Father Blum's reasoning is that all schools and all education are permeated with religion: there is no such thing as neutrality concerning God in the classroom. The public schools, he declares, have always been deeply religious, and are so now. From the beginning, they were Protestant in every sense of the word and remained so through most of the 19th century (64). Not only was the Protestant religion forced upon Catholic children against their vehement protests; physical punishment was inflicted to compel them to study and practice it. The courts upheld the practice of reading the King James version of the Bible; in Boston, a court even exonerated a teacher who flogged a Catholic child for refusing to read it (65).

Now, however, in a series of landmark decisions, says Father Blum, the Supreme Court has established a new state-enforced orthodoxy (71). The public schools are, indeed, no longer Protestant, but they are no less religious than before: they have embraced that fourth religion, known as Secularism, or Humanism. In the Protestant school, the Catholic child received a God-centered education, even though doctrines were inculcated totally in conflict with his own. In the secularist, he is taught silently, insidiously, and all but irresistibly that God is completely irrelevant (45). We have, therefore, as always, a state-subsidized religious establishment, in which the government intrudes into the very sanctuary of the child's soul and destroys his freedom of conscience and his right to religious integrity.

If the State can subsidize one kind of religion in the public schools, it is equally legal to subsidize another in a church-related school; and if it can subsidize secular instruction in one, it can do the same for another. For this reason, there can be no valid objection to granting vouchers, income-tax refunds, or other forms of aid, which parents may use as they see fit.

With the elimination of the three traditional God-centered religions, we have established in their stead a new man-centered faith. Secularists have a right to their own opinions, but not to force them upon Protestants, Catholics, and Jews. However, since the moral and religious values of this new faith now permeate the curriculum of all public schools, every child in them is forced to accept them. Every day, year in and year out, he

254

is exposed to this indoctrination (79). God-fearing parents, therefore, find themselves in a terrible dilemma: either they must submit to such perversion of their moral and spiritual integrity, or they must suffer the punishment of being forced to support a second educational system (80).

It is impossible, says Blum, for any intelligent teacher to instruct in literature, history, sociology, politics, economics, or even the physical and life sciences, without permeating and evaluating these courses with his own basic concepts, beliefs, and understanding—i.e., the philosophy and the religion by which he lives. It cannot be otherwise.

It is true that in a church-related school a specific denominational religion permeates every subject (86); however, since secular subjects are taught, the aid to religion is only incidental, and therefore irrelevant (89). The decisive question is not *who* is entrusted with public funds, but for *what* purpose they are expended. Since the church-related school performs a public service, it is entitled to public money (100).

Religious freedom, guaranteed by the First Amendment, is one of the most treasured of American rights; the individual has liberties which come, not from the state, but from a higher authority (46). The issue is simply whether a child shall have the right to pursue secular truth in association with religious conviction in a school of his own choice; without this right, religious freedom is constricted or destroyed.

This freedom means, for example, that Jews must be free without penalty to send their children to schools where the Talmudic law, in addition to secular subjects, is taught (49). Freedom of choice in education means that parents may send their children to any school they desire without assuming any additional burdens because they do so (50). In virtually all countries except the United States and those behind the Iron Curtain, such freedom is guaranteed (51).

When parents must assume an additional burden to exercise a religious freedom guaranteed by the First Amendment, their rights of conscience are violated (52); it is as if a fine were imposed upon them because of their religion. When Congress or a state denies public funds for religious schools, it is suppressing the freedom of conscience by indirection (60-61). When the state withholds public benefits from them and forcibly indoctrinates children in values which clash violently with those of their parents, it compels a conformity and uniformity which are most repugnant in a democracy and highly violative of the human personality (61). Such thought-control, found under Nazi and other authoritarian regimes, has no place in a free society (62).

In a larger sense, however, this whole question of equality for church-related schools is not a religious issue at all; it is one of civil rights, in the same sense and manner as it relates to Negro children when denied a decent school. Since the Constitution guarantees the freedom of choice in religion and since all children must receive schooling, it is a violation of basic civil rights even to ask whether a child attends a public or a religious school in order to qualify for public funds. This is a principle guaranteed by our Constitution as well as by the United Nations Declaration of Human Rights (118).

When the Masons and the Ku Kluxers forced a referendum in Oregon which closed religious schools, they made a concerted and vicious attack upon basic religious freedom (122).

The conformity of thought and belief now enforced in our public and monopolistic schools, stultifies, paralyzes, and destroys initiative and originality in the mind and spirit (125).[a] By adequately financing church-related schools, we will create a healthy rivalry and competition in education, precisely as has happened in Holland; this is the principle on which American industry operates and which enables it to pay high wages and produce superior products at competitive prices (137).

Father Blum indicates, however, that many Catholic laymen do not share his convictions. He states that they are of four kinds: (1) those who care only for material things; (2) the great number who have resigned all decision-making to their pastors and who show no interest in policy; (3) those who care, but will not do anything; and (4) the militant few who care and will fight to support the CEF (214-16). He admits that in city after city, he has found Catholic parents, particularly the better educated, becoming disenchanted with Catholic education and sending their children to the public schools (19). One odd result emerging from the financial crisis in Catholic education, he says, is the fact that some Catholics have become ardent advocates of a pedagogical dream: namely, that Sunday school and evening classes in religion could be substituted for the full-time school to the general advantage of the Catholic Church and its communicants (41).

7. General Criticism of the Public Schools

The critics of public education are legion: we hear that the schools are too permissive; that they make pupils into robots; that they are always experimenting with methods which do not produce results; that they are hotbeds of secularism or atheism; that they constitute a monolithic monopoly, stifle competition, and frustrate individual striving for excellence;

---

a.   We wonder what Father Blum thinks of the provisions relating to education in the Canon Law of the Catholic Church and of education in Spain, Portugal, Italy, Quebec, etc.

that they leave the brighter pupils bored; that they are too expensive; that teachers are interested chiefly in less work and higher salaries; that administrators have made themselves into oligarchs; that children do not learn to read or write.

The list is endless.

8. An Anonymous Anathema

There is an organization whose officers or promoters are unknown and which calls itself American United, doing business from a P. O. Box in Malibu, California, from which it conducts a national campaign against the public schools, denounced as The Child Seducers. It advertises for sale at the price of $4.95 a long-play recording by John Carradine giving "The best reason for the abolishment of public education." We are told that "The single most 'burning' issue in America today" is the destruction of our youth in the public schools. A brochure offers "The incredible account of how your child receives an indoctrination for world revolution. . . . How subversion, perversion, and pornography are being promoted by the Health, Education, and Welfare Department-financed S.I.E. C.U.S. sex-ploiters, with your money. — Why they promote 'unisex.' The new morality, the 'no morality,' the pernicious, lewd, and lascivious—reduction to the lowest common denominator of human existence. What every parent must know, now—the child you save may be your own."[a]

The Argument in Opposition

(In the following, we include a variety of viewpoints, ranging from those of loyal Catholics who see something that needs correction or reformation in the parochial schools or who wish to replace them with other methods of teaching religion; as well as those of Protestants and secularists who oppose them on principle and of educators who do so on philosophical grounds.)

---

a. It is interesting to note the similarity between this excoriation and the denunciations of the public schools emanating from Archbishop Hughes of New York in 1840-42.

By Catholics

The Most Reverend William R. McManus

Reverend McManus, Auxiliary Bishop of Chicago, discussing the situation of the Catholic schools in America, was certainly frank with his fellow-bishops when he declared: "Serious as are the schools' financial problems, they are not the main crisis. It is rather a crisis of confidence in the Catholic schools' future . . . a mixture of disenchantment . . . reluctance to make the immense investments needed. . . . If they wanted to spend it, Catholics have more than enough money to adequately finance the nation's fiscally strapped parochial elementary and high schools. But they apparently don't shell out because of a 'crisis of confidence' in the schools' future . . . and an uncertainty about the schools' direction in the post-conciliar Church, and an occasional conviction about the philosophical and theological premises for the Church's direct involvement in the work of the schools. If this crisis of confidence is not faced and solved soon, it may lead to a worse crisis, a shortage of students. We may find ourselves in the embarrassing predicament of having plenty of buildings, teachers, and money, but few pupils to educate. Declining enrollment is a sign that this crisis may have begun."[a]

A Catholic Woman Speaks Out

In her challenging book, *Are Parochial Schools the Answer?*,[b] the prominent Catholic writer, Mary Perkins Ryan, sets forth a thesis reminiscent of Orestes Brownson and even Jeremiah Crowley. She notes that even before 1963 some Catholic parents had removed their children from the parochial schools because they felt that a better religious formation could be achieved at home. Greater dissatisfaction, she declares, stems from the facts that (1) the pastor alone controls the school; (2) the nuns or other religious conduct it; and (3) the parents have nothing to say about educational policy (p. 52). She points out that nuns and priests are regarded as the only fully mature or responsible members of the Church; and that the school is a means of segregating Catholics from the general com-

---

a.   Statement in Houston, Texas, April 17, 1969, at a convention of Catholic educators; printed in the 1970 Catholic *Almanac,* p. 155.
b.   Holt, Rinehart, and Winston, 1963.

munity (54). Furthermore, while the public school must accept all who apply, the parochials can reject any applicant at will—something which public school teachers can hardly fail to resent (55).

Since Catholic laymen have been afraid of asking questions, they have developed the defensive attitude of the besieged (87). Mrs. Ryan implies that Catholic indoctrination creates nothing but a type of fossilized and perpetual youth (92), forever incapable of maturity, self-reliance, or independent thinking.

She ridicules the position held, for example, by Father Blum, that "secular" humanism may in any sense properly be called a religion; it may determine a person's attitude, but it does not teach any dogma nor does it offer a link between man and God (97).

What Catholics need now, she declares, is a church-centered system of instruction which shall be wholly religious, omit any attempt at secular instruction, and call for the personal thought and effort of the laity. It must not consist of catechetical indoctrination (112). We should have a multiphased and coordinated effort to awaken the Catholic community as a whole to the possibilities of communal worship (133); the laity must see that their role is not simply to keep their purses open and their mouths shut; on the contrary, they too must give of their intelligence, skill, and initiative for the work of the Father (134).

Mrs. Ryan concludes that, since it will be impossible for the Church to provide a full, secular education for all Catholic youth as well as total religious formation, it should concentrate on the latter (140-42); and parents should be helped and encouraged in their task of accomplishing this result (143). Since the Confraternity of Christian Doctrine was created precisely for this purpose, it should not be difficult to impart this help and instruction under the supervision of parish boards, where all Catholics, young and old, would enjoy the benefits of this apostolate (146).

The overriding reason for establishing schools in the first place was the fear that Catholic children attending public schools might lose their faith. Such anxiety, says the author, need no longer exist; for the children who graduate from the public schools are wholly as firm in their support of the Church as the products of the parochial (151-2).

Even if it were possible to provide a Catholic education for every Catholic child, Mrs. Ryan doubts that it would be desirable; for it offers only a sheltered, hothouse environment, and does not prepare the child for the impact of the secular atmosphere in which he must spend his adult life (157). In the public schools, on the contrary, he would come into contact with Jewish, Protestant, and secular thinking or people, all of which would be highly desirable for him (153).

The Team of Koob and Shaw

When Father C. Albert Koob and Mr. Russell Shaw criticize the Catholic schools almost in the spirit of Orestes Brownson, they certainly do so with the highest credentials. They are highly placed and fervently loyal Catholics, and what they say in *S.O.S. for Catholic Schools* assuredly deserves the most careful consideration. They declare that no one has cried more loudly than the Church that parents have the primary right to educate their children according to conscience; yet this "right" has meant only the abject surrender of their children to clerics, who have told the parents in no uncertain terms that their duty is to pay and say nothing (p. 13). In the Catholic schools, one-man or one-woman autocracy has always been and still remains the rule (35); no wonder, then, that the "crisis of confidence," so widely lamented, has become a general fact (40). The continuation of this kind of tyranny must lead to even greater disaffection among the educated, prosperous, and articulate members of the Catholic community (40). In the Church, the bishop and the religious orders own and operate the schools (44); laymen are rejecting the institutions for which they have paid so dearly but in the operation of which they have no influence whatever (46). And so, while the People of God are rejecting paternalism and authority, the schools continue to exercise their contemptuous tyranny in their historic manner (95-6). The authors point out that the Catholic schools cannot survive without the support of the laity; and that such support is unlikely to continue without decisive reforms.

Finally, the authors deny that the public schools are monolithic, except in the one fact that they exclude religious indoctrination (114); i.e., they are religiously neutral. Here again, we find prominent Catholics taking direct issue with the basic theories of Archbishops Hughes and Ireland and Father Blum.

Mr. Brown and Father Greeley

Can Catholic Schools Survive? is another valuable work by two prominent and loyal Catholics. The authors admit candidly that the number of Catholic students who are committed or well instructed Christians is "appallingly small." Since this is true, greater stress must be placed upon religion and the CCD apostolate (p. 101). Religious instruction, they say, cannot be left to the parents (67).

The authors agree with Crowley that the public schools were forced into religious neutralism through Catholic pressure (156): Catholics are therefore in no position to criticize them because they are non-religious.

And they ridicule in the strongest language the Blum thesis that the religious neutralism of the public schools constitutes a secularist religion or orthodoxy and that they are, consequently, actually sectarian institutions. Under such a definition, the absence of religion becomes a new religion—a preposterous conclusion; nor do the public schools, declare the authors, in any event, teach secularism even as a philosophy: "They are merely neutral toward religion" (155).

The authors are unsparing in their criticism: the laity have no voice in the operation of the Catholic schools (130); and, since they began withdrawing their children in large numbers even before tuition was charged, they did so for reasons other than financial (128). The schools do not publish any budgets; and have no plans to update the curriculum, the facilities, or the preparation of teachers (132).

We may well be surprised at other statements: obtaining tax-money, they say, will not solve the problems of the Catholic schools, even if they could obtain it (129); should they get partial support, they will demand more and more, and the government will supervise the instruction until its religious content is totally eliminated or destroyed (159). The universal tuition-voucher plan is pure nonsense, since the public schools are already free (159). The "double-taxation" argument, advanced by Catholic clerics, is totally without validity, for millions of other people who have no children in the public schools pay the general property tax and support education through other levies (174); and Catholics can scarcely expect Protestants who believe the Church of Rome to be the Whore of Babylon, willingly to supply money for the maintenance of her operations (163).

Nor will the People of God support the Catholic schools unless they are given more control and responsibility in their operation. The Catholic, like the public, schools must be tuition-free; they must become democratic; and at least 90% of all Catholic youth should, in time, be enrolled in them (145). The Catholic community can easily afford the expense if it wishes to assume it, now as it did for generations (177); it is not money that is presently driving Catholics away from their schools, but a lack of confidence in them together with the feeling that they do not belong to the people who paid and pay for them.

A Critical Jesuit

Among the sharp critics of Catholic schools, we must number Neil G. McCluskey, S.J., who declares in his *Catholic Education in America* that "four less than benevolent outcomes" resulted from the drive since 1884 to place every Catholic child in a Catholic school: (1) clerical domination;

(2) overcommitment to elementary education; (3) confusion of academic and pastoral purposes; and (4) the substitution of the school for the home and the church in the religious formation of the child (pp. 27-28). As for the plethora of small women's colleges that came into existence since 1935, "they condemn themselves, for the most part, to the limbo of mediocrity" (36).

Resolution of the National Association of
Catholic Laymen Concerning State Aid to
Parochial Schools

(After declaring that Catholic laymen contribute "vast sums of money" to the support of the Church but that no accounting is ever made of such funds, the Resolution states):

"The NAL reaffirms its position . . . calling for full and open financial disclosure, subject to public audit, by all church institutions on all levels...

"Increasing numbers of Catholics hold that the parochial system has outlived its usefulness and ought to be phased out. . . .

"There exist today strong indications that present efforts in religious education fail to 'build the Kingdom' in two ways. First, they fail directly the children they are predominantly designed to serve. . . . They fail also through a persistent dependence on the theory that knowing about 'religion' makes a 'religious' person. Secondly, they fail indirectly the entire Catholic community, because the priority they enjoy and the resources they demand militate against any real search for a relevant mode of parish life; one that would meet the needs of the individual Christian, his family and the broad community. . . .

"In view of this, we of NAL strongly urge that formal religious education programs cease and every resource presently used in such programs be redirected into a total comprehensive, to the human and religious needs of all; that every possible resource be directed to explore ways of establishing meaningful Christian community life."[a]

---

a.   The National Association of Catholic Laymen has (1971) 24 affiliates and 12,000 active members, which sent delegates to a national convention held in July, 1971, in La Jolla, California. The Resolution, quoted above, was embodied in a letter written by the Executive Vice President of the Association, Mr. Donald E. Nicodemus, and sent to Dr. Otto F. Krauschaar, Chairman of the Commission to Study State Aid to Non-Public Education, in Baltimore, Maryland.

By Protestants and Secularists

Dr. Leo Pfeffer

The eminent Constitutional lawyer and co-author of *Church and State in the United States,* Leo Pfeffer, declared that "Separation and religious freedom are aspects of a dual assumption upon which our whole democracy rests. One is the assumption of voluntariness in matters of conscience and spirit and in matters of man in his relation to God. This is as fundamental an element of the American democratic philosophy as anything can be . . . the use of tax-raised funds for religious schools violates the guaranty of religious freedom no less than the separation of church and state."[a]

Dr. George LaNoue

In his *Public Funds for Parochial Schools?,* George R. LaNoue declares that "If private schools were to be supported by tax funds, the practical effects would be that the American people would lose their actual control of the use of the taxes paid by all the people for purposes common to the whole society." This "could easily lead additional religious . . . or other groups to undertake full-scale parochial or private education with reliance on public tax support. This would destroy the public school system or at least weaken it so gravely that it could not possibly adequately meet the educational needs of all citizens. . . ." (pp. 1-2).

And again: "If the state supported parochial schools . . . the freedom of individual choice would be replaced by the coercion of taxation. This would affect not only the parochial constituent but, even worse, those of a different religion or of no religion. Theirs would be a true loss of religious liberty. The financial sacrifices made to send children to parochial schools are no different from the . . . sacrifices other people make to achieve their religious goals" (27-28).

Emmett McLoughlin, Ex-Priest

"Catholic parochial schools exist not because of the desire of Catholic parents or children for religious schools but because of the edicts of Canon Law, the encyclicals of the Popes, and decisions of the American Catholic hierarchy. . . .

---

a.   In "Freedom and Separation: America's Contribution to Civilization."

"The head of every parochial school is . . . the pastor of the adjacent sponsoring Church. Pastors are appointed by the local bishop . . . not because of their interest in education, or their ability as teachers or their pre-eminence in the arts and sciences. They are appointed because of their administrative skill, their success in raising money and their personal loyalty to the bishop and the hierarchy.

"The encyclicals of the Popes and the public statements of American bishops . . . constantly emphasize the rights of parents in education. In the parochial school, parents have no rights.   They have no voice in the location, the size or cost of the school building. They cannot vote for a school trustee (there are none), decide on a principal, or have a voice regarding the education or personality of a teacher. They have nothing to say regarding textbooks or curriculum. . . .

"In many American dioceses, where there are sufficient or nearly sufficient Catholic schools, the canon [No. 1374] is enforced under penalty of mortal sin and the refusal of absolution as long as children remain in a public school."[a]

Paul Blanshard, American Scholar and Author

"Under the Franco regime it is quite natural that the Caudillo's particular brand of fascism and the doctrines of Catholicism should be completely dovetailed in school textbooks. If there is a doubt in anyone's mind that the Catholic hierarchy itself opposes freedom, the doubts are instantly resolved when one reads the catechisms used by the children in Spanish national schools. They are naked and unashamed in their scorn of freedom of the mind. They are equally outspoken in condemning the institutions of Western democracy.

"In different parts of Spain I purchased several of the standard school textbooks which outline the moral basis of clerical fascism for young children. . . the Church textbooks used in Spain's national schools teach the Spanish children the identical, reactionary ideas of Pius IX's *Syllabus of Errors*. I found a number of young Spaniards who told me that they had been compelled by their teachers to memorize virtually all of this work from cover to cover when they attended the national schools. It is the political and moral Bible of Spanish elementary education."[b]

---

a.   *American Culture and Catholic Schools*, 1960, Lyle Stuart, pp. 43-45.

b.   *Freedom and Catholic Power in Spain and Portugal,* Beacon Press, 1962, pp. 112-113.

Editorial in the Washington *Post* (Sept. 30, 1971)

"Although there are those who seem to regard it as a restraint on religious worship, the First Amendment is, above all else, a guarantor of religious liberty. It reflects a recognition, as Mr. Justice Clark once put it for the Supreme Court, that 'the place of religion in our society is an exalted one, achieved through a long tradition of reliance on the home, the church and the inviolable citadel of the individual heart and mind. . . schools supported by public money and used by children of every faith and of no faith at all are not appropriate places for religious worship. . . .

"When men seek to use the public schools, which children attend by the requirement of law, to propogate faith, they confess a loss of faith in the home, the church, and the inviolable citadel of the individual heart and mind."

Editorial in the Washington *Evening Star* (Sept. 24, 1971)

"Religion in all its diversity is a vital element of strength in American life, and its erosion is a cause for deep concern. But it is folly to expect the schools to transmit it to the young, when many homes and churches are failing in that task, and to propose writing that desperate wish into the Constitution. Religious enrichment must flow from the family and the church; it cannot be legislated into being."

Loraine Boettner, Spokesman for Evangelical Protestantism

"The Roman Church not only promotes her own school system, but is strongly opposed to the American system of free public education. . . . This is true, first of all, because the Roman Church claims for herself and as a matter of right the privilege of supervising all education, so that the youth of the land can be efficiently directed toward that Church. . . .

"The ideal toward which the Roman Church strives is found in Spain where, under a concordat with the Vatican, the schools are financed by the government while the Roman Church supervises the curriculum, selects the teachers, and directs the education. . . . Protestant schools are prohibited. Why should anyone believe that the Roman Church in the United States would be satisfied with anything less ?"[a]

---

a.   *Roman Catholicism, op. cit.*, p. 368.

Gaston Cogdell, Director of Organization of
Americans United for Separation of Church and State

In a statement delivered April 27, 1971, to the Public Affairs Committee of the United States Senate: another "fallacy of the voucher plan is that a private citizen, the parent of a child enrolled in a sectarian private school, can do what a government agency itself cannot do—namely, authorize the giving of public funds to church institutions. By some magical and mystical process, the moral and constitutional strictures against the government using tax-money for sectarian enterprises is supposed to vanish when a piece of paper is given to a private citizen, a voucher certificate or coupon, that he gives to a church educational activity, which then presents it to the public treasury and presto! receives the public money. If it is wrong for the government itself to give tax money, taken by coercion from all citizens of all faiths, to enterprises owned and operated by the clergy and by the churches, then it is doubly wrong for a private citizen to assume this prerogative."

American School Administrators

At its 1971 convention, the American Association of School Administrators approved a resolution which declared in part: "Private and parochial schools . . . should not draw on the public treasury" because "the schools, traditionally operated in the public interest, would be removed from public to private control—control by each parent, which carries decentralization to absurdity; non-educational issues, such as race, background, or ideology could determine a school's income, hence its size, its ability to function effectively, and its survival; a massive bureaucracy would be necessary to enforce safeguards and regulations."

Edd Doerr, Director of Educational Relations
of Americans United

In testimony before the House Committee on Education and Labor on April 1, 1971: "Is it educationally sound to separate children—at public expense—by creed, race, ability, class, or the various prejudices and preferences of parents? . . .

"Hasn't the chief support for the voucher plan come from the same people who have long exuded hostility toward the idea of the common schools?"

266

A Militant Unitarian

The Reverend Paul R. Beattie, of All Souls Unitarian Church in Indianapolis, declared in a "Pulpit Editorial Against Looting the Public Treasury," of March 28, 1971: "The hierarchy of the Roman Catholic Church is showing its contempt and cynical disregard for the principles of American democracy. In state after state, the Church has been unrelenting in using its vast secular and financial power for the purpose of dipping its fingers into the public monies for the support of schools that the Catholics will not support. In assuming this posture, the Roman Catholic Church is fighting to destroy the historical principles which are the undergirding of the American experiment in democracy. Separation of church and state, freedom of religion, and universal education are all threatened by the sectarian drive for public funds."

Bishop Reuben H. Mueller, of the Indiana Area
United Methodist Church

"Private schools . . . exist because their patrons desire an educational dimension not provided in public schools. Supporters of private schools, therefore, desire specialized education. Further, private schools fail to serve in the public interest because they discriminate in enrollment policies. Public schools many not discriminate. Also, private schools are not subject to public regulation through elected or delegated representatives of the citizenry. Their policies are determined by small private associations . . . they are free to pursue educational policies with sectarian or partisan overtones. . . . State support of non-public schools could lead to a proliferation of private adventures into education, resulting in increased fragmentation and greater polarization of social and religious groups. . . . The selectivity practiced by non-public schools could cause the public schools to become the only agency responsible for the education of those who are economically, socially, and intellectually disadvantaged."

Resolution Dealing with Parochiaid of the 1971
Southern Baptist Convention

". . . regardless of the manner in which these funds are channeled into church schools" they would violate "the principle of religious liberty and . . . we hereby petition the federal and state governments to honor the principle of religious liberty and the constitutional position of separation of church and state inherent in the First Amendment to the U. S. Constitution. . . ."[a]

Statement of Elder R. R. Bietz, Vice President of
the General Conference of Seventh-Day Adventists

"The U. S. Supreme Court decision on public money for church schools has no effect on our schools. For Adventists, federal aid is out. We don't want it and we wouldn't take it. . . . One of the reasons we have schools is that we train young people to steep themselves in our religion, and this includes doctrine—in other words, the schools seek to make them good Adventists. . . . We believe in keeping church and state separate. Each can function better in its own sphere. To mix them would harm both."

Resolution Adopted by the Baptist Joint Committee
on Public Affairs, Washington, D. C., October 8, 1971

"We believe that the proposed voucher system will weaken rather than strengthen public education through the proliferation of inferior special interest schools which are essentially private schools. Although envisioned as an experimental program, we believe it will tend to become a continuing program . . . since its effects on public education are irreversible. We also express our concern that such a program will lead towards further polarization and fragmentation in the nation."[b]

Albert Shanker, President, New York Federation of Teachers

"The basic idea" of the voucher program "is to give each child (or his parent) the purchasing power to go into the free market and choose the public, private, or parochial school of his liking. . . .

"Like many other educational notions, vouchers are being sold as an 'experiment' . . . But not all experiments are alike. Some are harmless in that we try something new and, if we don't like the result, we go back to what was there before. . . . The voucher experiment is dangerous because it is irreversible. . . . Once great numbers of students depart from the public schools, there will be no schools for them to return to. . . . The result is inevitable—the end of public schools and the establishment of a system of tax-financed private education."[c]

a.   The Southern Baptist Convention with nearly 12 million members is the largest Protestant body in the United States.
b.   The Baptist Joint Committee represents about 25 million American Baptists.
c.   New York *Times* July 4, 1971.

"It is quite clear that the voucher idea, whether applied in New York City or throughout the United States, means the use of public moneys to educate the same children . . . but the schools will no longer be subject to control by the public through their democratically elected officials; nor will the students or parents in these voucher schools be guaranteed the constitutional rights which courts enforce in the public sector." [a]

"Blueprint for Disaster," Editorial in *Church and State*

(The Office of Economic Opportunity made two grants in 1969 and 1970 totalling $521,143 to the Harvard-based Center for the Study of Public Policy, with instructions to prepare a practical plan for financing elementary and secondary education through a system of voucher-payments. The group, headed by Director Christopher Jencks, in due course submitted a 219-page report called *Education Vouchers* in which seven plans are discussed. The following, from the October issue of *Church and State* is an analysis of the Jencks proposals.)

"The voucher system would" force all citizens "through taxation to support schools engaging in every sort of sectarian or political indoctrination, political and social action, and religious and political segregation. The Jencks report never mentions the fact that special kinds of indoctrination and discrimination are the main reasons for the existence of over 90% of all nonpublic schools. Not only would every citizen lose his right to support only the religious institutions of his free choice, but large established religious groups would derive proportionately more benefits than smaller groups with more thinly and widely scattered memberships. The voucher plan would 'establish' the largest church in any area. . . . .

"Community and interfaith harmony would disintegrate and America would become more like Northern Ireland or the Netherlands. The educational diversity and rich mix of children and teachers now found in our public schools would give way to competing institutions characterized by internal. . .rigidity. . . Academic freedom would vanish.

"Rather than promote economies, the voucher plan would destroy the economy and efficiency produced by the comprehensive public school and by a generation of public school consolidations . . . . school transportation costs would skyrocket. . . The proliferation of small, inefficient schools would drive the cost of education far higher than the cost of providing the very best public education for the children. . . .

---

a.   *Ib.*, July 11, 1971.

"The voucher system appeals principally to people who want education divided into enclaves where various kinds of indoctrination can take place, to people who cannot accept the ideal of a democratic public school system for children and teachers of all backgrounds and conditions, to people who are either too 'sophisticated' or ignorant to appreciate the fact that church-state separation and public education have made our nation great, and to those who are unwilling to sacrifice to operate private schools with special kinds of education inappropriate to public schools."[a]

By Those Who Believe In Public Funds for
Public Schools Only As an
Educational Philosophy

Democratically Governed School Districts

Those with motives to condemn the public schools are legion; their private counterparts are not subject to the same criticism, in part, at least, because they are not in the public domain. There are, in the United States, 19,169 public school districts controlled by boards of education elected by the people who control the purse-strings. If there is anything wrong with these schools, the voters can change them. If they are too lazy, ignorant, or indifferent to do anything about it, they can scarcely blame any one but themselves.

It is also a fact that school districts are as different from each other as the people who inhabit the various communities. Since each district is a self-regulative entity, it develops according to its own ethos and expresses itself in an *esprit de corps* peculiarly its own. The superindendent of public instruction and the legislature of each state do indeed exercise a certain authority; but in the last analysis and in the great majority of instances, local taxation is the principal source of income; and if grass-roots control is not effective, it is because the people show no sufficient desire to implement it.

---

a.　We should note that income-tax refunds and other similar plans, as passed in Minnesota and almost enacted in Wisconsin, are simply other methods of attempting to circumvent the obvious intent of provisions in state constitutions, the First Amendment, and various Supreme Court decisions. In every case, public money would be used to support sectarian schools and religious indoctrination as carried on in parochial education.

The Truly Monolithic System

On the other hand, if there is anywhere in the world a monolithic and monopolistic system of education, it is that operated by the Catholic Church. It teaches that it alone holds the keys to heaven and hell; that eternal salvation is impossible except through its mediation and ministrations; that absolute and ultimate authority has been placed in the hands of the pope by the Creator; that it only has the right to educate. Wherever it has been able to establish its total authority by means of concordats, non-Catholic schools are proscribed, or at the very least are forbidden to teach any religion except the Catholic. Under such a regime, there can be no variation, no questioning, no dissidence, no intellectual freedom whatever.

How Would a Voucher-System be Administered?

Would the federal government collect $40 or $50 billion from the American people to supply all parents with an annual check of, say, $800 or $1,000 for the education of each child according to uninhibited choice?

In that event, every church could set up its own school in its Sunday school wing; and if all vouchers were equal and sufficient to maintain an adequate institution, a small church could become wealthy on the profits. Every group—Communists, Black Panthers, Black Muslims, Jehovah's Witnesses, and several hundred other religious bodies—large and small—could establish their own schools. Those who preferred brown or yellow, or red, or some other complexion of skin, could send their children where they could mingle with others of the same color. There would be such fragmentation as has never been known in history.

If, on the other hand, every school were to be policed and placed under rigid regulations, there would be multiple discrimination and an army of bureaucrats would be required to administer the system.

The belief, or hope, however, that individuality could long survive under federal or even under state control is wholly fatuous. For we would be investing an utterly irresponsible central power with the tools of ultimate supremacy. All control would be removed from parents or localities. Is there anyone who believes that if such a system were established, it could fail to become a monolithic monopoly which would compel obedience and uniformity and finally mold every school that accepted any money into a slavish copy of a single model? Even if such power were conferred upon angels or saints, they would sooner or later become autocrats, destructive of all liberty, and do so in the name of welfare and humanity.

Would vouchers be denied those who desired schools segregated by religion or some other qualification? Would they first be denied to Humanists, since they do not believe in a personal deity? and then to Unitarians because they have no creed? then to Southerners because they believe in segregation? then to a dozen other kinds of dissidents? Before long, there would be warfare which would make all past confrontations seem like a convention of staid executives. Would the system finally grant vouchers only to the largest religious denominations in the country?

In a release dated February 6, 1971, the California Teacher's Association asks a series of searching questions, among which we find the following: (1) What will prevent economic, social, and religious stratification under a voucher system? (2) Under this system, who would transport a ghetto child to a school in a better area? (3) Could non-public schools expect to receive money without government controls? (4) What schools would accept children with low IQs or with behaviorial problems? (5) Would church schools continue to enroll virtually no children except those of their own faith? (6) Would non-public schools become subject to the same legal provisions that now apply to the public? (7) Who would pay for new buildings at schools where enrollments increased? (8) If extremist groups started their own schools, what would prevent them from brainwashing their students?

Precisely in what manner **would** a voucher-system operate? Would all funds from local property taxes, state and county equalization funds, federal subsidies, etc., now used for education, be pooled into a single treasury to be administered by a body of central super bureaucrats? It seems unlikely that any other system would be entirely practicable. But if this were done, all local control over education would be terminated. Absolute authority would be vested in an agency that could and certainly would establish an authoritarian system so absolute that it would surpass anything known in history. Children, the people of the future, would be molded into robots, brainwashed into slavery, and reduced into a generation of obedient automatons.

The Contribution of the Common School

The fact is that every proposal to fund private education with public funds leads directly back into that jungle, that insoluble controversy, from which the common schools, neutral toward religion and other bitter disputes, rescued the American educative process. Whatever their faults may be, they have welded heterogeneous races, creeds, and nationalities into a great nation; and have given the American people a proud and common heritage, which enables them to live at peace with each other. Elsewhere, even where people are ethnically homogeneous, they have still found causes for deadly conflict, as, for instance, in Ireland. In our country, where a hundred disparate groups might easily have fragmented into warring minorities, we have become a united nation. For this, above all else, we can be thankful to the common school for having conferred so great a blessing.

The Place of the Private School

The private secular-elite school certainly has its place and an unquestioned right to exist. Perhaps it is superior in certain respects to the public school; but it is also a fact, first, that it is far too expensive for the great majority; and, second, that it does nothing that a public school, organized for the purpose, could not do at far less cost. Let those who prefer and can afford it, send their children to private day or boarding schools; however, they have no right to expect the ordinary taxpayer to underwrite the expense.

Nor do those who wish their own creed or special interest to be the dominant element in education have the right to ask those who do not share their specific views to pay for their propagation. Every system of dogma or doctrine is intended to aggrandize the group or power structure which promotes it. We cannot channel public money into any ecclesiastical polity without destroying the most sacred heritage bequeathed by our Founding Fathers.

The Educative Process

The common school exists to *educate*, a word which comes from the Latin *educere*, to draw forth. This is a process which enables the growing youth to call upon his own resources and ultimately to think and judge for himself. Education does not indoctrinate; it does not lay down Truth by authority. It is based upon facts, upon the research of scientific inquiry, and upon results which no rational or unprejudiced person will deny or question. The Pythagorean Proposition is demonstrable; its truth is universal. But the Truths embraced by 250 religious bodies in the United States are in a different category altogether; for this reason, religious teaching should, as President Grant once declared, be left to the home and the church; and so long as it does not obtrude in the schoolroom or on the campus, it can coexist in the midst of a hundred disparate ideologies without harm or conflict in the body politic.

Two factors are therefore the *sine qua non* in the American common school if it is to serve our people in the future as in the past; public funds must be used for public purposes only; and teachers in schools supported by taxation must be neutral in regard to speculative or controversial opinions, doctrines, creeds, and dogmas which form the bases of individual churches, of most private schools, and of a multiplicity of other organizations. Since to inculcate a special ideology is the *raison d'etre* of most private schools, it is their privilege to do so; but it is NOT their right or privilege to receive public funds for the purpose; and no such doctrine may be taught in a publicly-supported institution.

The Ideals of the Founding Fathers

When our Founding Fathers wrote our Constitution, it was against the backdrop of 500 years of religious wars which stemmed directly from a union of church and state and specifically from powers accruing to ecclesiastical polities through the use of public money to advance their own interests. When these men met in solemn conclave to write our national charter, they established the most revolutionary principle known in modern times: namely, that on American soil there would be complete separation of church and state and that no public money should ever be used for sectarian purposes.

The Economy of Consolidation

Public education is the only kind which can be universally acceptable; it is also far more economical. We know that in thousands of school districts consolidation has taken place. The 1-room, 8-grade, 1-teacher country school has given way to the centralized facility with a thousand pupils. In 1930-31, there were 127,531 school districts in the United States; as late as 1947-48, there were 94,926; but in 1969, these had been reduced to 18,244 operating units.[a] Universal experience has demonstrated that in spite of the cost of bussing pupils to a central location, the consolidated school not only offers far better schooling but does so much more economically. For example, in Montana, we found that the per-pupil cost in the rural areas was far higher than Helena or Butte. In the larger school, teachers can specialize and there are enough pupils to fill every class. A single adequate library serves every one, as does the science labora-

---

a.   Cf. 1970 *Digest, op. cit.,* p. 44.

274

tory, the athletic field, and many other facilities. If a small school were to attempt to supply all these, the per-pupil cost would be enormous—as it is in the elite seculars.

If schools were to be fragmented on the basis of creed, color, or any of a hundred other bases, the cost of supplying adequate facilities would mount into the stratosphere, since the price of duplication would multiply the expenditures; or, if proper equipment and teachers were not available, the quality would descend to the level once found in the one-room country school.

Universal Tyranny and Uniformity

In addition to fragmentation without limit, a voucher-system controlled by a federal or even a state bureaucracy would necessarily lead to universal tyranny, conformity, and uniformity; freedom or individuality could not hope to survive. To quote Albert Shanker in one of his articles published in the New York *Times*: "The real impact of the voucher scheme is readily apparent; what remains unclear is why some who profess support of constitutional rights, civil liberties, and equality of educational opportunity can continue to promote it."

Declarations of the United States Supreme Court

Pierce v. Society of Sisters, 1925: an Oregon case which invalidated a referendum abolishing sectarian schools in the state, but only with the proviso that such schools must always be supported entirely by voluntary contributions.

Cochran v. Board of Education, 1930: a Louisiana case, in which the right of the state to supply free textbooks to pupils in parochial schools was upheld (but without reference to the First Amendment) on the theory that this was aid to the child and not to the school: in short, the child-benefit theory.

Everson v. Board of Education, 1947: a New Jersey case, in which the Court upheld a statute which authorized bus transportation for parochial pupils on the basis of the child-benefit theory. However, aid of any kind to the school itself was strictly forbidden.[a]

---

a.   In this case, in which the vote was 5 to 4, Mr. Justice Douglas voted with the majority. Later, however, he changed his mind and stated that if he had another opportunity, he would reverse himself.

McCollum v. Board of Education, 1948: an Illinois case, in which the Court declared that religious instruction may not be given in a public schoolroom.[a]

Zorach v. Clausen, 1952: a New York case in which the Court upheld a statute permitting the release of pupils during school hours for religious instruction elsewhere than on public school premises.

In making its decision, the Court declared: "Neither a state nor the Federal Government can set up a church. Neither can pass laws which aid one religion, aid all religions, or prefer one religion over another. Neither can force nor influence a person to go to or remain away from church against his will or force him to profess a belief or disbelief in any religion. No person can be punished for entertaining or professing religious beliefs or disbeliefs, for church attendance or non-attendance. No tax in any amount, large or small, can be levied to support any religious activities or institutions, whatever they may be called, or whatever form they may adopt to teach or practice religion. Neither a state nor the Federal Government can, openly or secretly, participate in the affairs of any religious organization or group or vice versa. In the words of Jefferson, the clause against establishment of religion by law was intended to erect 'a wall of separation between church and state'."

Having voted with the minority in Everson, Mr. Justice Rutledge declared in a dissenting opinion: "The reasons underlying the First Amendment's policy have not vanished or diminished in force. Now, as when it was adopted, the price of religious freedom is double. It is that the Church and religion shall live both with and upon that freedom. There cannot be freedom of religion, safeguarded by the state, and interference by the church or its agencies in the state's domain or dependence on its largesse. . . . The great condition of religious liberty is that it be maintained free from sustenance, as also from the interference by the state. For when it comes to rest upon that secular foundation, it vanishes with the resting. Public monies devoted to payment for religious costs, educational or other, brings the quest for more. It lays too the struggle of sect against sect for the larger share or for any. Here, one by numbers alone will benefit more; there another. This is precisely the history of societies which have had established religion and dissident groups. . . . The end of such strife cannot be other than to destroy the cherished liberty. The dominating groups will achieve the dominant benefit; or all will embroil the state in their dissensions."

a. In his concurring opinion in the McCollum case, Justice Frankfurter quoted Judge Jeremiah Black, who had written in 1856: "The manifest object of the men who framed the institutions of this country, was to have a *State without religion* and a *Church without politics.* . . . For that reason they built up a wall of complete and perfect partition between the two."

Engel v. Vitale, 1962: another New York case in which the recitation of a prepared Regent's Prayer in the classroom of a public school was declared unconstitutional.

Abingdon v. Schempp-Murray, 1963: a case in which Bible reading and the recitation of the Lord's Prayer in a public schoolroom were declared unconstitutional. [a]

Flast v. Cohen, 1968: a New York case in which the Court held that an individual can bring suit to challenge federal expenditures on grounds that they violate the principle of church-state separation.

Walz v. The Tax Commission of New York, 1970: a case in which the Court declared, in effect, that the exemption from taxation of a church sanctuary is valid since it has been in existence so long; however, the clear implication of the decision is that such exemption must be left to the several states and their political subdivisions; and, further, that it is not a right but rather a privilege which can be granted or withdrawn by the local authorities.

DiCenso v. Robinson, 1971: a Rhode Island case in which the Court declared unconstitutional an arrangement under which the state was to pay 15% of the salaries of teachers who taught secular subjects in parochial schools. In this, a lower court was upheld.

Lemon v. Kurtzman, 1971: a Pennsylvania case in which the Court declared unconstitutional a plan under which the state used money derived from horse racing and cigarette excises to purchase the services of teachers of secular subjects in parochial schools. In this the Court overturned a lower court decision.

---

a.   In arriving at its decision in the Schempp case, the Court declared: "The public schools are supported entirely, in most communities, by public funds—funds exacted not only from parents, nor alone from those who hold particular religious views, nor indeed from those who subscribe to any creed at all. It is implicit in the history and character of American public education that the public schools serve a uniquely *public* function; the training of American citizens in an atmosphere free of parochial, divisive, or separatist influences of any sort—an atmosphere in which children may assimilate a heritage common to all American groups and religions. This is a heritage neither theistic nor atheistic, but simply civic and patriotic."

In a concurring opinion, Mr. Justice Douglas declared: "The most effective way to establish anything is to finance it. . . . Financing a church either in its strictly religious or other activities is equally unconstitutional . . . the institution is an inseparable whole . . . What may not be done directly, may not be indirectly, lest the Establishment Clause become a mockery."

These two cases, which were heard together by the Court, are of such crucial importance that we quote somewhat extensively from them in a footnote.[a] Their great significance rests upon the fact that here the Court finally grappled with and made a definitive determination concerning the basic nature of the parochial school—namely, that the religion of the sponsoring church or Order permeates every subject, that the entire enterprise is sectarian and that ultimately there can be no separation of the religious from the secular elements in the curriculum of the school. *DiCenso* and *Lemon*, therefore, probably constitute the most important and far-reaching decisions which the Court has ever made in the field of church-state relationships.

---

a.   In the decision written by Chief Justice Burger, the Court declares: "The two legislatures . . . have . . . sought to create statutory restrictions designed to guarantee the separation between secular and religious educational functions and to ensure that State financial aid supports only the latter. . . . We need not decide whether these legislative precautions restrict the principal or primary effect of the programs to the point where they do not offend the Religion Clause, for we conclude that the cumulative impact of the entire relationship arising under the statutes in each State involves excessive entanglement between government and religion. . . .

"The church schools involved . . . are located close to parish churches. This understandably permits convenient access for religious exercises since instruction in faith and morals is part of the total educational process. The school buildings contain identifying crucifixes, religious paintings and statues either in the classrooms or the hallways. Although only approximately 30 minutes a day are devoted to direct religious instruction, there are religiously oriented extracurricular activities. Approximately two-thirds of the teachers in these schools are nuns of various religious orders.

"On the basis of these findings, the District Court concluded that the parochial schools constituted 'an integral part of the religious mission of the Catholic Church. . . .' The various characteristics of the schools make them 'a powerful vehicle for transmitting the Catholic faith to the next generation'. . . . In short, parochial schools involve substantial religious activity and purpose.

"The substantial religious character of these church-related schools gives rise to entangling church-state relationships of the kind the Religion Clauses sought to avoid. . . .

"Our decisions . . . have permitted the States to provide church-related schools with secular, neutral, or non-ideological services, facilities, or materials . . ."but "teachers have a substantially different character than books. . . .

"The schools are governed by the standards set forth in a 'Handbook of School Regulations,' which . . . states that 'Religious formation is not

confined to formal courses; nor is it restricted to a single subject area.'
Finally, the Handbook advises teachers to stimulate interest in religious
vocations and missionary work. . . .

"The teacher is employed by a religious organization, subject to the
direction and discipline of religious authorities, and works in a system
dedicated to rearing children in a particular faith. These controls are not
lessened by the fact that most of the lay teachers are of the Catholic faith.
. . .

"We simply recognize that a dedicated religious person, teaching in a
school affiliated with his or her faith and operated to inculcate its tenets,
will inevitably experience great difficulty in remaining religiously neutral. .
. . With the best of intentions such a teacher would find it hard to make a
total separation between secular teaching and religious doctrine. . . .
Further difficulties are inherent in the combination of religious discipline
and the possibility of disagreement between teacher and religious authorities over the meaning of the statutory restrictions. . . .

"The State must be certain, given the Religion Clauses, that subsidized
teachers do not inculcate religion. . . ." Therefore "A comprehensive,
discriminating, and continuing State surveillance will inevitably be required to ensure that these restrictions are obeyed. . . . Unlike a book, a
teacher cannot be inspected once so as to determine the extent and intent
of his or her personal beliefs. . . ."

(The preceding refers to the decision of the Rhode Island Court, with
which the United States Supreme Court agreed.)

"The Pennsylvania statute also provides state aid to church-related
schools for teachers' salaries . . . the very restrictions and surveillance
necessary to ensure that teachers play a strictly non-ideological role give
rise to entanglements between church and state. . . .

"The history of government grants of continuing cash subsidy indicates that such programs have almost always been accompanied by varying
measures of control and surveillance. The government cash grants before
us now provide no basis for predicting that comprehensive measures of
surveillance and controls will not follow. . . .

"A broader base of entanglement of yet a different character is presented by the divisive political potential of those state programs. In a
community where such a large number of pupils are served by church-
related schools, it can be assumed that state assistance will entail considerable political activity. Partisans of parochial schools . . . will inevitably
champion this cause and promote political action to achieve their goals.
Those who oppose state aid . . . will inevitably respond and employ all of
the usual political campaign techniques to prevail. Candidates will be
forced to declare and voters to choose. It would be unrealistic to ignore
the fact that many people confronted with issues of this kind will find
their votes aligned with their faith. . . .

"The highways of church and state relationships are not likely to be one-way streets, and the Constitution's authors sought to protect religious worship from the pervasive power of government. The history of many countries attests to the hazards of religion intruding into the political arena or of political power intruding into the legitimate and free exercise of religious belief. . . .

"The potential for political divisiveness related to religious belief and practice is aggravated in these two statutory programs by the need for continuing annual appropriations and the likelihood of larger and larger demands as costs and populations grow. . . .

"Under our system the choice has been made that government is to be entirely excluded from the area of religious instruction and churches excluded from the affairs of government. The Constitution decrees that religion must be a private matter for the individual, the family, and the institutions of private choice, and that while some involvement and entanglement is inevitable, lines must be drawn."

In a concurring opinion, Mr. Justice Douglas and Mr. Justice Black declared: "What is palpably a sectarian course can be marked for deletion. But this problem only starts there. Sectarian instruction, in which, of course, the State may not indulge, can take place in a course on Shakespeare or in one on mathematics. No matter what the curriculum offers, the question is, what is taught? We deal not with evil teachers but with zealous ones who may use any opportunity to indoctrinate a class. . . . One can imagine what a religious zealot, as contrasted to a civil libertarian, can do with the Reformation or with the Inquisition. Much history can be given the gloss of a particular religion. I would think that policing these grants to detect sectarian instruction would be insufferable to religious partisans and would breed division and dissension between church and state."

In another concurring opinion, Mr. Justice Brennan declared: "The picture of state inspectors prowling the halls of parochial schools and auditing classroom instruction surely raises more than an imagined spectre of government 'secularization of a creed.' "

Appendix

Resolutions Adopted
by
The Third Plenary Council of the American Catholic Church

Convened November 9, 1884, in Baltimore

I. That near every church a parish school, where one does not yet exist, is to be built and maintained *in perpetuum*, within two years of the promulgation of this Council, unless the bishops should decide that because of serious difficulties a delay may be granted.

II. A priest who within this time prevents the building or maintenance of such school through his serious neglect, or after repeated warnings by the bishop does not discharge his responsibility, deserves to be removed from the church.

III. The mission or parish which neglects to aid the priest in erecting or maintaining the school, that on account of this supine negligence, the school cannot exist, is to be reprimanded by the bishop and induced by more effective and prudent means to bring forth the necessary support.

IV. That all Catholic parents are bound to send their children to the parish school, unless it is evident that a sufficient training in religion is given either in their own homes, or in other Catholic schools; or when, because of a sufficient reason, approved by the bishop, with all due precautions and safeguards, it is licit to send them to other schools. What constitutes a Catholic school is left to the decision of the bishop.

Provisions of Catholic Canon Law Dealing with Education[a]

Canon 1113. Parents are under a most serious obligation to provide to the best of their ability for the religious, moral, physical, and civic education of their children, and also to provide for their temporal welfare.

Canon 1372. (1) From childhood, all the faithful must be reared so that they are taught nothing contrary to faith and morals, but so that religious and moral training have the primary place. (2) Not merely parents, as in Canon 1113, but all who take their place, have the right and the serious duty to provide a Christian education for their children.

Canon 1373. (1) In every elementary school, religious instruction suitable to the age of the children, must be imparted. (2) Students at secondary schools or colleges must be given more complete instruction in religion. The bishops must see to it that this be done by priests conspicuous for zeal and learning.

Canon 1374. Catholic children may not attend non-Catholic, neutral, or mixed schools, that is, those which are open also to non-Catholics. It is for the local bishop to decide, in accordance with the instructions of the Holy See, under what circumstances and with what precautions against the danger of perversion, attendance at such schools may be permitted.

Canon 1375. The Church has the right to establish schools of every grade, not only the elementary, but secondary schools and colleges.

Canon 1379. (1) Where there are no Catholic schools, as envisioned in Canon 1373, provisions must be made for founding them, especially by the local bishops. (2) If the public universities are not imbued with Catholic doctrine and ideology, a national or regional Catholic university

---

a.   These sections of Canon Law dealing with education are translated from the *Codex Juris Canonica* published 1949, by the Newman Press, pp.374, 470-473. The wordings here given have been compared with other translations found in *Canon Law: A Text and Commentary,* by T. Lincoln Bouscaren, S.J., and in *A Practical Commentary on the Code of Canon Law* by Reverend Stanislaus Wayward, O.F.M.

should be established. (3) The faithful must lend their help for the establishment and support of Catholic schools, according to their means.

Canon 1381. (1) The religious training of youth in all schools is subject to the authority and inspection of the Church. (2) The local bishops have the right and responsibility of seeing to it that nothing contrary to faith and morals be taught in any schools within their territory. (3) The bishops have also the right to approve teachers of religion and religious textbooks; also, to demand the removal of either teachers or texts in the interests of religion and morality.

TABLE I[a]

Costs and Enrollment in Public Schools

| | Totals | Below | in | Thousands | | Actual Amounts | |
| | | | | | | | |
Year	Popula- tion	Enroll- ment	ADA	Total Cost	Per-Pupil Oper.	Cost Total	
1870	39,818	6,872	4,077	$63,397	$9.37	$15.55	
1890	62,948	12,723	8,154	140,000	16.57	17.23	
1910	91,972	17,814	12,827	426,250	27.85	33.23	
1920	105,711	21,578	16,150	1,036,051	53.32	64.16	
1930	122,775	25,678	21,265	2,316,790	86.70	108.49	
1940	131,699	25,434	22,042	2,344,049	88.09	105.74	
1950	150,697	25,111	22,284	5,837,643	208.83	258.85	
1960	179,323	36,067	32,477	15,613,255	375.14	472.17	
1965	193,795	42,835	39,154	26,248,026	537.35	653.81	
1968	197,863	43,891	40,829	32,977,182	658.25	786.84	
1970	203,185[b]	45,904[c]	43,000[d]	43,300,000[e]	858.00	954.00[f]	

a.   Data through 1968, from the 1970 *Digest of Educational Statistics*, pp. 28-29, published by the Office of Education; population from census reports.

b.   From 1971 *Statistical Abstract*, p. 14.

c.   *Ib*. p. 107.

d.   Estimated.

e.   *Ib*. p. 102.

f.   *Ib*. p. 98.

TABLE II[a]

Teachers, Salaries, and ADA's in Public Schools

Year	Staff	Classroom Teachers	Average Salary	Staff to Enroll.	Staff to ADA	PTR
1869-70		201,000	$189	34.2		20.3
1889-90		364,000	252	34.9		22.4
1909-10		523,000	485	34.1		24.3
1919-20	678,000	657,000	871	31.8	23.8	24.6
1929-30	880,000	843,000	1,420	29.2	24.2	25.3
1939-40	912,000	875,000	1,441	27.9	23.9	25.2
1949-50	962,000	914,000	3,010	26.1	23.2	24.4
1959-60	1,464,000	1,387,000	5,174	24.7	22.2	23.4
1965-66	1,885,000	1,786,000	6,935	22.7	20.7	21.9
1967-68	2,071,246	1,957,000	7,905	21.2	19.9	20.9
1969-70	2,184,000[b]	2,061,115[c]	8,560[d]	20.9	19.7	20.9
1971			9,265[e]			

a. Data through 1967-68 from *Digest,Op. cit*., pp. 28-29.
b. Estimated.
c. 1971 *SA* p. 116.
d. *Digest, op. cit*., p. 41.
e. 1971 *SA*, p. 122.

TABLE III[a]

Enrollment in Elementary and Secondary Schools

Year	Total	Public	Private	Catholic	% Cath.
1880	10,600,000	9,867,000		405,234	
1890	13,650,000	12,733,000		633,238	
1900	16,961,249	15,503,110	1,351,722	854,523	5.0
1910	19,643,933	17,813,852	1,676,837	1,237,251	6.3
1920	23,463,898	21,579,316	1,699,481	1,701,213	7.3
1930	28,551,640	25,678,015	2,651,044	2,464,467	8.6
1940	28,257,000	25,433,542	2,611,047	2,396,305	8.5
1946	28,458,625	25,618,964	2,839,667	2,619,003	9.2
1950	28,660,250	25,111,427	3,380,139	3,066,387	10.7
1955	34,623,000	30,528,323	4,094,677	3,988,900	11.6
1961	42,012,076	36,086,771	5,674,943	5,369,540	12.8
1965	48,779,976	42,173,764	6,304,772	5,662,328	11.6
1969	51,901,000	46,531,000	5,370,000	4,843,188	9.3
1970	51,432,313	45,904,000	5,528,323	4,429,323	8.6
1971-72				3,800,000[b]	7.5

a. Data from 1970 *Digest, op.cit.*, pp.2-3, except for 1970, which are from pp.24 and 33. Catholic enrollments from the *Official Catholic Directory* and its predecessors for the years indicated.
b. Estimated.

TABLE IV[a]

Enrollment in Non-Catholic Private Elementary and Secondary Schools

Control	1891	1946	1961-62	1965-66	1968-69	1970
Secular			239,951	341,270	366,157	
Baptist			16,574	25,189	23,671	
Ch. Reformed			39,964	42,275	45,852	63,000
Friends				10,572	12,164	14,968
Jewish			39,830	52,589	66,724	
Lutheran			161,045	188,521	195,690	
(Mis. Syn.)	(118)	(80,058)	(150,440)	(172,536)	(166,809)	(163,753)
Methodist				5,622	5,374	
Presbyterian				4,766	4,732	
Prot. Epis.			30,516	48,582	54,122	
SDA	255	32,647	59,684	65,920	69,399	68,770
Other Church			39,189	41,458	59,899	
Assembly of God						8,341
Total			626,753	826,764	903,784	1,099,000[b]
Total Ch.-Related			386,802	485,494	537,632	

a. All data for Missouri Synod Lutheran, Seventh-Day Adventist, and Assembly of God schools supplied by these denominations directly. Data for 1970 for Christian Reformed and Friends' schools directly from these denominations. Other totals for 1961-62 from the 1966 *SA*, p. 128. Data for 1965-66, from *Digest, op. cit.*, p. 31. Data for 1968-69 from *Directory of Nonpublic Schools,* published by the Office of Education in 1971.

b. Estimated.

TABLE V[a]

Early Growth of the Catholic Church in America

Item	1808	1830	1840	1845	1850	1860	1880	1891
Dioceses	1	11	16	21	30			
Bishops	2	10	17	25	27		55	
Archbishops							12	
Priests	68	232	482	683	1,081	2,235	5,989	8,778
Churches	80	230	454	675	1,073	2,385	6,407	7,631
Chapels, Stations			358	592	560	1,128	1,706	
Seminaries	2	9	13	22	29	48	24	
Students							1,186	
Boy's Colleges	2	8	12	15	17	89		
Female Academies	2	20	47	63	91	202		
High Schools							663	624
Male Relig. Insts.						100		
Female Relig. Insts.						166		
Parochial Schools							2,246	3,277
Pupils							405,234	665,328
Asylums						183	373	
Communicants					1,233,350		6,143,222	8,579,966

a.   Data for 1808 through 1850 from *The Metropolitan Catholic Almanac and Laity's Directory* of 1850-51, published by Fielding Lucas, Jr., in Baltimore. Data for 1860 from *ib.* of 1860-61, published by John Murphy and Co. Data for 1880 and 1891 from *Sadlier's Catholic Directory*, published in New York.

TABLE VI[a]

Catholic Membership, Churches, Parochial Schools and Enrollment

Year	Membership	Enrollment[b]	Churches, Parishes	Elementary Schools	% Parishes with Schools
1880	6,143,222	405,234	6,407	2,246	35.0
1884		490,531	6,626	2,464	37.2
1890	8,301,367	654,838	7,420	3,209	44.6
1891	8,579,966	665,328	8,631	3,277	42.9
1896	9,410,790	796,348	9,501	3,361	35.4
1900		903,980	10,427	3,812	36.5
1905	12,462,793	1,031,378	11,387	4,235	37.2
1920	17,735,553	1,701,213	10,608	5,852	55.2
1930	20,203,702	2,248,571	12,413	7,225	58.3
1936	20,735,189	2,212,260	12,720	7,490	58.9
1940	21,403,186	2,108,892	13,132	7,597	55.3
1945	23,963,671	2,029,012	14,302	7,493	52.3
1950	27,766,141	2,477,741	15,292	7,914	51.7
1955	32,575,702	3,253,608	16,139	8,843	54.2
1961	42,104,899	4,502,410	16,996	10,503	61.8
1965	44,837,371	4,566,616	17,445	10,902	62.5
1971	48,214,729	3,413,610	18,244	9,271	50.8

a.   All data from the *Official Catholic Directory* and its predecessors.
b.   It should be noted that the totals here given for enrollment include only the elementary.

288

T A B L E   VII[a]

The Catholic Church in America Since 1900

Category	1904	1920	1936	1946
Communicants	11,877,317	17,735,553	24,402,124	44,847,371
Priests--Clergy	13,267	21,019	31,108	38,908
Brothers				6,721
Sisters				139,218
Parishes--Churches	11,186	10,608	12,720	14,523
High Schools	825	911	1,809	2,413
Students			195,821	477,190
Elementary Schools	4,001	5,852	7,490	8,036
Pupils			2,212,260	2,141,813
Total: El. and Sec.	986,088	1,701,213	2,408,081	2,619,003
Teaching Religious				86,807
Lay Teachers				8,435
Released Time Pupils				812,998
Total under Instruction				3,451,725

	1955	1961	1965	1971
Communicants	32,573,702	42,104,899	45,640,619	48,214,729
Priests	46,970	54,682	58,632	58,161
Brothers	8,752	10,928	12,271	10,156
Sisters	158,069	170,438	179,954	153,645
Parishes	16,035	16,996	17,637	18,244
High Schools	2,399	2,433	2,465	1,954
Students	639,607	886,295	1,095,519	995,713
Elementaries	9,385	10,594	10,931	9,606
Pupils	3,349,293	4,502,410	4,566,806	3,413,610
Total: El. & Sec.	3,988,900	5,388,705	5,662,328	4,419,323
Teaching Relig.	106,357	115,793	123,653	83,285
Lay Teachers	24,907	52,884	75,103	106,844
Pub. Sch. Pupils under Rel. Inst.	2,104,634	3,472,176	4,590,227	5,484,498
Total Instructed	6,093,534	8,860,881	10,252,555	10,374,116

a.   All data from the P.J. Kenedy *Official Catholic Directory* for the year indicated, except the statistics for 1904, which are from its predecessor.

TABLE VIII[a]

Enrollments and Staff in Catholic Schools [b]

Year	Enrollment	Staff	Pupil Ratio	No. of Religious	No. of Lay	%Lay
1920	1,925,521	49,516	38.8	45,563	3,943	7.9
1930	2,464,467	72,552	33.9	65,601	6,951	9.5
1945	2,546,697	95,796	26.5	86,922	8,874	9.3
1950	3,066,387	106,777	27.9	93,300	13,477	12.6
1955	3,988,900	131,264	30.1	106,357	24,907	18.9
1961	5,388,705	168,677	31.3	115,793	52,884	31.3
1965	5,662,328	198,756	28.5	123,653	75,103	37.7
1971	4,429,323	200,438	22.1	93,594	106,844	53.4

a. Data for 1920 and 1930 from the 1967-69 *Data Bank, op. cit.*, p. 5; for 1945-71, from the *Official Catholic Directory*.

b. These ratios are substantially too low, because "staff" includes the entire personnel, a great many of whom are part-time employees. The *Data Bank, op. cit.*, shows that in 1967-68, in a staff of 205,400, 28,200 were part-time employees, which produced a true ratio of 26.4, instead of the 22.1 shown above.

TABLE IX

Corrected Pupil-Staff Ratios in Catholic Schools

Schools	Enrollment	Staff	Pupil Ratio
Elementary			
1962-63[a]	4,342,273	103,779[b]	36-40[c]
1967-68[d]	4,105,805	116,400+13,400	33.4
1969-70[d]	3,607,168	113,800+19,400	29.2
Secondary			
1962-63[a]	1,009,081	39,809[b]	26.0
1967-68[d]	1,072,521	50,900+7,100	20.0
1969-70[d]	1,050,930	53,400+8,800	18.0
Combined			
1962-63			37.9
1969-70			26.4

a. Enrollments for 1962-63 from *Catholic Schools in Action*, Neuwien, Notre Dame Press, p. 33.

b. *Ib.*, p. 82. This includes about 95% of total enrollment and assumes that the remainder is comparable.

TABLE X

Enrollment, Staff and Ratios in Catholic Schools

Dubuque

Year	Enrollment	Staff	Pupil-Teacher Ratio	No. of Religious	No. of Lay	% Lay
1905	2,585	64	40.4	62	2	3.1
1920	3,445	92	37.5	88	4	4.3
1930	4,297	148	29.0	137	11	7.6
1940	4,289	179	23.9	171	8	4.5
1950	5,873	213	27.6	189	24	11.3
1961	8,789	308	28.5	238	65	21.1
1965	10,428	366	28.5	255	111	30.3
1971	8,901	308	25.7	145	163	52.9

St. Paul

Year	Enrollment	Staff	Pupil-Teacher Ratio	No. of Religious	No. of Lay	% Lay
1905	7,457	166	45.9	165	1	.4
1920	8,943	206	43.4	206	0	.0
1930	16,415	443	37.1	422	21	4.7
1940	13,912	452	30.8	417	35	7.8
1950	18,488	526	35.5	438	88	16.7
1961	31,183	807	38.6	603	204	25.3
1964	33,318	1,026	32.6	600	388	37.8
1971	20,811	866	24.0	372	494	57.0

Milwaukee

Year	Enrollment	Staff	Pupil-Teacher Ratio	No. of Religious	No. of Lay	% Lay
1892	9,981	151	66.2	137	14	9.0
1900	13,818	260	47.4	249	11	4.2
1910	19,029	405	46.9	402	3	.8
1920	22,378	480	46.6	471	9	1.5
1930	30,442	760	40.0	760	0	.0
1940	31,558	862	36.9	832	30	3.5
1950	35,800	1,153	31.1	1,094	49	4.3
1955	42,756	1,201	35.7	1,006	195	16.3
1961	51,532	1,525	33.8	1,087	438	28.7
1964	52,097	1,505	35.3	906	499	33.3
1970	31,504	1,274	24.8	586	688	54.1

c. *Ib.*, p. 97.
d. Data for 1967-68 and 1969-70 from the 1967-70 *Data Bank, op cit.*, p. 8, 12, and 14. The added numbers under "Staff" are the part-time teachers.

TABLE XI

Negro Enrollment in Public and Catholic Schools [a]

Year	*Public* Total	Negro	% Negro	*Catholic* Total	Negro	% Negro
1969-70	45,618,578	6,615,000	14.5	4,089,658	197,940	4.84
1970-71				3,938,090	183,818	4.66

a. Data for public schools for 1969-70 from Feb. 1971, *Church and State*, p. 7; for Catholic, from 1967-70 *Data Bank, Op. Cit.,* pp. 55-56; for 1970-71, from 1970-71, *ib.*, Appendix D. It should be noted that statistics in *Data Bank* include only schools covered in survey, which are considered representative of all.

TABLE XII

Academic Status of Catholic Teachers in 1969-70-71 [a]

	Elementary	Secondary
Full-Time: Total	92,179	40,196
Certified	57,747	28,528
Uncertified	34,432	11,668
Ratio	37.4%	29.2%
Part-Time: Total	9,600	6,482
Certified	5,469	4,047
Uncertified	4,141	2,435
Ratio	43.0%	30.2%
Teachers in 1970-71 [b]		
Less than B.A.	26.2%	2.5%
With B.A.	62.2%	54.9%
With Master's	11.5%	41.8%
Earned Doctorates	.1%	.8%

a. *Data Bank* of 1967-70, *op cit.,* p. 16, represents about 87% of total.
b. *Data Bank* of 1970-71, p. 20.

TABLE XIII

Salaries of Catholic Teachers

Category	1958	1961-62	1967	1968	1969-70	1970-71
Sisters:[a]						
In S.F.	$900[b]	$1,200[b]	$1,285	$1,450[c]	$1,695[c]	$1,995[c]
Youngstown	750	1,000				
Lay		3,547[d]				
Lay Elem.[e]		3,150			5,138	5,575
Lay Sec.[f]		4,500			7,200	7,813

a. It should be noted that in addition to their salaries, sisters receive housing, transporation, and certain other fringe benefits. The Church also invests considerable sums of money in their education and preparation, which Bartell estimated at $9,350 in 1963, cf. *op. cit.,* p. 208.

b. Cf. Bartell, *op. cit.,* p. 40.

c. Cf. 1970-71 *Data Bank, op. cit.,* p. 31.

d. Cf. Bartell, *op. cit.,* p. 109. Salaries of lay teachers in Catholic schools in Ohio were $2,388 less than their counterparts received in the public schools in 1963.

e. Cf. 1970-71 *Data Bank, op. cit.,* p. 30 and 34.

f. *Ib.*

TABLE XIV[a]

Per-Pupil Costs in the Catholic Schools of Two Cities

S.F. Diocese	1959	1961	1962	1963
Elem. Oper.	$69.04	$80.63	$85.57	$90.09
Cap. Outlay	28.33	31.98	50.83	36.21
Total	97.37	112.61	136.40	126.30
Augmented[b]				223.26
Central H.S.				
Operational	232.64	228.15	242.23	262.54
Cap. Out.	10.75	12.10		
Total	243.39	240.25	242.23	262.54
Contributed	102.24			111.85
Total Augmented	$345.63			$374.39
Youngstown Second.				
Operational	161.63	174.17	186.04	187.20
Capital Outlay	21.52	44.84	52.71	229.01
Cont. Services	107.00			115.45
Value of Plant	67.77			119.45
Total Augmented	357.92			651.11

a. All data in this table from Bartell, *op. cit.*
b. Augmented means that cost includes contributed services of religious personnel.

TABLE XV

Sources of Revenue and Costs in Catholic Schools[a]

Elementary	1958	1963	1967-68	1970-71
San. Fran.				
Tuition	$6.00	$6.00		
Fees	35.86	43.88		
Parish Subsidy	27.08	41.95		
Youngstown				
Tuition	000.000	000.000		
Parish Subsidy	67.88	92.39		
Nationally: Per-Pupil Operational Cost: Cash			$145.00	$240.71
Value of Contributed Services[b]			101.00	68.64
Total			$246.00	$309.35
Sources of Income:				
Tuition			32.48	57.58
Fees			9.42	12.46
Parish Subsidies			88.31	129.14
Public Aid				10.23
Other			14.79	31.10
Secondary: Per-Pupil Operational Cost in Cash:			$335.00	481.00
Diocesan				
Contributed Services[b]			244.50	168.85
Total			$579.50	$650.85
Sources of Income				
Tuition			182.25	243.32
Fees			22.10	41.18
Subsidies			72.35	127.29
Public Aid				20.67
Other			58.30	48.54
Private: Per-Pupil Operational Cost in Cash:				612.57
Contributed Services[b]				207.06
Total				$819.63

Elementary Tuition in 1969-70[c]

Schools Charging Less Than $50		42.8% about	1,500,000 Pupils
	From $50 to $99	21.5% about	775,000 Pupils
35.7% about	Over $99	35.7% about	1,285,000 Pupils

---

a. Data for 1958 and 1963, Bartell, *op. cit.,* p. 145 for 1967-68, 1967-70 *Data Bank, op. cit.,* p. 21; for 1970-71, *ib.* 1970-71, p. 24.
b. Data for contributed services for 1967-68 from 1967-70 *Data Bank, op. cit.,* p. 21; for 1970-71, from *ib.* of 1970-71, p. 32.
c. *Data Bank* of 1967-70, *op. cit.* p. 21.

TABLE XVI[a]

Enrollments and Schoolrooms in U.S. Public Schools

Year	K-8	Secondary	New Rooms	Rooms in Use
1955-56	22,060,000	8,472,000	67,088	1,043,000
1958-59	26,581,000	8,258,000	69,543	1,263,000
1959-60	27,602,000	8,485,000	69,400	
1960-61	28,439,000	8,821,000	72,214	1,332,000
1961-62	28,686,000	9,566,000	72,089	1,385,000
1962-63	29,374,000	11,372,000	65,300	1,438,000
1963-64	29,915,000	11,110,000	69,300	1,497,000
1964-65	30,652,000	11,628,000	65,200	1,549,000
1965-66	31,177,000	12,658,000	72,600	1,595,000
1966-67	31,766,000	12,132,000	71,000	1,653,000
1967-68	32,495,000	12,581,000	71,000	1,709,000
1968-69	32,871,000	12,972,000	71,000	1,764,000
1969-70	33,249,000	13,282,000	64,000	1,836,000
1970-71	27,269,000	18,712,000 [b]		1,864,000

Rooms Constructed: 1955-56 to 1969-70	1,126,385
Rooms Abandoned: 1958-59 to 1969-70	333,385
Net Increase in Rooms	793,000
Increased Enrollment: 1955-1970	15,448,842
Added Pupils Provided with Desks at 25 Per Room	19,825,000
Enrollment: 1970-71	45,981,000
Number that Could be Schoolhoused at 27 Per Room	50,328,000[c]

a. Data for 1955-56 from 1956 *SA* p. 116. Enrollment data for remainder of years from 1970 *Digest, op. cit.,* p. 24–25. Data for new schoolrooms and rooms in use from *ib.,* p. 49 and from 1971 *SA* p. 114.
b. The large increase in secondary and the corresponding decrease in K-8 pupils in 1970-71 was due to the fact that a great many 7th and 8th graders were classified as secondary pupils in junior high schools in that year for the first time.
c. With 25 pupils per room, the 1,864,000 stations could accommodate 46,600,000.

TABLE XVII [a]

Live Births and School Enrollment

Year	Live Births	Entering Sch. at Age Six	Enrollment[b] K-12
1955	4,104,000		
1956	4,181,000		
1957	4,255,000		
1958	4,204,000		
1959	4,245,000		42,012,076
1960	4,258,000		
1961	4,268,000	3,981,000	
1962	4,167,000	3,956,000	
1963	4,098,000	4,127,000	46,957,190
1964	4,027,000	4,078,000	
1965	3,760,000	4,118,000	48,779,976
1966	3,606,000	4,130,000	
1967	3,521,000	4,140,000	
1968	3,502,000	4,042,000	
1969	3,571,000	3,975,000	51,904,000
1970	3,718,000	3,906,000	51,432,000
1971		3,647,000	50,961,000
1972		3,498,000	50,319,000
1973		3,415,000	49,594,000
1974		3,397,000	48,949,000
1975		3,464,000	48,511,000
1976		3,596,000	47,900,000
1977			47,450,000
1978			47,050,000
1979			46,855,000[c]

a.   Data on live births from 1963 *SA* p. 52 and *ib*. 1971, p. 48. The number entering school at age six assumes a dropout and infancy death-rate of 3%.

b.   Totals given here assume a death and dropout rate of about 4%.

c.   Since the number of births during 1955-62 totalled 33,682,000 and those during 1963-70 29,302,000, we know that school enrollment in 1979 must be at least 4,380,000 less than in 1970.

T A B L E XVIII[a]

The School Lunch Program

Year	Fed. Subsidy	State Sub.	Local Sub.	Children's Payment
1947	$67,900,89	$20,616,000	$17,532,000	$112,540,000
1950	119,709,503	39,000,000	31,553,000	177,336,000
1955	169,291,476	68,991,000	53,908,000	336,362,000
1960	303,548,820	92,608,000	127,522,000	555,707,000
1965	497,091,114	113,682,000	178,700,000	797,572,000
1968	540,206,839	161,973,000	278,551,000	995,756,000
1969	597,131,349	154,979,000	320,276,653	1,041,241,376
1970	697,131,968	184,296,944	355,371,620	1,093,788,221
1971	1,012,722,000	205,000,000	416,400,000	1,215,455,000
		1950	*1965*	*1971*
Total Cost		$367,598,503	$1,587,045,114	$2,849,577,000
State-Fed. Sub.		158,709,503	610,773,114	1,217,722,000
Catholic Share[b]		15,000,000	70,000,000	90,000,000

---

a. All information in this table supplied by the U.S.D.A.
b. estimated.

298

Index

178-179; 240, 247, note 293, 295

Beary, D. H.,Asst. Administrator of Boise School District, 56

Beattie, Rev. Paul R., Unitarian, opposed to parochiaid, 267

Behr, Rev. Joseph J., Supt. of Pueblo Cath. schools, 125

Bennett, James Gordon, statement of, concerning Catholics, 202

Bernard, Elmer, Administrator of Grants in Duluth, 68

Bible Missionary School, Boise, 55

Biennial Report, Mont. State Supt. of Public Instruction, note 11

Bill for Establishing Religious Freedom in Virginia by Jefferson, 196-197

Bill for the More General Diffusion of Knowledge in Virginia by Jefferson,198

Bill of Rights,198

Birth rate, the falling, 5, note 10, 18, note 86; 105, 118, 145; and the Great Depression, 169-192; in Iowa, 169-170; and abortion 170; note 171; 178; and school enrollment,192

Births, Live, and School Enrollment in the U. S.,297

Bishop Kelly High School in Boise, 55-56

Black, Judge Jeremiah, 276

"Blaine Amendment", 223-224, note 223

Blanshard, Paul, on Catholic schools in Spain, 264

Blum, Father Virgil, 114, 179, 188, 208; argument of, for parochiaid, 253-256, note 256; 259, 261

Boettner, Lorraine, critic of Cath. schools, 234-235, 265

Bohman, Allan, Supt. Fairview Junior Academy (SDA) in San Bernardino, 160

Boise, 4, analysis of, 53-59; 172, 177

Boise Valley Elementary School (SDA),55

Bond issues: in Helena, 10; Butte 19, note 20; Albuquerque, 42; Scottsdale, 49, 52; Boise,53, 57; Fargo, 61; Duluth,68; Green Bay, 75; Dubuque, 86; Kansas City, 94; St. Paul, 102; Milwaukee, 117, 121; Pueblo, 127, 134; Detroit,137, 148

Bouscaren, T. Lincoln, note 282

Brennan, Mr. Justice, note 280

Brown, William, 185, co-author of *Can Catholic Schools Survive ?,* note 185; 240, 260

Brownson, Orestes A., critic of parochial schools, 225-226; editor, *Quarterly Review,* note 225; 229

Bureau of Indian Affairs,182

Burger, Chief Justice, opinion of, in *Lemon* and *DiCenso,* note 278-280

Burns, Father Ernest, Cath. schools in Helena, 11-12; 14

Bussing, 14, 55, 68-69, 85, 89, 92, 104, 113, 128, 140, 141, 142

Buswell, The Most Rev. Charles A., Bishop of Pueblo diocese, statement of, 124, 130

Butte,5, analysis of, 17-23; 81, 172, 175, 176, 274

Butte Vo-Tech,18, 21

California Association of Christian Schools, teachings of, 194-195, 233

California Teachers' Association on vouchers,272

Calvinists,199, 211

Can Catholic Schools Survive?, by Brown and Greeley, 240, statements in, 260-261

Cannard, Dave R., Accountant of Bakersfield Academy, 161, 162

Canon Law: A Text and Commentary, note 282

Canon Law on education, 237, note 252; 282-283

Carolita, Sister, ESEA director in Milwaukee Cath. schools, 113

Carroll, Charles, of Carrollton, 207

Cathedral (Cath.) High School, Duluth, 66, 69, note 69-70

Catholic Almanac, The, note 258

Catholic children without schooling, 203; indoctrination of, 213; perils of, in public schools, 218-219

Catholic Church, growth of, 215, 216; loss of communicants, 217; controversy in, over property, note 222; declarations of, on education, 237; since 1900, 289

Catholic Ecumenical Council, Declaration of, on Religious Freedom, 251; on Christian Education, 251; of Conscience, 252

Catholic Education in America, Neil McCluskey, note 193, 204, 213, 241, 261

Catholic Education in the Western World, James Michael Lee, 243

Catholic education, monolithic, 271

Catholic enrollment, true cause of decline in, 115-117, 187-188

Catholic immigrants refused to establish schools, 184; left Church, 184

Catholic laymen: disillusioned with parochial schools, 12, 35, 115-117, 125, 184-185, 187-188; contributions of, to Church, 45, 78, 100-101, 116, 125; savings of, by phasing out parochial schools, 14, 21-22, 28, 34, 45, 77-78, 100-101, 105-106, 124-125, 130-131, 142

Catholic Membership, Churches, Parochial Schools, and Enrollment in U. S., 288

Catholic Mirror, The, 217

Catholic philosophy of education, 241-242

Catholic Provincial Councils, seven, 1829-1848, 184; declarations of, 211-215

Catholic pupils absorbed by public schools, 10-11, 13-14, 19-20, 21-22, 85-87, 145-146, 172-179

Catholic school finances, 186-187, note 187, 244-245, 293, 294, 295

Catholic schools, costs and salaries of teachers in, 244-245, note 245; comparative, 245-247, 293, 294, 295

Catholic Schools in Action by Reginald Neuwian, 243, note 290

Catholic schools, lack of accountability in, 116, 243, 262

Catholic schools, names of, 233-234

Catholic schools, nature and purpose of, 232-236

Catholic schools, operation of, 238-239

Catholic schools, PTRs in, 244, 290, 291

Catholic share of federal subsidies, 182

Catholic teachers, salaries of, see study of each city; in U. S. 293

Catholic Yearbook of 1828, note 199

Catholics in Maryland, 197; in early America, 199-200

Center for the Study of Public Policy, 269

236, 240

Public Money for Parochial Education, by V. P. Lannie, note 203

Public School Society, 200; encouraged Scripture reading, 201; 202, 203, 204, 205, 206; position of, at hearing before New York City Council of Aldermen, 208-209; abolished, 210, 211

Public schools condemned by Hughes, 203-204; by Cath. councils and clerics, 217-218, 221; by Father Virgil Blum, 253-256; by various critics, 256-257

Public schools facing loss of enrollment, 5, note 10; 18, note, 86; 105, 118, 145, 169-170, note 171, 192, 297

Public schools, names of, 233

Pueblo *Chieftain* 124

Pueblo schools, 5, analysis of, 124-134; 172, 173, 177, 178

Quakers, 196, 200, 211

Quarterly Review of Orestes A. Brownson, 225

Quigley, Archbishop Hames, of Chicago, statement of, 220

Racial composition of schools, 92, 111-112, 123; 138-139, 149

Raisch, William, Supt. of W. Delaware School District in Iowa, 89

Reitan, Walter R., Administrator of Oak Grove Lutheran High School in Fargo, 157

Released- or shared-time programs: none in San Bernardino, 25, Bakersfield, 34, or Albuquerque, 43, 44; released time only for Mormons and Catholic pupils in Pocatello and Idaho Falls, Ida., 54, 188-189; permitted but not used in Fargo, 63; none in

Duluth, 68 or Green Bay, 76; shared time only widely used in Dubuque, 85; none in Kansas City, 94; both used to some extent in St. Paul diocese, 104-105; none in Milwaukee, 113, Pueblo, 128, or Detroit, but shared time only used in diocese outside city, 142, 189; extent of, according to the *Official Catholic Directory*, 188

Religious News Service, note 69-70

Rhode Island, parochiaid struck down, 182, 277

Roberts, Larry, Principal, Bible Missionary School in Boise, 55

Roberts, Neil, ESEA administrator in San Bernardino, 26

Rogers, Virgil M., educator, 7

Roman Catholicism, by Loraine Boettner, note 235, 265

Roosevelt, Theodore, 223, on parochiaid, 224-225

Rutledge, Mr. Justice, 276

Ryan, Mary Perkins, author of *Are Parochial Schools the Answer?* 185; statements of, 258-259

Sadlier's Catholic Directory, note 287

St. Francis School in Bakersfield, 35

St. James Church, meeting at, 204-205

St. John's Lutheran School in Bakersfield, 34, 163

St. Patrick's Cathedral in New York, note 207; 211

St. Paul, 5, analysis of, 98-108; 137, 172, 173, 175, 177

St. Paul Vo-Tech, 103, 105, note 106

St. Paul's Academy, secular prep. school, 162-163

Salaries of Cath. teachers, 244-245,